OPERATION GRATITUDE
SENDING CARE PACKAGES TO U.S. MILITARY

W9-BCP-358

*Thank you for your service!*

# The Top 200
# Sportscards
## In The Hobby

## An In-Depth Guide
## For The Card Collector

by Joe Orlando
Editor of *Sports Market Report*
Foreword by Tom Candiotti

**ODYSSEY PUBLICATIONS**
A Collectors Universe Company
NASDAQ: CLCT
www.SportsMarketReport.com

Publisher:  Odyssey Publications
          A Collectors Universe Company
          NASDAQ: CLCT

Author: Joe Orlando
Foreword:  Tom Candiotti
Contributing Editor:  Brian Seigel
Cover Design:  Jeffrey Mercer
Typography & Design:  Jackie Floyd of Type "F"
Production Coordinator:  Alice Ensor
Graphic Design:  Prax Cruz, Don Hallack, Phil Jordan, Celia Mullins

Printed in the United States of America
First Edition, First Printing
10 9 8 7 6 5 4 3 2 1

ISBN# 0-9669710-8-6

Library of Congress Catalog Card Number: 2002106996

Odyssey Publications
A Collectors Universe Company
510-A So. Corona Mall
Corona, CA  92879-1420

1-800-996-3977 or 909-734-9636

www.SportsMarketReport.com

Printed in the United States

# Foreword

*By Tom Candiotti*

Card collecting has been and always will be a passion of mine. It not only enables me to relive memories from my childhood, but it seems to give me a link to the greatest players and sports heroes from yesteryear. I can hold a sportscard and remember the stories that my dad would tell me about the player. I can vividly recall sharing my childhood collection with my father. I would watch him pick up a Stan Musial card and, with a twinkle in his eye, show me how Stan "The Man" used to hold the bat at the plate.

It is absolutely amazing when you think about the journey some of these cards had to endure in order to reach collector hands today. What were the odds that some of these vintage cards could survive the ages? When you consider that many

of these great cards survived through two World Wars, paper drives, flipping contests, bicycle spokes and your mother's house cleaning, it makes you realize how special they truly are. When a high-grade example of one of these precious, little treasures emerges in the market, it tends to boggle the mind. Just the opportunity to look at one of these gems, with your own eyes, is an experience in itself. The opportunity to own one is an opportunity to own a little piece of American history.

Collecting can be enjoyed by people of all ages from every walk of life. Whether you pluck an Alex Rodriguez card from a $2.50 modern pack or stress, sweat and agonize over spending, what a lifetime of earnings is for many, on the best Mickey Mantle rookie card in existence, the joy is the same. I have been privileged to share in each experience as my collection has evolved over time. The thrill of the search and the conquest of the purchase can almost be as exhilarating as standing on the pitcher's mound and hearing the roar of the crowd after floating a knuckleball by a helpless-looking Barry Bonds for strike three!

This book will illustrate the most important sportscards in existence today, from Ruth to Ryan to Rodriguez. Whether you are an advanced collector or a beginner, this book will give the reader valuable insight and analysis for each and every card on the list. You will travel back in time and learn a little about each athlete and the cards they are featured on with every flip of the page. This guide will be an essential hobby tool for generations of sportscard collectors as an unrivaled reference. If this guide doesn't get you excited about collecting the classics of American sport, I'm not sure what will. I hope it can spark the collector inside of you as it has done for me.

Happy Collecting,

Tom Candiotti

# Table of Contents

# Acknowledgements

To the countless contributors that helped make this book possible, thank you. Thank you to all the collectors and dealers who put up with my endless questions about which cards should make the list and which ones shouldn't. Thank you to all the collectors who kindly shared their prized cards with us so the world can now enjoy and learn about them. Thank you to all the PSA graders who shared their knowledge about the cards.

Thank you to Tom Candiotti for giving his time and energy not only to the making of this book, but to the hobby in general as an advocate for sportscard collecting. Thank you to Alice Ensor who put in a ridiculous amount of time helping me make changes to the book over and over and over again and for not committing me to Cuckoo's Nest. Thank you to Jackie Floyd for working into the wee hours of the morning on layout and design, putting all the pieces together.

Thank you to all those at Collectors Universe, Inc. who put in hours upon hours scanning cards, constructing ads and designing the cover for this book. Thank you to Brian Seigel who is not only a helpful editor and knowledgeable collector, but a good friend as well. Thank you to David Hall for his support and encouragement along the way. Thank you to everyone at Odyssey Publications for giving me the opportunity to share my enthusiasm for this hobby with all the collectors out there.

Thank you to my parents. I wouldn't be where I am today without their support. Last but not least, thank you to my wife who put up with my long nights over the last few months. If anyone is happy that this book is finished, it's her, trust me.

Enjoy the book!

Joe Orlando

# Introduction

When I was younger, I thought I knew everything about this hobby. As you might imagine, I was terribly wrong. The one thing I quickly realized is that no matter how much you think you know about sports collectibles, you can never know enough. The hobby is so vast that it is impossible to be an expert in all the respective fields.

What I have tried to do over the years is to absorb as much as I possibly can in reference to all areas of the hobby. I also don't like to use the word "expert" with reckless abandon. To be considered an expert in any field, you have to basically master the respective area in question. While I do not con-sider myself to be an expert in all fields, I have done my homework over the years and I have a passion for this great hobby of ours.

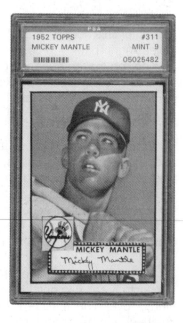

There were times, in my early collecting days, when dealers took advantage of me. Whether I paid too much for one item or bought another one that turned out to be altered or counterfeit, there were times that I wanted to just quit collecting altogether. After more thought, I realized that the problem didn't really lie with me. I was just a kid and, even if I wasn't a kid, there just simply wasn't a great deal of avail-able information out there for collectors to refer to. With the exception of the basic price guides, which never seemed to be reflective of actual market val-ues, there weren't many quality guides available to inform the collector. This is where I would like to help.

No one person has all the answers when it comes to hobby questions. Many times, it comes down to mere opinion but I want to help educate collectors because an educated collector is a happy one. The more you know about what you are buying, the more comfortable you will be when you are considering a purchase. The more available knowledge there is, the more this hobby will flourish and mature. It is a benefit to everyone involved, collectors and dealers alike. The end result is increased commerce.

The good news is that the concept of third party grading has helped elevate the hobby. In the past, cards were subject to overgrading and an inherent conflict of interest that could not be avoided. When it came to the buying and selling of sportscards, the dealer or seller was the one who possessed the majority of the control. Today, the playing field has been leveled between the collector and the dealer.

The fact that a disinterested party has now authenticated and graded the card helps solve many of the problems the hobby endured 10 or so years ago. I can remem-ber buying cards from a dealer in Near Mint condition one minute and returning with those same cards, only minutes later, to have the dealer tell me that the cards were somehow magically lowered now to mere Excellent condition when it came time for him to buy. I am sure some of you have had similar experiences.

With the Internet becoming such a popular venue for sportscard transactions, grading has been the key. It has taken the guesswork out of the equation. The seller has a very liquid product and the above mentioned conflict has diminished quite a bit since the grade has been determined by the third party. The buyer has received piece of mind because, as he or she becomes familiar with the grading standards, they will know exactly what they are paying for. As an extreme example of how the hobby has changed as a result of third party grading, sight-unseen sales have risen dramatically in recent years.

More and more collectors, new and formerly disgruntled ones, have entered the hobby because the hobby has never been as safe and fun as it is today. This is only the beginning and, as more collectors understand the value in self-education, the better it will be for all of us. I hope that you are able to use this book as a reference in helping to assemble your collection. I also hope that you enjoy this great hobby.

I have enjoyed collecting sports memorabilia for over 20 years. I have shared the ups and downs that most collectors experience so I understand the joy and frustration that people go through at times. The key is to make your collecting experience as fun as possible. I hope, in some small way, my book can help you reach that goal.

Sincerely,

Joe Orlando
Author

## About the Author

Joe Orlando has been an advanced collector of sportscards and memorabilia for nearly 20 years. Joe has established himself in the hobby as a re-spected authority on sportscards, game-used equipment and autographs with a concentration on high-end vintage material. Joe attended Westmont College in Santa Barbara, California where he studied communications and was a team captain and catcher for the baseball team. After a brief stint in the minor leagues, Joe obtained a Juris Doctor from Whittier Law School in Southern California in the spring of 1999.

During the last three years, Joe has authored several collecting guides and dozens of articles for Collectors Universe, Inc. Currently, Joe is the Vice President of PSA and he has appeared on several radio and television programs as a hobby expert including ESPN's award-winning program *Out-side the Lines* as the featured guest. He is also Editor of the company's nationally distributed *Sports Market Report*, the most comprehensive and respected monthly price guide for sportscards and memorabilia.

# A Note About The Sports Guide 200

The Sports Guide 200 is a listing of the top 200 sportscards in hobby history. Some of the top collectors and dealers in the country helped select the 200 cards on our list. Each contributor was asked to choose their top 200 sportscards and this list is the result of the poll. I would like to personally thank each and every person for his or her help in compiling this tremendous list.

Photo Courtesy of Troy Kinunen

## Subjectivity

The bottom line is that, if you ask 200 different people to produce a list of what they believe are the 200 most important cards, you would get 200 different lists. That is part of what makes this hobby fun; it always comes down to an opinion. It stems from those playground arguments you might remember from your childhood. "Willie Mays is better than Hank Aaron," one kid shouts but his friend interrupts with a laugh and says, "Mickey Mantle is better than both of them." Sportscards are like the heroes they feature; they are dear to collectors and each one is subject to debate.

Photo Courtesy of Troy Kinunen

What I can assure the readers of is that this list was compiled with that dilemma in mind and a great deal of care was used in making the selections. Believe it or not, it was hard to narrow it down to a top 200 list. There are so many fabulous sportscards to choose from. From the early tobacco cards to the modern day technological miracles, there is something for everyone on this list. I found myself struggling, day after day, with the realization that 200 slots were a very limited number to work with. When I started working on

Photo Courtesy of the National Baseball Hall of Fame Library, Cooperstown, N.Y.

this guide, I thought it might be a challenge to fill those 200 slots. By the time I finished, my mind had been changed completely.

## Criteria

There were several factors used in determining the top 200 sportscards. Popularity of the card and player, market value, historical value, athletic accomplishment, rarity and eye-appeal were just some of the criteria used when selecting these cards. For instance, a 1985 Topps Mark McGwire rookie card is not nearly as rare as a 1935 Diamond Star Mickey Cochrane but the popularity of the McGwire card is overwhelming, therefore, the McGwire rookie makes the list despite the fact that it is truly a common card. This list is not necessarily a guide to the 200 cards with the best investment potential either. The factors were weighed against each other in order to make a final determination.

One area that confuses most collectors is the area of athletic accomplishment and popularity. Most people would assume that both go hand in hand but nothing could be further from the truth. Athletic accomplishment is definitely a factor in determining values of any sports collectible but popularity is even more important. Take, for instance, Eddie Murray. No one will argue that he isn't one of the greatest baseball players to ever play the game but the fact remains that he is not as popular as some players who have accomplished much less throughout their careers.

In fact, Murray was one of my personal favorites growing up. At the time of publishing, Murray was one of only three men to ever reach 500 home runs and 3,000 hits with Hank Aaron and Willie Mays being the others. How could I leave Murray off the list? Well, poor Eddie wasn't ex-

actly a charmer. His relationship with the media was poor at best and, because of that, Murray was portrayed as an unfriendly man to the public. Was it merely the result of shyness? Perhaps. Was the media unfair? Maybe. Sometimes the perception of the player is unjustified but, whatever the perception is, it will affect the popularity of his or her collectibles. In some cases, personality and perception can be just as important to valuation as touchdowns and home runs are.

One area where I am sure to get a lot of criticism is the lack of rare common or semi-star players included on the list. Many sportscard books would include cards like the 1933 Goudey Benny Bengough, the 1952 Topps Johnny Sain or Joe Page errors on their lists strictly based on market value and rarity. I disagree. The reality regarding rare commons and semi-stars is that there is a very limited audience for those cards. If you are trying to assemble the world's finest 1933 Goudey or 1952 Topps set, then those cards will become a priority but, if you are not a set builder, those cards become unimportant. I want to appeal to the majority of collectors out there and the majority of collectors could care less about cards that fit that description.

The logic behind such a bar on these types of cards was simply this: If the average collector had $25,000-$100,000 to spend on sportscards, would they spend it on an obscure player just because the card is rare or would they spend it on a major player like Babe Ruth or Jackie Robinson? I think the answer is very clear. Most people care about the icons of sport or at least the recognizable stars from the past and present, not about the Benny Bengoughs of the world. On the other hand, if I were to compile a list purely

based on popularity, the list would be nothing more than a checklist for players like Mantle and Jordan. Popularity is a major factor but only one of several that were used in creating this list.

Again, this is not a personal criticism of those cards because advanced collectors realize how tough they are. It is just the reality of our hobby; the market for obscure players, no matter how rare the card, is very limited. That is why high-grade examples of those obscure rarities sell for huge dollars while the mid-to-low grade examples have a hard time finding a home. Once the high-grade set builders acquire a satisfactory example, there are not too many potential buyers for those cards at high price levels. It's not really an opinion; it's a fact. If someone offered you a Near Mint to Mint T205 Gold Border Ty Cobb at the same price as a 1933 Goudey Benny Bengough in the same grade, which one would you take?

## Trends and the Truth

As the sportscard market matures, collectors begin to see the truth behind the hype of certain cards. Like most collectible fields, the sportscard hobby has its share of trends that make headlines today and disappear a few weeks later. The key for collectors, who want to make sure that they are receiving a solid value, is to focus on quality. To me, quality sportscards are those cards that have the best chance of retaining long-term popularity because the demand for the item should remain stable regardless of general market swings.

Even when an overall market seems weak, the quality items still sell. For instance, if the overall market is slow but one of the finest Mickey Mantle cards comes up for sale, the card will still bring good money. A great case in point was the sale of a 1952 Topps Mickey Mantle grade PSA Gem Mint 10, the finest grade available. During a time when the overall market was best described as slow, the card sold for a record $275,000. The same cannot be said for lower quality examples. When the overall market suffers, it's the average material that struggles the most. If you are looking for security in your

Photo Courtesy of the National Baseball Hall of Fame Library, Cooperstown, N.Y.

purchases, learn as much as you can about the quality of the item you are buying.

Now, on the other hand, there are those risk takers who choose to climb aboard the bandwagon and they enjoy the thrill of speculation. This is also a fun aspect to the hobby. I am sure most of you can remember holding on to the rookie cards after opening wax packs and hoping that those players would become superstars someday. Some of those players were Mike Schmidt and Nolan Ryan while others turned out to be Greg Brock and Ron Kittle. It's part of the speculation game, it's a gamble. "Could this guy be a future Hall of Famer?" It's a question all collectors ask and, many more times than not, their prayers are not answered.

This list, for the most part, does not address the modern players or cards that would fit this description. We have decided to include, in proportion to the vintage card selection, a few modern stars because of their overwhelming popularity but the reality of the modern market is that most of the cards are overproduced at best and, while there are some tremendous athletes playing today, their careers have yet to blossom. Most sports analysts claim that a player's legacy is more defined by the last quarter of their career than by the first quarter, keep that in mind. All of us can speculate about a modern card but, if a career-ending injury hits some prospect or player who only has a few years under his belt, the dream is over.

Another question that some readers might have, especially those new to the hobby, is why baseball cards dominate the list. It doesn't seem to matter if another sport is actually more popular than baseball today; the overwhelming majority of collectors focus on baseball.

The answer is, to some degree, a simple one but there are a few reasons behind the answer.

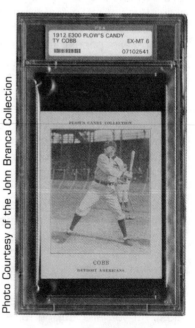

Photo Courtesy of the John Branca Collection

First of all, baseball goes back in our country's history further than the other major sports do. It's part of the reason why baseball is labeled as America's pastime. No other sport can claim to compete with baseball's rich history. Football, basketball and hockey were all sports that just started to catch on with the general public in the latter half of the 20th Century. In fact, even boxing may arguably have a richer history than those sports.

Prize fighting certainly has deeper roots in our nation's history and championship matches were regarded as major events well before the general public fell in love with touchdowns, rebounds and slap shots. Boxers, much like the baseball legends of the pre-war era, were regarded

as major celebrities. Remember that some of baseball's biggest legends, like Babe Ruth and Lou Gehrig, played before the widespread availability of television. Without a great deal of video footage, our imaginations can run wild about these stars. It adds to the mystique of the game.

Secondly, there is something about baseball that captures the child in all of us. There is an almost magical quality about baseball that the other sports don't seem to possess; I can't explain it fully but it's true. When polled, most sports fans and collectors will tell you that, when they dream about sports, it always seems to involve baseball. Hitting a home run in the bottom of the ninth inning to win the game is probably the most universal sports fantasy that exists. Remember that scene from the movie *The Natural?* That's exactly what I'm talking about.

Finally, baseball fans place such an emphasis on statistics and milestones that collectors seem to flock to baseball cards. The 3,000 Hit Club, the 500 Home Run Club and the 300 Win Club are all major collecting themes in the sportscard world. Each card captures a season, a moment in time for the player. For some reason or another, the other major sports do not have the loyal collector following that baseball has. As time goes on, maybe that fact will change. Eventually, the other sports will build a rich history of their own like baseball and maybe more collectors will gravitate towards those sports but, until then, baseball remains the king of the hobby by a large margin.

## Vintage Cards

A Few Things to Keep in Mind about Cards from the Past

All vintage cards are tough to find in true high-grade. When browsing through the top 200 list, this is something that I suggest you keep in mind. The manufacturing process was so poor and the cards were packaged so carelessly that, in most cases, the cards didn't even come direct from the factory in high-grade. If you don't believe me, go out and buy a vintage pack of baseball cards and open it up. The cards were constantly manufactured off-center with a variety of print marks, staining (from candy, gum, tobacco, or oils) and other condition obstacles.

The interesting thing is, even if a collector was fortunate enough to open a pack and find a high-grade card in days past, few seemed to care enough about the cards to protect them. Cards were mishandled often because they weren't valued like they are today. Where's a time machine when you need one! Cards were placed in rubber bands, shoeboxes, bike spokes and used in a variety of games like "flipping" where collectors would literally toss their prized gems across the room for fun. In fact, card protection did not become a major concern until the mid-1980's. Finally, collectors started

to care for their cards by placing them in plastic sleeves and a variety of holders.

Card grading has changed over the years and it has become a more defined science with more factors to consider than ever before. The paper these cards were printed on was, for the most part, extremely fragile and paper collectibles are more susceptible to the elements, such as humidity and sunlight, over time than just about any other major collectible I can think of. Keep that in mind when you find a vintage card that has somehow survived in pristine condition over half a century. How some of these treasures survived in high-grade is mind-boggling but that is what makes the quality vintage Sportcards so desirable. Each and every vintage card on the Top 200 list is tough in comparison to any modern production and, with each card, there is a story.

## The Future of the Top 200

As you might imagine, this list will inevitably change over time but the majority of the cards featured on the list will be a part of the top 200 for generations. Staying power was another key factor in determining the top 200 sportscards. As time goes on, the legends will grow. The majority of the sports figures on this list have solidified their place in history. Ted Williams doesn't need to raise his career batting average and Jim Brown doesn't have to gain another yard; they have left their mark already. In addition, not too many people bothered to protect their vintage cards so, unless a giant "find" of pristine vintage cards surfaces in the next few years, a hoard so large that it completely alters the current supply and demand status, this list should provide a great representation of the best sportscards for years to come.

## Guide Layout

The guide contains three major sections for each sportscard.

The purpose of each section is explained below, these types of questions will be answered:

**Importance:** Why is this particular card important to the hobby? Why is the athlete featured on the card important to sports history?

**Difficulty:** What unique flaws, if any, make this card tough to find in high-grade or tough to find at all? In comparison to other cards on the list, how tough is this card?

**Comments:** What is the outlook for this card? What factors should enable this card to remain on the Top 200 list in the future? Why was this card chosen over, perhaps, another comparable issue or player?

## 1887 N172 Old Judge Cap Anson

### Importance:

The rarity of this issue cannot be underestimated. Seldom seen in any grade, these Anson Old Judge cards have few rivals in terms of rarity, especially the *In Uniform* variation. In fact, most collectors, even advanced ones, have yet to see an example of this variation in person. To illustrate the point, an ungraded example sold in excess of $60,000 in the last couple of years and that card was estimated to be in merely Very Good to Excellent condition.

Anson, during his 27-year career, would reach a .300 batting average 24 times and hit .380 or better three times. He also showed occasional power at the plate despite playing during the "Dead Ball Era" and, in fact, he became the first man ever to club three consecutive homers in one game. Without question, this is the most elusive and desirable issue of baseball's first superstar player.

Photo Courtesy of Lew Lipset

### Difficulty:

All Old Judge cards are nearly impossible to find in nice shape but the Anson *In Uniform* variation takes difficulty to the next level. Not only is it a condition rarity due to the inherent problems associated with the issue but it is also a general rarity, tough to locate in any grade. Packed in Old Judge and Gypsy Queen cigarette packs, these cards had to avoid a number of obstacles to reach us here today, over 100 years later.

Just about every condition obstacle you could imagine affects this issue such as toning, staining, general wear and print defects. Keep in mind just how fragile baseball cards are. They are made of mere paper and paper is at the mercy of the elements such as temperature and humidity unlike some other collectibles or antiques. It's a wonder how some of these cards survived the long journey without being obliterated, let alone being found in high-grade. This issue ranks near the very top of overall difficulty.

1887 N172 OLD JUDGE CAP ANSON

## Comments:

It may sound like a broken record but, as time goes on, rarity will become an increasingly important factor to collectors in the marketplace. It is really the principle that governs all other collectible fields and it is natural that this factor will have more and more influence in the sportscard market as time passes. The key here is that this issue is not only rare, it features a Hall of Famer. Anson, while not a household name to the average collector or baseball fan, was really the first superstar in the sport. There were players who technically had better skill but Anson had marquee value. If you were looking for the ultimate Anson, especially the *In Uniform* variation, this would be it.

# 1887 N28 Allen & Ginter Cap Anson

## Importance:

The first mainstream tobacco issue featuring one of the most significant figures from baseball's early days. Cap Anson was not only a Hall of Fame caliber baseball player; he was also considered an innovative manager.

As a player, he was the first man to collect 3,000 hits (he collected exactly 3,000), had a career batting average of .329 and led the league in RBI's 9 times. As a manager, he was the first man to require spring training for players in order to get them into shape. Even though he was not well liked for his antics on the field, Anson remains a key figure in baseball history. The Old Timers' Committee elected him to the Hall of Fame in 1939.

## Difficulty:

When a card is over 100 years old, you know there will be obstacles. The main problem is finding the card at all. Generally speaking, this card has a number of typical flaws. First, look out for print defects in the pure white background, mainly black print spots. Second, the reverse is usually found with some degree of toning so make sure it isn't too bad, otherwise, it may be a detractor. Third, the reverse of the card features a checklist so don't be surprised if you find examples with handwritten notations on them.

Finally, with these ancient cards you have to realize that most of them have soft corners and edge wear because they were packed in cigarette boxes. There were no screw downs or plastic sleeves to protect the cards back then so general wear is a problem. Overall, this is a very tough card to find in high-grade.

## 1887 N28 ALLEN & GINTER CAP ANSON

**Comments:**

When you combine Anson's early impact on the game and the rarity of the issue, the outlook is solid for this N28 card. As collectors become more advanced, rarity becomes more of a focus. I will guarantee you this; there will never be an abundance of this card in any grade let alone high-grade. Anson was one of only 10 baseball players selected for the set and that says a lot about his impact. As collectors learn more about the history of the game, they will gravitate towards attractive, early cards like this. Anson will never be anywhere near as popular as Ruth or Mantle but his place in history is secure.

## 1888 N162 Goodwin Champions Cap Anson

### Importance:

This is an incredibly tough and beautiful 19th Century issue featuring baseball's first superstar. This card, one of 8 baseball cards featured in the set, is arguably more attractive (with beautiful colors) than his N28 issue and more difficult to find.

With Anson's four batting crowns, twice hitting over .400, his ability as a hitter was never questioned. He also took somewhat of a scientific approach to the game, an approach never seen before. Anson taught others how to generate power at the plate by learning to drive the baseball with authority at all times, however, not merely to hit home runs. This card is one of only a few to feature one of baseball's most significant figures of the 19th Century, Cap Anson.

### Difficulty:

Again, here's a card that is so old that it is bound to have major problems. These cards were inserted into packages of Old Judge and Gypsy Queen Cigarettes to start so staining can be an issue. Like the N28's, the reverse features a checklist so beware of notations made on the reverse by those set builders from days past. The inclusion of more color can also make it easier for print defects to surface. The blue background will reveal any dark print marks so keep that in mind.

Finally, general wear might be the biggest obstacle for most early issues and this one is no exception. Keep in mind just how fragile baseball cards are. Baseball cards are made of paper, which is fragile and are at the mercy of the elements of time, sunlight, humidity and temperature. All of this in addition to the touch of human hands.

PSA

1888 N162 GOODWIN CHAMPS    #
CAP ANSON                NM 7
07042659

ANSON,
(1st Base, CHICAGO.

CHICAGO

OLD JUDGE & GYPSY QUEEN CIGARETTES

## 1888 N162 GOODWIN CHAMPIONS CAP ANSON

## Comments:

The addition of increased color has a great affect on any baseball card and there is a significant difference between this Anson card and most of his other examples. The combination of color and rarity gives this card a lot of appeal. Like the comparison between the 1941 Play Ball Ted Williams and the 1939 Play Ball Williams rookie card, the more colorful cards (due to eye-appeal) seem to enjoy increased demand over time no matter the age. Players from this era will never get the attention that players from the 1920's or 1950's receive but demand should remain solid as collectors learn more about the history of the game.

# 1888 N162 Goodwin Champions King Kelly

## Importance:
This is a key card of one of the most popular players of the 19th Century. Mike "King" Kelly was known as much for his wild ways off the field as he was for his wild ways on the bases. Despite the fact that Kelly did not possess incredible numbers, Kelly entertained fans everywhere he went and he was part of several pennant-winning teams. Kelly did lead the league in batting twice and runs scored three times but his popularity was more a product of his colorful character than his baseball skills.

Just before the 1887 season, the Chicago White Stockings sold him for a record $10,000 to the Boston Beaneaters. Oh my, how things have changed. The Old Timers' Committee inducted Kelly into the Hall of Fame in 1945.

## Difficulty:
These early 19th Century cards are bound to have major problems. These cards were inserted into packages of Old Judge and Gypsy Queen Cigarettes to start so the potential for staining exists. Like the N28's, the reverse features a checklist so beware of notations made on the reverse by those set builders from days past. The inclusion of more color can also make it easier for print defects to surface. The blue background will reveal any dark print marks so keep that in mind.

Finally, general wear might be the biggest obstacle for most early issues and this one is no exception. Keep in mind just how fragile baseball cards are. They are made of mere paper and paper is at the mercy of the elements such as temperature, humidity and the human hand unlike some other collectibles or antiques. It's a wonder how some of these cards survived the long journey without being obliterated. This card provides a major challenge.

1888 N162 GOODWIN CHAMPIONS KING KELLEY

## Comments:

Kelly is considered a bit overrated by many baseball historians but remember that popularity, in many cases, will override a player's performance. Likewise, if we based demand on strict player performance then Eddie Murray cards would be more sought after than Derek Jeter cards and so on. Forget the numbers, Kelly is a significant figure in the game and this is one of the earliest star cards you can find. He was an entertainer and that is a large part of what an athlete should be. Fans pay to be entertained and Kelly was a master at that. The future for this card is solid, not only for the rarity, but also because he is one of the few recognizable names from baseball's beginnings.

# 1909 T204 Ramly Cigarettes Walter Johnson

## Importance:

This is the key card in one of the most beautiful sets produced in the early part of the 20th Century. This card is as stunning as it is rare. The black and white portrait of Walter Johnson is surrounded by gold embossed borders on the front, giving this card the ultimate antique feel. The reverse of the card provides the ultimate contrast to the lavish front, simple without an ornate frame. There are a few rare variations in the 121-card set but the "Big Train" card is the most desirable. Johnson is widely regarded as one of the most dominating pitchers of the 20th Century. He won 20 or more games 12 times with two 30-win seasons mixed in.

His greatest season on the mound, and perhaps the greatest season by any pitcher, took place in 1913 when Johnson went 36-7 with a 1.14 ERA. During his great campaign, he would also lead the league in strikeouts and post 11 shutouts. No card in the set comes close in importance, even the other Hall of Famers in the set rank a distant second.

## Difficulty:

When it comes to pure difficulty, this Johnson classic has few rivals on the list. Tougher than the legendary T206 issue and even more elusive than the incredibly tough T205 Johnson, it's the toughest card of the hard-throwing righty in the top 200. If there was one condition obstacle to be most concerned with, it would be those pesky gold borders. Much like the T205 issue, the gold borders are extremely susceptible to chipping and edge wear. Please beware of re-colored or re-touched examples in the marketplace.

Card "doctors" will often perform "surgery" in order to conceal the damage along the sides. The slightest touch will reveal the white cardboard underneath, which creates an immediate eyesore if serious wear is present. Staining is also very common as these cards were packaged along with tobacco cigarettes. In general, it is truly amazing to think how any of these cards could have survived the long journey of nearly 100 years. This is, without a doubt, an extraordinarily difficult card and one you will have a hard time finding in any grade.

## 1909 T204 RAMLY CIGARETTES WALTER JOHNSON

**Comments:**

Most baseball experts feel that he may have been the greatest strikeout pitcher ever because he played during an era when hitting was a game of methodical contact and not free-swinging power. Johnson's career strikeout mark (3,506), taken in context, is truly amazing. The fact that he was part of the first group elected to the Hall of Fame in 1936 gives collectors one more reason (not that they needed any) to collect his cards. The original inductees are often used as a theme for many collections. This Ramly Johnson, at first, was left off the list for fear that it might be too obscure. After further thought, the beauty, rarity and significance of the card were overwhelming.

# 1909-11 T206 White Border Ty Cobb
(Green Portrait, Red Portrait, Bat off Shoulder and Bat on Shoulder)

## Importance:

A legendary quartet of a legendary player. The T206 set is one of the hobby's most desired sets. The beautiful stone lithography artwork captures the game and its participants from a day long past. The four Cobb cards featured in the set are collected like a mini-set of their own much like the four Babe Ruth cards found in the 1933 Goudey set. While the T205 Cobb is more difficult to find in high-grade, these Cobb cards are the most popular of the fiery competitor and not easy to find in nice shape by any means.

The demand for the portrait versions (Green and Red) has always been exceptional due to the fact that many collectors prefer to collect the portraits because of their outstanding visual appeal, however, in terms of demand, the two Cobb with bat variations have traditionally enjoyed more attention than the Red Cobb due to their multi-colored presentation. All four Cobb cards featured in this subset are, without question, near the top of this list in terms of pure importance with the Green Portrait leading the way.

## Difficulty:

The four Cobb cards range in difficulty with the Green Portrait Cobb being the toughest by far. Often found with terrible centering, the Green Cobb is very rarely seen in unqualified top grades if at all. The other three, in terms of pure difficulty, would rank as follows: Bat on Shoulder, Bat off Shoulder and Red background. Stored in tobacco packs, it is amazing that any of these cards survived in decent shape. Subject to staining, toning and inconsistent printing quality, these cards are virtually impossible to find in high-grade. The inconsistent printing quality led to a range in boldness of color and focus problems on many of the cards.

One unique problem with the Red Portrait Cobb is that it is often found with an orange background instead of red. The Orange Background Cobb is seemingly more common than the bold red version. Examples that feature deep color and a sharp image are in high demand in the hobby. Trimming is also something to be wary of as many of these cards were naturally cut with variance in size, allowing card "doctors" some leeway to work with. The centering, as with most T206 cards, is very inconsistent as well. Due to the "Southern Find," some fresh examples do exist but not in any type of quantity.

1909-11 T206 TY COBB

## Comments:

These cards, if the list were ranked by strict importance, would be near the top for sure. This quartet is only second to the four Ruth cards that anchor the 1933 Goudey set. With the exception of the few major rarities in the T206 set, these Cobb cards are the four keys to the set. As a collector, you just can't ignore his astounding numbers and, as time goes on, those numbers will continue to enhance the desirability of his cards. Pete Rose may have the career hit record, but Cobb had the dominance. As the key cards in perhaps the most popular set in the hobby, the demand for these cards should always be strong.

## 1909-11 T206 White Border Walter Johnson
(Hands at Chest and Portrait)

### Importance:
Perhaps the most popular issue featuring the "Big Train." Walter Johnson was so dominant that it's hard to imagine. With 417 victories and an incredibly puny ERA of 2.17, his career numbers are remarkable. Johnson was one of the first five men to be elected into the Hall of Fame in 1936. That elite and memorable group consisted of (along with Johnson) Babe Ruth, Ty Cobb, Christy Mathewson and Honus Wagner. Wow! He is still regarded as the best right-handed pitcher in baseball history.

Finding either card in high-grade is as tough as hitting his slingshot fastball. The portrait variation, as with most of the cards in the set, is considered the most desirable of the two. The Johnson portrait is one of the more visually appealing cards on the list.

### Difficulty:
The T206 cards are tough simply by virtue of their age and general wear is a big problem. You have to look very closely at the cards because corner wear can be hard to detect because of the design and whiteness of the borders. Often, you will see the tips of the corners, under magnification, with paper loss but you have to look close to see it. The centering problems, associated with the issue, are common as well, particularly the Hands at Chest example.

In addition, look for a wide range of color quality. Watch out for examples with a "washed out" look. Trimming is also something to be wary of. The Johnson Portrait is slightly more popular than the Hands at Chest variation, however, due to the "Southern Find" of T206's, the portrait seems to be more plentiful in top grades.

T206
WALTER JOHNSON
HANDS AT CHEST
PSA
NM-MT 8
02076870

JOHNSON, WASHINGTON

T206
WALTER JOHNSON
PORTRAIT
PSA
NM-MT 8
03386187

JOHNSON, WASHINGTON

## 1909-11 T206 WALTER JOHNSON

## Comments:

The T206 set is considered to be one of the finest sets ever produced and for good reason. The cards are popular, colorful, difficult and the set features so many Hall of Famers (76 variations) it's scary. The portrait is the example that collectors seem to always be drawn to. Many collectors will try to assemble portrait subsets instead of attempting to assemble the entire T206 set, which would take hoards of money, and overwhelming time. Before there was Ryan and Clemens, there was a man they called "The Big Train." Some may surpass Johnson's strikeout totals, but it's hard to imagine any modern pitcher approaching his ERA or win totals. This Johnson issue should enjoy increased demand by future generations of collectors.

# 1909-11 T206 White Border Christy Mathewson
(Dark Cap, White Cap and Portrait)

## Importance:

This is one of Christy Mathewson's most visually attractive is-sues. The T206 is certainly regarded as one of the hobby's most desirable sets and for good reason. The Christy Mathewson cards are among several keys to the set. The portraits have always been more popular than the other variations or poses in the set due to their visual beauty, the Mathewson example is no exception. Four times in his illustrious career, Mathewson would win 30 or more games with a career-high of 37 in 1908.

The key to his success was a specialty pitch that, by today's baseball lingo, would be called a screwball. The pitch could fool left-handed and right-handed hitters alike. He could start the pitch over the plate and have it fade away to a lefty or start it off the plate outside and have it come back to nip the outer edge of the plate on righties. With an ERA of 2.13 for his entire career, it's hard to imagine how anyone could hit him.

## Difficulty:

The T206 cards are tough simply by virtue of their age and gen-eral wear is a big problem. You have to look very closely at the cards because corner wear can be hard to detect because of the design and color of the whiteness of the borders. Often, you will see the tips of the corners, under magnification, with paper loss but you have to look close to see it. The centering problems, associated with the issue, are common as well.

In addition, look for a wide range of color quality. Watch out for examples with a "washed out" look. Trimming is also something to be wary of. While all three variations are tough, the White Cap Mathewson card appears to be the hardest to find. Due to the "Southern Find," some fresh examples do exist but not in any type of quantity. The Mathewson Portrait is one of the toughest portraits from the set to find in high-grade.

**1909-11 T206 CHRISTY MATHEWSON**

## Comments:

The T206 Mathewson cards are, quite possibly, his most popular examples. Like the other Hall of Famer cards in the set, the portrait is clearly the most desirable of all the poses. So, the demand for the Mathewson portrait will probably always be slightly higher than the other variations in the set. That's not to say that the portrait is more difficult; collectors are simply drawn to cards with the best eye-appeal. The demand for these examples is great for a multitude of reasons, as Mathewson is an upper echelon Hall of Famer.

# 1909-11 T206 White Border Eddie Plank

## Importance:

This is the second most desirable card from the famed T206 set and the only pose featuring the Hall of Fame pitcher. Eddie Plank ranks as one of baseball's best left-handed pitchers. Plank amassed 327 wins and he remained the all-time leader (for lefties) for nearly 50 years until Warren Spahn surpassed him in the early 1960's. Plank won 20 or more games in 8 different seasons and still holds the all-time record for most shutouts by a lefty with 69. Not this time Mr. Spahn!

Plank's array of off-speed pitches and unusual demeanor on the mound caused many hitters to become frustrated. Despite entering the league at age 26, Plank was still able to accumulate impressive career numbers. Plank was elected to the Hall of Fame in 1946 and this is, without question, his most valuable card.

## Difficulty:

The Plank example is much scarcer than the majority of the other cards in the set, but hobby experts still don't have a clear explanation for the rarity. In fact, at the time of publication, PSA has graded almost the identical number of Planks as they have Wagners. The most common belief is that the card suffered damage due to a poor printing plate and, therefore, many of the Plank cards were discarded due to their inferior printing quality.

The T206 cards are tough simply by virtue of their age and general wear seems to be a big problem. You have to look very closely at the cards because corner wear can be hard to detect because of the design and whiteness of the borders. Often, you will see the tips of the corners, under magnification, with paper loss but you have to look close to see it. The centering problems, associated with the issue, are common as well. In addition, look for a wide range of color quality. Watch out for examples with a "washed out" look. With this card, all of the above problems, especially the color problem, are taken to the next level. Trimming is also something to be wary of.

Photo Courtesy of the Tom Candiotti Collection

PSA
T206
EDDIE PLANK
NM-MT 8
02044145

PLANK, PHILA. AMER.

## 1909-11 T206 EDDIE PLANK

## Comments:

As long as the T206 set is popular, this card is going to receive a great deal of attention. I guess that means this card is going to be popular for a very long time. Plank was not on the same level as Mathewson or Johnson as a pitcher, but this card is one of the most valuable rarities in the hobby. The key here is that the card features the combination of rarity and a Hall of Famer. Often times, rarities are limited to obscure players who the average collector lacks interest in but, here, Plank wasn't only a star, he was the best lefty in the game for a long while. The outlook is solid on this card and, if rarity continues to be a dominant force in demand, then this card could gain more attention. Time will tell if this Plank is actually tougher than the Wagner.

## 1909-11 T206 White Border Tris Speaker

### Importance:

The only T206 card to feature the legendary Tris Speaker and, perhaps, Speaker's most desirable card overall. Tris Speaker, also known as "The Grey Eagle," collected over 3,500 hits and was considered to be the best defensive center fielder of his era. Speaker was truly a defensive innovator as he was the first man to implement the "shallow" approach to playing the outfield. During the dead-ball era, other center fielders were able to copy Speakers style of play because long drives were a rarity.

By the 1920's, a new power game was being played and no center fielder could continue to play such a shallow position with the exception of Speaker. He was so fast and got such great jumps on the ball that he continued to use his innovative technique. By the way, he hit .344 for his career and is the all-time leader in doubles with 793.

This beautiful card, which captures Speaker looking to strike the ball with his lethal bat, is the only one featuring Speaker in the entire set. While some dispute whether or not this is Speaker's technical rookie card, most acknowledge it as his rookie.

### Difficulty:

When a card is nearly 100 years old, you know it's tough. The T206 cards are commonly found off-center and, due to this and other condition obstacles, the card can be found trimmed or altered. One key to look for on this issue is deep color. The blue background can be a tremendous asset if the color is bold but beware of "washed out" backdrops. Toning along the edges and toning or tobacco staining on the reverse are common. With the exception of a few small "finds," these T206's were packaged with tobacco so I am sure you can imagine the potential for damage. This card is very tough in near mint or better condition. Due to the "Southern Find," (where some virtually uncirculated gems were discovered) some fresh examples do exist but not in any type of quantity.

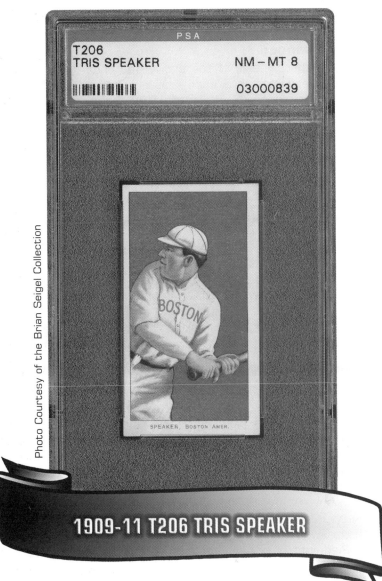

## 1909-11 T206 TRIS SPEAKER

**Comments:**

Tris Speaker does not have the name that some other players have like Ty Cobb or Babe Ruth but his accomplishments speak for themselves. He is certainly regarded as an upper-tier Hall of Famer (elected in 1937) by baseball historians. Speaker is the kind of player who should gain more respect as time goes on and collectors start to focus on his incredible numbers. The T205 Speaker is tougher and the Cracker Jack Speaker is, perhaps, more attractive but no other Speaker card has such mass appeal. As one of the many keys to the incredibly popular T206 set, this card should always enjoy solid demand.

# 1909-11 T206 White Border Honus Wagner

## Importance:

This is the pinnacle of the entire sportscard hobby. Of all the sportscards ever produced, this one is considered the ultimate piece of cardboard. The rumors have changed over the years, regarding the reason for the great rarity, but most experts believe that Wagner did not want to promote tobacco use by children and, hence, had the card removed from production. Documentation has recently surfaced to support this theory, including newspapers from the day. In addition, Wagner was a great shortstop, 3,000 Hit Club member and one of the original inductees to the Hall of Fame in 1936.

## Difficulty:

It is believed that approximately 50 copies of this Wagner card exist. Many of the surviving copies are, unfortunately, in terrible condition. A few mid-grade copies exist with only one known NM-MT example to surface. That famous copy fetched over $1,200,000 at auction making it the highest price ever paid for a sportscard by a large margin. If that doesn't tell you about the difficulty and legendary status of this card, I don't know what will.

Aside from the fact that T206's had to survive two paper drives of WWI and WWII, along with "attic cleaning," handling and other environmental hazards, the T206 Wagner was printed in very short supply in 1909. As a result, it is no wonder why, over 90 years later, only about 50 or so still survive with only a handful known in Excellent or better condition.

Keep in mind that the vast majority of the surviving Wagners have Sweet Caporal backs. One of the two known Wagners with a Piedmont back happens to be the legendary PSA NM-MT 8.

PSA

T206
HONUS WAGNER
McNALL/GRETZKY

NM-MT 8

00000001

WAGNER, PITTSBURG

## 1909-11 T206 HONUS WAGNER

## Comments:

This card has always been the "crown jewel" of the sportscard hobby. There are other cards that are arguably more scarce but this one has such a compelling story behind the rarity combined with Wagner, one of the finest players of his day and an inaugural HOF inductee. Now that we know of the great harm that tobacco use can cause, it makes this card even more interesting. It's amazing in retrospect but sometimes lost in the compelling story is the fact that Wagner was such an outstanding ballplayer. He was a 8-time NL batting champion, a record stil unsurpassed today. Let's not forget that.

# 1909-11 T206 White Border Cy Young

(With Glove, Bare Hand and Portrait)

## Importance:

This is the most popular issue to feature Cy Young, the standard by which all other pitchers are now measured. While it is debatable whether Cy Young was actually the best pitcher ever, it is his name that graces the ultimate pitching award. Imagine this, to win 500 games; you would have to win 20 games every year for 25 years! In order to match Cy Young's total, you still need an extra 11 wins!

The bottom line is that Cy Young was on the mound for all 511 wins and that is what baseball is all about; you either win or lose the game. No one was better, in that regard, than Mr. Young. Young was so incredibly durable that he completed 749 games during his career and threw 7,357 innings, both all-time records. Young's three career no-hitters and 2.63 ERA just add to his legacy.

## Difficulty:

The Young variations, especially the portrait, are seen far less often than other star cards in the set. You definitely will see more Cobbs and Johnsons (due to the "find" years ago) on the market than Young portraits. The T206 cards are tough simply by virtue of their age and general wear is a big problem as a result of human handling and a variety of environmental hazards.

You have to look very closely at the cards because corner wear can be hard to detect because of the design and whiteness of the borders. Often, you will see the tips of the corners, under magnification, with paper loss but you have to look close to see it. The centering problems, associated with the issue, are common as well. In addition, look for a wide range of color quality. Watch out for examples with a "washed out" look. Trimming is also something to be wary of. Due to the "Southern Find," some fresh examples do exist but not in any type of quantity.

1909-11 T206 CY YOUNG

## Comments:

Cy Young, just by virtue of the annual pitching award, will remain in the minds of baseball fans forever. Not every fan knows exactly how many wins Young has or what teams he played for but they all know that he must have been darn good to have the award named after him. These three poses are all popular but, once again, the portrait steals the spotlight. The lush, green background is very attractive, much like the background on the Green Portrait Cobb in the same set. The classic feel and attention to detail make these cards true cardboard art. For several reasons, you just can't go wrong with a T206 Young card. Who the heck is going to break his record of 511 wins?

## 1911 T205 Gold Border Ty Cobb

### Importance:

This is the most sought after card in the tough but beautiful T205 set. Ty Cobb was widely considered the greatest player of his day and his career numbers are astounding. The only thing greater than Cobb's numbers was his desire to succeed. In some cases, his desire went too far. He would sometimes brawl with spectators and often practice so hard that his would tear his own body apart. In addition, Cobb would often sharpen his spikes before the game in order to inflict a little extra pain on those daring enough to tag him out. If that doesn't tell you about his fiery nature, I don't know what will.

In 1911, Cobb enjoyed, perhaps, his best overall season. He set career-highs in batting (.420), hits (248), doubles (47), triples (24), RBI's (127), runs (147) and slugging average (.621). Cobb led the league in each of those categories as well as stolen bases (83) but his career-high was 96 swipes. What a season!

The misconception is that Cobb was merely a singles hitter (a .367 lifetime batting average, some say .366 depending on the source) and nothing else. Cobb drove in nearly 2,000 runs in his career, had 892 steals, was a fine defensive player and had occasional "pop" in his bat. While the T206 set, along with the four Cobbs, is more popular, the T205 Cobb is perhaps more desirable due to its scarcity and condition sensitivity.

### Difficulty:

This card is as tough to find in high-grade as Cobb was tough on the field. The gold borders are extremely susceptible to chipping and wear. The slightest touch on a corner will reveal the white paper underneath the gold coating and, because of this, many examples are found re-colored. In addition, centering has always been a problem with this issue as many examples were produced with strikingly uneven borders. This Cobb is definitely one of his toughest cards and tougher than any of the four Cobb examples found in the T206 set, including the Green Portrait Cobb.

Photo Courtesy of the Brian Seigel Collection

PSA

T205 GOLD BORDER
TY COBB                    NM-MT  8

                          05012073

TIGERS

TY COBB DETROIT AM.

**1911 T205 TY COBB**

## Comments:
Advanced collectors realize how tough this Cobb really is. While the T206 Cobb examples are popular, the T205 Cobb is really not too far behind. This card has an enormous amount of desirability because it is actually superior to the T206's in difficulty and, arguably, in visual appeal. With all the modern technology used in the production of sportscards today, I will take little pieces of art like this every single time. One reason this Cobb issue was chosen over some of his other tough cards, like the E93 Caramel Cobb, because this set, while extremely tough, is more mainstream. The amount of ingenuity and talent that went into designing this card is really remarkable. Wow!

# 1911 T205 Gold Border Walter Johnson

## Importance:

This is a key card in one of the toughest issues on this list. Walter Johnson was the first true power pitcher to dominate on the mound. Johnson would reach back to harness that unmatched power and propel his arm forward like a slingshot to the plate. In fact, he threw so hard that he didn't bother to develop a curveball until the last few years of his career. After winning 417 games, including 110 shutouts, it was obvious to all that he didn't need one.

This card, like the Cobb, is a beautiful piece of artwork. The aesthetics and difficulty make this one very popular. While not as popular as the T206 Johnson examples, the demand outweighs the supply even more so with this card. With all of his incredible pitching numbers, did you know he was also one of the greatest hitting hurlers of all-time? He slugged 24 homers in his brilliant career.

In 1911, Johnson enjoyed a typical "Train-like" season. He would lead the league with 36 complete games and six shutouts en route to 25 total victories. At that point in Johnson's career, the 25-win total was his best ever but, the very next season, he would reach 33 victories and then 36 in 1913. The "Big Train" was in full force.

## Difficulty:

This Johnson card is almost never found in high-grade. The gold colored edges are prone to chipping and the slightest edge wear is easily detected. Beware of examples that have been re-colored. In addition, centering has always been a problem with this issue as many examples are found with significantly uneven borders. Keep in mind that this card, while not quite as popular as the T206 Johnson varieties, is significantly more difficult. All in all, this card is one of the toughest on the list.

PSA

T205 GOLD BORDER     #
WALTER JOHNSON     NM-MT 8

08136088

# 1911 T205 WALTER JOHNSON

## Comments:

Again, this card is not as popular as his T206 examples (like Cobb) but rarities such as this Johnson card are picking up a lot of steam in the sportscard market. As collectors become more advanced, they tend to flock towards the rarities. I can't remember the last time I saw one of these Johnson cards in a respectable grade. This is, without a doubt, one of the toughest Johnson cards on the list. As time goes on and new pitchers rise to stardom in the modern era, they are all, inevitably, compared to the likes of Walter Johnson. Cy Young may have reached an unthinkable career win total but it is Johnson who many baseball experts feel was actually the superior pitcher.

# 1911 T205 Gold Border Christy Mathewson

## Importance:

This is one of "Matty's" toughest and most desirable cards. The combination of rarity and beauty make this card a major winner. Like the Johnson card in the same set, can you remember the last time you saw a nice example of this card for sale? It has probably been a long time and it might be even longer until you find one.

Christy Mathewson was a dominant pitcher and a fan favorite. His life story is a study in triumph and tragedy. This card shows a smiling Mathewson, a smile that would fade much too quickly as he passed away in his mid-40's from accidentally inhaling poison gas during World War I. He was the first superstar pitcher of the sport, appealing to more than just the diehard baseball fan, and a gentleman as well much like Walter Johnson.

As one of the original members selected to the Hall of Fame in 1936, his cards take on extra importance. His 373 victories, including three consecutive seasons of 30 or more (1903-1905), place Mathewson in rare company. In 1911, he would lead the league in ERA (1.99) while posting a 26-13 record including 29 complete games. This card is an early, wonderful piece of artwork that is extremely popular with advanced hobbyists.

## Difficulty:

As mentioned before, these gold-bordered cards are very tough to find in high-grade due to easily chipped edges. As a result, many examples have been re-colored or touched-up along the gold border in order to conceal wear. The Mathewson example, as well as some of the other cards in the set, also suffers from poor centering. In fact, of the few high-grade examples I have seen in circulation, the majority of them seem to be off-center. This card is a tremendous condition rarity.

**1911 T205 CHRISTY MATHEWSON**

## Comments:

The great aspect of a card like this Mathewson is, while there may be a tougher or more obscure Mathewson issue out there, this one is both tough and mainstream enough to keep its popularity growing. Christy Mathewson, along with Walter Johnson, are two legends whose names will be repeatedly mentioned as all-time pitching staffs are assembled. One key to consider is that very, very few early baseball players have the kind of name recognition that Mathewson has and this is a factor that cannot be underestimated as future generations of collectors enter the market. Mathewson's name and legacy will stand the test of time.

# 1911 T205 Gold Border Cy Young

## Importance:

This is the toughest Young card on the list and one of the keys to the set. Cy Young was so good that MLB named the annual pitching award after him. That says a lot about the type of pitcher Young was. MLB doesn't even have an award named after Babe Ruth! After winning 511 games, including 15 seasons with 20 or more victories (5 seasons of 30 or more), it is easy to see why they chose Mr. Young to stand for mound excellence, starting the award in 1956.

In 1911, Young came to the end of his career. Limited to 18 starts overall (7 with Cleveland and 11 with Boston), Young would win a total of 7 between the two clubs. Young did manage to throw two shutouts and complete 12 of his final 18 games, a testament to his incredible durability even though he was well past his physical prime.

Young was elected to the Hall of Fame, one year after Christy Mathewson and Walter Johnson, in 1937. This is a great early card of the pitching icon and a tough one as well. There are not too many cards from Young's playing days and this one ranks up there with the best, even rivaling the beautiful T206 Young portrait.

## Difficulty:

When these cards are found with minimal chipping, they look outstanding. Unfortunately, these cards are almost never found with minimal chipping. The colored borders reveal white with the slightest touch so beware of re-colored examples.

In addition, centering has always been a problem with this issue with the vast majority of known examples, even the few high-end ones, having noticeably uneven borders. Overall, this is a tremendously difficult card, rarely offered in any grade.

PSA
T205 GOLD BORDER
CY YOUNG
NM-MT 8
02017094

1911 T205 CY YOUNG

## Comments:

Cy Young's name will always be with us because of the award that bears his name. Having 511 wins, a threshold that I cannot imagine any modern pitcher ever approaching, results in long-lasting power for his cards. Young may not have been the most dominant pitcher but, like Hank Aaron, consistency was his trademark. In the end, Young's consistency made him a legend. The demand for this entire issue has risen dramatically over the years and for good reason. The T206 issue is a classic, there's no denying that but, as collectors advance and gravitate towards scarcity; the T205 issue becomes more and more appealing. As a tough, key card in a great set, this Young example should enjoy high demand for years to come.

## 1912 T202 Hassan Triple Folders Ty Cobb Steal Third (w/Jennings)

### Importance:

This is quite possibly the most attractive pre-war baseball card issue ever produced and Cobb was the key. There are several different cards in the set that feature Ty Cobb and, while each of them is desirable, this one is considered the most valuable because it is the only one that features Cobb along with another Hall of Famer (Hughie Jennings). The large design and beautiful artwork on these cards make them one of the most aesthetically appealing cards ever.

The large design also made it tough to preserve the condition of these beauties. The two images, along the sides, surround an action shot in the middle of the card. Here is where we can appreciate the intensity of Cobb. That intensity made Cobb the first man ever to be elected to the Hall of Fame, ahead of Ruth, in 1936. Cobb would lead the league in hitting (.367 career average) ten times and six times in steals (892 altogether). Cobb got on base a lot, ran a lot and scored a lot. That was his job and no one did it better during his era.

### Difficulty:

The first thing that comes to mind here is that these cards were meant to be folded. With that in mind, it is hard to believe that many high-end examples could exist. "Spider" wrinkles will usually be found along the folding borders and will not harm the overall grade too much as long as it is not

Photo Courtesy of the Joe Verno Collection

severe. The fact of the matter is that this card may be one of the real "sleepers" on the list because of the inherent difficulty. With the complicated and oversized design, this card has its share of print and general wear problems. Don't overlook this issue, it is extremely tough.

## 1912 T202 HASSAN TRIPLE FOLDERS TY COBB

**Comments:**

Cobb has been surpassed by Rose in hits and Henderson in runs but neither one of them were as dominant as Cobb was, they reached those numbers by virtue of longevity. The one number hard to imagine anyone approaching is Cobb's career batting average of .367. Even the best modern hitters fail to reach that number in their best years so, for a career, you can basically forget about it. The bottom line is that these cards are beautiful and Cobb dominates the set. The artwork on these cards, which is strikingly similar to the T205's, is simply fantastic and, if you like Cobb, you have to own this card. Look for increased demand on this issue as time goes on and collectors become more familiar with the set.

## 1914/15 Cracker Jack #30 Ty Cobb

### Importance:

Arguably, this is Cobb's most attractive card and one of two major keys to the set. The image of Cobb on this 1914/1915 Cracker Card is fantastic. Cobb is pictured glaring out at the pitcher, almost taunting the pitcher to put one over the plate. With Cobb's track record at the plate, chances are that he's going to make it to first base or beyond after an extra base hit.

No, Cobb did not possess home run power. He even chastised Ruth for trying for the home run but Cobb was no "Judy" hitter. Cobb led the league in slugging average, one of the most significant statistics in all of baseball, 8 times. His relentless drive to win made Cobb a loner for most of his life. It is a tradeoff he was willing to make. When you are willing to win at all costs, you have little time to make friends. For Cobb, that goal was met at both ends.

### Difficulty:

The 1914 Cracker Jack issue is incredibly tough because the only way to acquire these cards was to pull them from candy boxes. There was no "find" and no redemption program available from the company. Caramel staining, from the candy, will usually be located on the reverse but it can also affect the front. On the other hand, there may have been a "find" of 1915 Cracker Jack examples and a redemption program (you could send away for a set and album) but don't let that fool you, these cards are still very tough.

The same problems that disturb the quality on the 1914 Cracker Jacks can affect these examples. The two problems that are found most frequently with the 1915 examples are centering (the Cobb seems to be found off-center even more frequently than the rest of the cards in the set) and border toning. In addition, try to find examples that have bold red backgrounds and try to avoid examples that have an orange appearance to them.

In addition, with both the 1914 and 1915 issues, some examples are found with glue damage on the reverse. Collectors would often place these cards in albums so this type of defect is fairly common. Keep in mind that the only two ways to tell the 1914's from the 1915's is the fact that the 1915's feature a reverse that is turned upside down and the 1914's were printed on thinner paper. This issue is one of the toughest on the list.

PSA

1915 CRACKER JACK #30
TY COBB MINT 9
01000544

Cracker Jack
BALL PLAYERS

COBB, DETROIT - AMERICANS

## 1914/15 CRACKER JACK TY COBB

## Comments:

The Cracker Jack Cobb is an awesome card in every respect. The set is popular, the card is very attractive, the card is difficult and the image of Cobb holding his lethal weapon is a special one indeed. It jumps right off the red background and exemplifies Cobb's intensity better than any of the T206 cards. To say the outlook is great for this card is an understatement; it would rank high on the list of pure importance. Forget about Cobb's personality, his numbers alone will keep him at the top of most wantlists, not just the wantlists of those diehard Detroit Tigers fans. There are several Cobb cards on this list but this one just might be his best card overall.

# 1914/15 Cracker Jack #57 Walter Johnson

## Importance:

This is a key Cracker Jack of one of the best pitchers in baseball history. The 1914 and 1915 Cracker Jack Walter Johnson cards are important on a number of levels. First, both cards are major keys in the set along with Joe Jackson, Ty Cobb, Honus Wagner and Christy Mathewson. Second, the cards are somewhat unique in that most of the star cards feature a portrait-style photo or close-up pose of the player. Both Johnson cards differ in that they feature the "Big Train" in a full windup and in a full body pose.

Finally, the importance of Johnson as a player is undeniable. This issue was produced right in the middle of his prime. After having back-to-back 30-win seasons (33 and 36), Johnson won 28 and 27 games respectively in 1914 and 1915 to lead the league. He finished with well over 400 victories in his career and, from 1910-1919, he never won fewer than 20.

## Difficulty:

The 1914 Cracker Jack issue is incredibly tough because the only way to acquire these cards was to pull them from candy boxes. There was no "find" and no redemption program available from the company. Caramel staining, from the candy, will usually be located on the reverse but it can also affect the front. On the other hand, the 1915 Cracker Jacks, while not quite as tough as the 1914 examples, are still very tough. The cards are very susceptible to border toning and, because of the way the 1914 cards were packaged (literally placed in boxes of Cracker Jacks); sharp corners are hard to find as well.

A "find" of 1915 cards surfaced a few years back and you could also send away for the 1915 cards via postal mail so nice copies do exist, just not in large quantities. In addition, with both the 1914 and 1915 issues, some examples are found with glue damage on the reverse. Collectors would often place these cards in albums so this type of defect is fairly common. Keep in mind that the only two ways to tell the 1914's from the 1915's is the fact that the 1915's feature a reverse that is turned upside down and the paper stock of the 1914's is thinner.

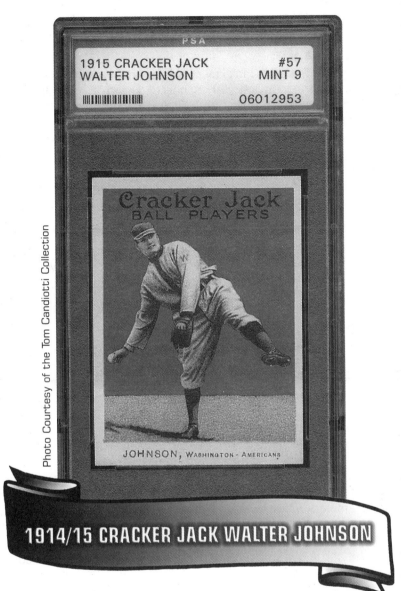

PSA

1915 CRACKER JACK #57
WALTER JOHNSON MINT 9
06012953

Cracker Jack
BALL PLAYERS

JOHNSON, WASHINGTON - AMERICANS

## 1914/15 CRACKER JACK WALTER JOHNSON

## Comments:

This card is of major importance because of the Cracker Jack appeal and the historical significance of Johnson. That's why this card made the list, pure and simple. Does this card exhibit the eye-appeal of the Mathewson or the Cobb? No. The image of Johnson is shown from a distance and, traditionally, collectors prefer the close-up shots of their heroes. That being said, when a pitcher leads the league in strikeouts 12 times, is widely considered the greatest right-handed hurler ever and the card is one of only a few major keys in one of the most popular issues of all-time, you can't deny its place. This is not Johnson's toughest or most popular card but it was clearly important enough to make this top 200 list.

# 1914/15 Cracker Jack #68 Honus Wagner

## Importance:

This is a Cracker Jack key of the legendary Pirate shortstop. All right, so Honus Wagner is better known for his famous T206 baseball card than his baseball skill. While this may be true, it is a shame because Wagner was one of the best players in baseball history. Let's take a look at his numbers. Wagner hit .327 for his career, had over 1,700 RBI's, over 700 steals, 3,418 hits and he did it all as a shortstop.

Wagner would also be crowned N.L. Batting Champion 8 times in his career, a feat still unsurpassed. When he retired, Wagner held many offensive records including career hits and RBI's but they have since been broken. With the exception of pure power numbers, no other shortstop has come close to Wagner's numbers. This card is one of the toughest cards in the set to find in high-grade making it a major key.

## Difficulty:

The 1914 Cracker Jack issue is incredibly tough because the only way to acquire these cards was to pull them from candy boxes. There was no "find" and no redemption program available from the company. Caramel staining, from the candy, will usually be located on the reverse but it can also affect the front.

On the other hand, there may have been a "find" of 1915 Cracker Jack examples and a redemption program but don't let that fool you, these cards are still very tough. The same problems that disturb the quality on the 1914 Cracker Jacks can affect these examples. The two problems that are found most frequently with the 1915 examples are centering and border toning. When the borders are clean, the image in the center really jumps off the card. When the borders are toned, it can really reduce the eye-appeal of the card.

In addition, try to find examples that have bold red backgrounds and try to avoid examples that have an orange appearance to them. The deeper the red, the more attractive the card can be. In addition, with both the 1914 and 1915 issues, some examples are found with glue damage on the reverse. Collectors would often place these cards in albums so this type of defect is fairly common. Keep in mind that the only two ways to tell the 1914's from the 1915's is the fact that the 1915's feature a reverse that is turned upside down and the 1914's were made with thinner paper.

PSA

1915 CRACKER JACK #68
HONUS WAGNER NM-MT 8

07059222

Cracker Jack
BALL PLAYERS

WAGNER, PITTSBURGH - NATIONALS

## 1914/15 CRACKER JACK HONUS WAGNER

## Comments:

This card is no match for the most famous Wagner card (the T206) but, like the Mathewson and Johnson cards in the same issue, it is certainly one of the keys to the Cracker Jack set and this example is one of the toughest cards in the set. What did I just say? Let's repeat. He's a recognizable Hall of Famer (an elite member of the inaugural group of five in 1936), the set is extremely popular and the card is one of the toughest in the set. Case closed.

# 1914/15 Cracker Jack #88 Christy Mathewson

## Importance:

This is one of the keys to the set and, arguably, the most attractive "Matty" issues in the hobby. Mathewson was the only major star to have two entirely different poses (pitching versus portrait) in the 1914 and 1915 Cracker Jacks set. While both variations are tough, the 1914 example is, without question, the tougher of the two. Much like New York Yankee slugger Lou Gehrig, Mathewson possessed the class of a gentleman, the mind of a professor and the determination of a Pit Bull.

The unfortunate similarity between the lives of Mathewson and Gehrig was the tragic end to their lives. For Gehrig, it was a rare disease that took his life at a young age. For Mathewson, it was poison gas inhalation during WWI. As a pitcher, the man compiled 300 wins by age 32! He won 20 or more games for 12 straight seasons and won over 30 games on four different occasions. Mathewson had a season-high of 37 in 1908. His screwball was his "money" pitch and it will take a lot of money to buy either card in high-grade.

## Difficulty:

Here, we have two cards with two different levels of difficulty. The key with the 1914 issue is that, unlike the 1915 Cracker Jacks, there was no "find" or redemption program that helped high-grade copies come to light. This particular card is rarely seen in any grade. All of the 1914 Cracker Jacks were packaged in candy boxes so you can imagine the frustration of trying to locate nice examples. Staining from the candy, general wear from the packaging, toning on the edges and reverse and centering problems all affect these red background beauties.

There may have been a "find" of 1915 Cracker Jack examples and a redemption program but don't let that fool you, these cards are still very tough. The same problems that disturb the quality on the 1914 Cracker Jacks can affect the 1915 examples like poor centering and toning. In addition, try to find examples that have bold red backgrounds and try to avoid examples that have an orange appearance to them. The deeper the red, the more attractive the card.

Finally, with both the 1914 and 1915 issues, some examples are found with glue damage on the reverse. Collectors would often place these cards in albums so this type of defect is fairly common. This issue is one of the toughest on the list.

Photo Courtesy of the Peter Garcia Collection

1914 CRACKER JACK
CHRISTY MATHEWSON
PSA
#88
PR-FR 1
07116515

1915 CRACKER JACK          #88
CHRISTY MATHEWSON     MINT 9
                      02024485

## 1914/15 CRACKER JACK CHRISTY MATHEWSON

## Comments:

The 1915 set may be more popular because it is actually feasible to complete a set, however, I don't think the easier 1915's affect the 1914 star cards, like this Mathewson, much. Maybe the 1915 Cracker Jack commons and semi-stars will outperform the 1914's in the long run, but look for the tougher 1914 star cards to pick up major steam in the near future. The 1915 Cracker Jack Mathewson card really captures the persona of the athlete. Mathewson is shown poised and well groomed; he was considered the gentleman of the game. The card, while not as tough as the 1914 issue, has greater visual appeal, creating tremendous demand for the card.

## 1914/15 Cracker Jack #103 Shoeless Joe Jackson

### Importance:

If you consider the overall popularity of the set and the incredible story behind the man, this card becomes extremely important. The 1919 Black Sox scandal will forever be a scar on the game but the role that Jackson played is still up for debate. Jackson supposedly accepted $5,000 to "throw" the World Series, however, Jackson hit .375, drove in 6 runs and played flawless defense. What do you think? Because of this, Jackson was banned from baseball and Hall of Fame consideration.

Perhaps Jackson's greatest compliment would come from another baseball legend, Babe Ruth. Ruth often said that he tried to model his swing after Jackson's because he felt that "Shoeless" had the best swing he ever saw. It's too bad baseball fans were unable to see that swing over the course of an entire career. Despite the scandal, Jackson's card is still very popular and the key to both the 1914 and 1915 sets.

### Difficulty:

The 1914 Cracker Jack issue is incredibly tough because the only way to acquire these cards was to pull them from candy boxes. There was no "find" and no redemption program available from the company. Caramel staining, from the candy, will usually be located on the reverse but it can also affect the front. On the other hand, the 1915 Cracker Jacks, while not quite as tough as the 1914 examples, are still very tough. The cards are very susceptible to border toning and, because of the way the 1914 cards were packaged (literally placed in boxes of Cracker Jacks); sharp corners are hard to find as well.

A "find" of these cards surfaced a few years back and you could also send away for the cards via postal mail so nice copies do exist just not in large quantities. The Jackson, like the Cobb, is more likely to be found off-center (side to side) than not. In addition, with both the 1914 and 1915 issues, some examples are found with glue damage on the reverse. Collectors would often place these cards in albums so this type of defect is fairly common. Keep in mind that the only two ways to tell the 1914's from the 1915's is the fact that the 1915's feature a reverse that is turned upside down and the 1914's were printed on thinner paper stock.

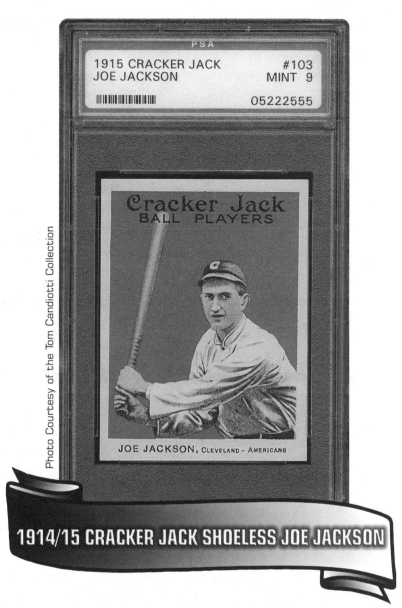

PSA

1915 CRACKER JACK     #103
JOE JACKSON     MINT 9

05222555

Cracker Jack
BALL PLAYERS

JOE JACKSON, CLEVELAND - AMERICANS

## 1914/15 CRACKER JACK SHOELESS JOE JACKSON

## Comments:

This card will always remain popular due to the compelling story that accompanies Jackson and the great artwork in the set. These cards are considered by many to be amongst the most attractive cards ever designed. The red background and fine image of Jackson make for a great combination. Is "Shoeless" holding his legendary "Black Betsy" bat? That bat eventually sold at auction for well over $500,000 in 2001. Even in strict mint condition, this card would only cost you a fraction of that price. No matter what happens to Jackson's baseball status in the future, this card is a key. Who needs the Hall anyway?

# 1915 (M101-5) Sporting News #86 Joe Jackson

## Importance:

This is one of the few mainstream cards to feature "Shoeless" Joe and the second most valuable card in the set. After all, it does hold Babe Ruth's official rookie card and a great card of Jim Thorpe. This set, while not entirely mainstream, is certainly more appealing to the average collector because of the other keys in the set and the semi-familiarity with the issue.

Despite being banned from the game, collectors are drawn to the incredible story of "Shoeless" Joe Jackson. He is treated, much like Pete Rose, as a Hall of Famer anyway. Before his banishment, Jackson stole over 200 bases and made his mark as a well-rounded hitter with a .356 batting average and a .517 slugging average.

His swing was even copied by another famous hitter named Babe Ruth. I can't think of a better compliment than to have the greatest player in baseball history copy your swing. The Sporting News issue has never been extremely popular but the set has a few major keys, including this card.

Image Courtesy of A.K. Miller

## Difficulty:

The card is difficult for a few reasons. First, the Sporting News cards are tough to locate in any grade let alone high-grade. Second, the card is very susceptible to black print spots in the face of the card. Third, these cards are traditionally found with horrible centering (usually 70/30 or worse). Finally, Jackson was one of the stars of the set (at the time) so it was probably handled more often than most other cards. All in all, this is a very tough card.

Photo Courtesy of the Tom Candiotti Collection

**1915 (M101-5) SPORTING NEWS JOE JACKSON**

## Comments:

Jackson does have more popular and more visually attractive cards but this one is no slouch. Perhaps more obscure than the others, this card still has a lot going for it. It's scarcer than other Jackson cards on the list and the set, while somewhat obscure, is gaining in popularity. This card is seldom offered in high-grade so the potential for increased demand is here. I chose this Jackson over his E-90-1 "rookie" card because of the extreme rarity and obscurity of that particular issue. Just give this one some time. When it comes to Jackson, you don't have many choices.

# 1915 (M101-5) Sporting News #151 Babe Ruth

## Importance:

This is the rookie card of the greatest player in baseball history. That's a pretty good reason to have this card on the list, don't you think? With so many great things going for it, you have to wonder why it hasn't received more attention. A young Ruth is pictured firing the ball as a pitcher for the Boston Red Sox.

As a pitcher, Ruth's numbers were outstanding. Ruth compiled a 94-46 record (.671 winning percentage) with 107 complete games, 17 shutouts and a career ERA of 2.28. In the World Series, his pitching record is even more impressive. Ruth went 3-0 with an ERA under 1.00. Are you kidding me?

Image Courtesy of A.K. Miller

After three full seasons on the hill (1915-1917), the Red Sox began to put Ruth in the outfield part-time in 1918. The rest is history. When Boston traded the great slugger, little did they know that the trade would lead to a World Series Championship drought that would last till this day. As the only mainstream issue to feature Ruth as a member of the Red Sox, this card is extremely important.

## Difficulty:

The card is difficult for a few reasons. First, the Sporting News cards are tough to locate in any grade let alone high-grade. Second, the card is very susceptible to black print spots on the face of the card. Third, these cards are traditionally found with horrible centering (usually 70/30 or worse). Finally, Ruth wasn't the "Sultan of Swat" at the time the card was made so most people didn't care for this card even when they did find it. All in all, this is a very tough card.

PSA
1915 M101-5 SPORTING NEWS #151
BABE RUTH
P.-BOSTON RED SOX NM-MT 8
02061501

BABE RUTH
P.—Boston Red Sox
151

## 1915 (M101-5) SPORTING NEWS BABE RUTH

## Comments:

The future for this card, in my opinion, looks extremely bright. Rarity and population are becoming more and more significant as the hobby evolves and this card should fall right into the new collector focus. The only thing stopping this card from having a monumental price tag is that it resides in a set that is so tough that it is only mildly popular. The lack of color in the design may also be a reason that this card is somewhat overlooked, at least when taken in context. Sometimes, difficulty can be a curse but "The Curse" is what this card symbolizes. It's Babe Ruth's rookie card! What else does one need to say?

# 1915 (M101-5) Sporting News #176 Jim Thorpe

## Importance:

This is the only mainstream card to feature Jim Thorpe as a baseball player. As one of the greatest all-around athletes of the 20th Century, Thorpe has been elevated to legendary status and, here, he is pictured as a baseball player. Do any of you remember what Michael Jordan looked like when he tried to play baseball? Now, many people consider Jordan to be amongst the greatest athletes of the modern generation, which makes Thorpe's ability to excel in so many different sports a wonder.

While Thorpe was inducted into the NFL Hall of Fame in 1963, his baseball career was not quite as memorable. As a baseball player, Thorpe would only hit .252 in his major league career, which spanned 289 games (from 1913-1919) but that is not important in the overall scheme of things. It was Thorpe who paved the way for two-sport stars like Bo Jackson, Brian Jordan and Deion Sanders. This card is of the utmost significance due to the importance of Thorpe's contributions.

## Difficulty:

While not quite as popular as Thorpe's 1933 Goudey Sport King, this card is certainly tougher. The centering and print problems are the common obstacles associated with the issue. Most examples, if you are lucky enough to find one, are centered in the neighborhood of 70/30. The contrast between the black and white colors on the card will only prove to make the centering look even worse than it technically is when measured. Centered copies do sell for a premium. In addition, the print defects are usually found in the light-colored borders (usually black print specks). In conclusion, the main difficulty here is finding the card at all as all 1915 M101-5 Sporting News cards are scarce. It may not be Thorpe's best looking card in terms of visual appeal, but it certainly is his toughest on the list.

PSA

1915 M101-5 SPORTING NEWS #176
JIM THORPE                    NM-MT 8
BLANK BACK
07002143

JIM THORPE
R. F.—New York Giants
176

Photo Courtesy of the Tom Candiotti Collection

## 1915 (M101-5) SPORTING NEWS JIM THORPE

## Comments:

The Sporting News set is not the most popular set in the world but Thorpe, as perhaps the 20th Century's greatest pure athlete, should have a lot of staying power for years to come. This issue, a brutally tough one, is the only mainstream example that captures Thorpe as a baseball player and that is important. Full of stars and Hall of Famers, this set has a great chance of gaining increased acceptance as the hobby matures. Despite a very small find of these cards a few years back, there is a very limited amount of Thorpe examples in circulation. For these reasons, this card should enjoy solid demand long into the future.

## 1932 US Caramel #11 Rogers Hornsby

### Importance:

This is the toughest and earliest issue to feature the greatest right-handed hitter of his era and, maybe, ever. Rogers Hornsby was able to hit for average and power during a time when few baseballs cleared the outfield walls. He had a .358 career batting average including a season in which he hit an amazing .424 (still a NL record today). In fact, Hornsby would hit .400 or better three times in his career to go along with 7 batting titles (6 or them consecutively from 1920-1925).

Hornsby also clubbed 301 homers in his career and led the league twice in that department. His ability to hit for power and average led to two Triple Crown Awards and two MVP's. Like Ty Cobb and Cap Anson, Hornsby was a fiery, disliked figure from his day but his accomplishments are legendary. Hornsby was elected to the Hall of Fame in 1942.

### Difficulty:

As mentioned above, this set is ridiculously tough. If it were not for a "find" of 1932 U.S. Caramels a few years back, there probably wouldn't be any high-grade copies in existence. Amazingly, no Hornsby cards materialized from that famous "find." At the time of this writing, only a handful of high-grade copies were known.

Major toning problems, inconsistent print quality and general wear issues make any of these U.S. Caramels a virtual impossibility in high-grade. Many of these examples are seen with very bland color and, due to the packaging process, the cards never seem to be found sharp. They are believed to be scarce partly due to the fact that the cards themselves could be redeemed for baseball equipment. I am sure the cards are worth a lot more than the balls or gloves are today but who knew? The Hornsby card is seen far less frequently than other major stars in the set like Foxx or Cobb.

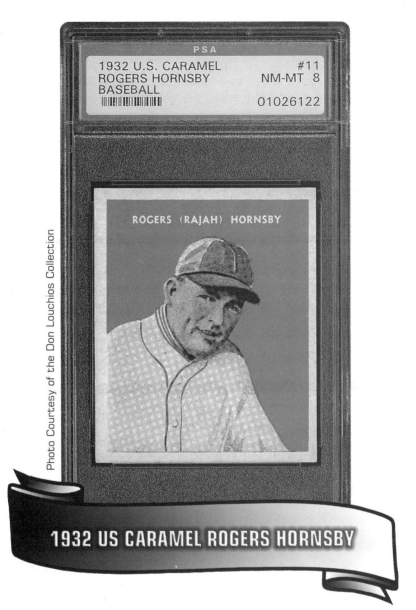

PSA
1932 U.S. CARAMEL     #11
ROGERS HORNSBY     NM-MT 8
BASEBALL
01026122

ROGERS (RAJAH) HORNSBY

## 1932 US CARAMEL ROGERS HORNSBY

## Comments:

I have to admit, the more I read about this guy, the more I am intrigued and realize how underrated he is. Just look at his numbers! This guy was no "slap" hitter. Hornsby hit with power and his ability to hit for average is, to this day, legendary. His fierce competitive nature made him a bit of an outcast but so was Cobb. This set, as a whole, has really become a collector favorite because of the incredible difficulty in finding quality examples. It's not as attractive as his Goudey example but it is tougher. Like Joe Jackson, you don't have much of a choice with Hornsby; this is one of only a few available cards that feature this great hitter.

## 1932 US Caramel #14 Ty Cobb

### Importance:

This is a key card in one of the toughest issues on the market. Even though this card was made after his playing days, the card is still very important. The set is tremendous, featuring top athletes from different sports. There are boxers and golfers but the majority of the set is devoted to baseball players. The set featured many legends such as Lou Gehrig and Babe Ruth but the difficulty is what separates this set from the rest. The visual appeal and selection of athletes helps make this Cobb example a very important card.

In 1936, when the Hall of Fame first opened its doors, Cobb received the highest percentage of votes, even more than the legendary Babe Ruth. The only thing Cobb couldn't do in his career, although I think it might be more appropriate to say didn't do, was hit the long ball. Cobb excelled in almost every facet of the game and he made that the focus of his life.

### Difficulty:

As mentioned above, this set is ridiculously tough. If it were not for a "find" of 1932 U.S. Caramels a few years back, there probably wouldn't be any high-grade copies in existence. Major toning problems, inconsistent print quality and general wear issues make any of these U.S. Caramels a virtual impossibility in high-grade. Many of these examples are seen with very bland color and, due to the packaging process, the cards never seem to be found sharp.

They are believed to be scarce partly due to the fact that the cards themselves could be redeemed for baseball equipment. I am sure the cards are worth a lot more than the balls or gloves are today but who knew? The Cobb card, as a part of this set, is one of the tougher cards on the list.

PSA
1932 U.S. CARAMEL #14
TY COBB MINT 9
BASEBALL
02017105

TYRUS (TY) COBB

1932 US CARAMEL TY COBB

## Comments:

As the hobby matures, there is an increased focus on rarity. It becomes a more significant factor in demand as collectors search for the challenging issues. The Cobb example is part of a very interesting set and is extremely difficult. As mentioned with regards to other issues, rarity can sometimes be a problem if an issue is too rare. Some collectors will just give up on a set or card if they think they have no chance at acquiring it. In this case, I think the attractiveness of the issue will outweigh the collector frustration and the frustration will turn into demand.

## 1932 US Caramel #26 Lou Gehrig

### Importance:

As the first mainstream card of Lou Gehrig, this card is of extreme importance. While Lou Gehrig does not technically have a rookie card, this is the first key Gehrig card. While not as popular as his 1934 Goudey examples, this card does have age and difficulty on its side. While Babe Ruth often overshadowed Gehrig, Gehrig's numbers are astounding. In addition to his "Iron Horse" streak of 2,130 straight games, Gehrig was a feared slugger and run producer.

At the time of his death, Gehrig's 493 career homers placed him 3rd behind only Jimmie Foxx and Babe Ruth. He also finished with 1,995 RBI's, still 3rd behind Hank Aaron and Ruth at the time of publishing. You often hear baseball experts talk about "what could have been" in regards to Ted Williams, but what about Gehrig? If Gehrig did not fall ill to such a devastating disease, what would his numbers look like? He was one of the very best to ever play the game.

Photo Courtesy of National Baseball Hall of Fame Library, Cooperstoown, NY

### Difficulty:

These 1932 U.S. Caramels can give collectors a headache! If you want a high-grade copy, you better have a lot of patience and a lot of money because the demand certainly outweighs the supply on these condition rarities.

Toning and poor print quality make these cards difficult but the Gehrig is also found off-center most of the time. They are believed to be scarce partly due to the fact that the cards themselves could be redeemed for baseball equipment. This is truly one of Gehrig's toughest cards, far tougher than his more popular Goudey examples.

Photo Courtesy of the Don Louchios Collection

PSA

1932 U.S. CARAMEL      #26
LOU GEHRIG
BASEBALL      NM-MT 8

07006097

HENRY (LOU) GEHRIG

1932 US CARAMEL LOU GEHRIG

## Comments:

This card reminds me a lot of the 1939 Play Ball Ted Williams card. The 1939 Play Ball Williams was never as popular as his 1941 Play Ball card because it wasn't as visually appealing (the 1939 card is black and white while the 1941 was produced in color). Slowly but surely collectors realized that, despite the difference in eye-appeal, the 1939 issue was the first Williams card and demand picked up. The 1932 U.S. Caramel Gehrig has so many things going for it that it should enjoy more demand as time goes on.

# 1932 US Caramel #32 Babe Ruth

## Importance:

This is the last card and the key to an extremely tough set. After a long drought in the mainstream card market, Babe Ruth came back to us in the form of the 1932 U.S. Caramel card. Ruth had been featured in several different candy and tobacco issues over the years but most of them are considered oddball cards today. This card was produced during an era when Ruth was still a very productive player, some years launching home runs at a faster rate than some entire teams did.

This would also be the year that Ruth would hit the famous "called shot" against the Chicago Cubs in the World Series. Some dispute the authenticity of the moment, claiming that Ruth never pointed at the bleachers in center but that he was merely waving his hands at the Chicago dugout as he let two strikes go by. The Chicago players were giving Ruth a very hard time, ragging him relentlessly. Whether Ruth called his shot or not, he sure shut those guys up on the third pitch. A tape measure blast into the centerfield bleachers will do that from time to time. This is one of only a few different mainstream issues available on Ruth. Any card of Ruth is important and this one is no exception.

## Difficulty:

I remember attending shows as a youngster and looking for this card, not to buy, but just to look at it. Show after show went by and I never saw one up close. When I finally did get a chance to see one, it looked like my dog picked his teeth with it! This card is very, very tough. They are believed to be scarce partly due to the fact that the cards themselves could be redeemed for baseball equipment.

With commonly seen border toning, poor centering and horrible eye-appeal (due to inconsistent print quality), this card is a treasure in high-grade. The difference between the visual appeal of a high-grade example and a standard example is so vast that you would think they are different cards entirely.

Photo Courtesy of the John Branca Collection

PSA

| 1932 U.S. CARAMEL | #32 |
| BABE RUTH | NM-MT 8 |
| BASEBALL | |
| | 07029624 |

GEORGE (BABE) RUTH

**1932 US CARAMEL BABE RUTH**

## Comments:

When you combine the rarity of the card and the popularity of Ruth, I don't see how this card could ever lose demand. There just are not enough of these examples in existence to satisfy the growing numbers of collectors. This card is actually much, much tougher than any of the four Goudey Ruths, including the Yellow #53 example, and it was produced a year earlier. As collectors advance and move on to bigger and better collectibles, they tend to focus on the true legends of the game. Ruth has set the standard that all other athletes are judged by.

## 1933 Delong #7 Lou Gehrig

### Importance:

As one of only a few available mainstream cards featuring Gehrig, this card is immediately placed into extremely important status. The Delong Gehrig card, when it comes to pure rarity, is right there with the 1932 U.S. Caramel card. In fact, many experts feel that this card is even tougher than the 1932 U.S. Caramel card. The unique and attractive design of the Delong set makes this Gehrig card very desirable. Gehrig's powerful swing graces the front of the card, a swing that put Gehrig into the record books.

In 1933, Gehrig would have a typical Gehrig-like year. He would hit .334 with 32 homers, drive in 139 runs and score a league leading 138 runs. To put Gehrig's ability to drive in runs in perspective, his 1933 total of 139 was his 9th best total in his career. For most Hall of Famers, 139 RBI's would be a career-high. For Gehrig, it was below his average.

The only thing about Gehrig that was more powerful than his swing was his appeal to the average fan. Gehrig was never boastful or arrogant; he just went about his business like most other hard-working Americans. His big heart and gentle demeanor just made it that much tougher to watch Gehrig retire as a result of a rare, terminal illness that now bears his name.

### Difficulty:

This card might be the toughest Gehrig issue in the hobby. These Delongs have very narrow borders so, if the card is centered just a tad one way or the other, the centering appears to be much worse than it actually is. Much like the 1933 Goudey cards, the name box at the base will sometimes be offline with the rest of the image, causing many examples to be considered technically off-center.

In addition, the borders always seem to be found with toning and appear to have a dirty appearance. Mild toning is usually acceptable with most vintage issues as long as the toning is not found in patches or severe, hindering the overall eye-appeal of the card. On pure difficulty, this card ranks up there with the best of them, far tougher to find than the Goudey issue. Forget about high-grade examples, when was the last time you saw one of these in any grade?

Photo Courtesy of the Tom Candiotti Collection

PSA

1933 DeLONG                    #7
LOU GEHRIG            NM-MT 8

02112755

LOU GEHRIG
NEW YORK YANKEES

1933 DELONG LOU GEHRIG

## Comments:

Who will ever forget July 4, 1939, when a tearful Gehrig uttered those famous words, "Today, I consider myself the luckiest man of the face of the earth." With dignity and grace, Lou showed all his fans that even the "Iron Horse" was human. Forget about his numbers, if there were a Hall of Fame based on class, Gehrig would be first in line. This card, considering its combination of difficulty and beauty, seems to have great potential for future demand and the hobbyist who can make claim to a high-grade example might be the luckiest collector on the face of the earth.

# 1933 Goudey Jimmy Foxx (#'s 29 and 154)

## Importance:

As the first two Goudey examples featuring "The Beast," these cards instantly become important. During the 1920's and early 1930's, most of the headlines went to those two sluggers in New York (Ruth and Gehrig). There was a right-handed power hitter that could hit the ball as far as Ruth and who possessed the genial nature of Gehrig; his name was Jimmie Foxx.

In 1933, Foxx proved his worth. After hitting .356 with 48 homers and 163 RBI's, Foxx earned the Triple Crown and was awarded MVP in the American League. Interestingly enough, those numbers were actually inferior to his 1932 MVP output of .364, 58 homers and 169 RBI's. Now do you think Foxx could hit? Both of these cards are considered high on the list of keys for the 1933 Goudey collector.

## Difficulty:

While the #29 Foxx ex-ample is considered the tougher of the two due to its inclusion in the rare low number series, both cards represent a challenge. Each card suffers from "bleeding" on the reverse which can be a real eye-sore. When the sheets of cards were laid on top of each other, the moist ink would sometimes stick to the reverse of the cards above. One major condi-tion obstacle would be the edges and borders that are very susceptible to toning and discoloration.

Image Courtesy of A.K. Miller

Another problem with Goudeys is that these cards were often discarded during the paper drives of World War II, so finding them in any condition is tough in itself. On difficulty alone, each card would rank high on the list.

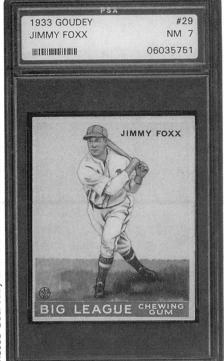

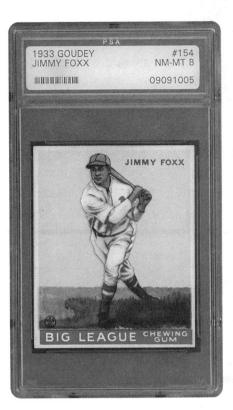

1933 GOUDEY JIMMY FOXX

## Comments:

Jimmie Foxx has a very loyal following in the hobby. During his playing days, he was overshadowed but he seems to be getting more and more popular as time goes on. Each of these Foxx cards which are identical in appearance are considered keys to one of the most popular sets in existence. Many collectors actually feel that this card is far more visually attractive than the Gehrig cards in the same set and that is starting to reflect in the price as both Foxx cards have slowly been closing the price gap in recent years. The 1933 Delong or 1932 U.S. Caramel Foxx cards may be tougher, but the 1933 Goudey Foxx cards are definitely more popular.

## 1933 Goudey Babe Ruth (#'s 53, 144, 149 and 181)

### Importance:

The Sultan of Swat is the dominating force behind the 1933 Goudey set. Ruth remains the symbol of baseball, as he was the first international superstar to put on a uniform. He wasn't just the most recognizable face in the game; he was the most recognizable face on the planet! The four cards that feature Ruth represent the most desirable subset in the hobby. All four cards are different with the #53 and #149 examples having the closest resemblance.

Each card is known, not only by card number, but also by name. The #53 card (Yellow Ruth), #144 card (Full Body Pose Ruth), #149 card (Red Ruth) and the #181 card (Green Ruth) are all keys to the 1933 Goudey set. While Ruth was featured in earlier issues, these Goudeys are considered by many to be his most important cards.

### Difficulty:

Each of the four cards are difficult but the #53 Ruth is clearly the toughest, followed by the #149 card, then the #144 card and finally the #181 Ruth. The #149 Ruth is not far behind the #53. The resemblance between both cards goes beyond the appearance; they are both very comparable when it comes to rarity and condition obstacles. Both have similar centering and print problems. The #144 Ruth, while it is a double printed card and more common than the #181 Ruth, is tougher to find in high-grade than the #181 card.

There are two versions of the #144 card. One has a focused image and one is slightly out of focus with the unfocused version being much more common. For each card, look for centering problems, toning on the light colored borders and edges, and "bleeding" on the back. When the sheets of cards were laid on top of each other, the moist ink would sometimes stick to the reverse of the cards above. It can make for a real eyesore if the "bleeding" is significant. Another problem with Goudeys is that these cards were often discarded during the paper drives of World War II, so finding them in any condition is tough in itself.

## 1933 GOUDEY BABE RUTH

## Comments:

All four cards are difficult, colorful, popular and feature the biggest name in baseball history. Even though the listed cards are not ranked in order, if they were, these Goudey Ruths would rank high on the list. Any of the four Ruth cards would be considered the centerpiece of a collection. Forget about Ruth's astonishing numbers, his legacy will remain strong as records are broken decades from now. It is hard to imagine anyone dominating a sport the way Ruth did during the 1920's and that domination is reflected quite well in this issue. Only one man was given four cards, the "Sultan of Swat." I just can't say enough about this famous quartet.

## 1933 Goudey Lou Gehrig (#'s 92 and 160)

### Importance:

These are the first two Goudey examples that feature the "Iron Horse" and both cards rank high on the list of keys to the 1933 Goudey set. These two 1933 Goudey cards represent the beginning of Gehrig's reign in New York. During the 1920's and early 1930's, it was Ruth who would dominate the New York headlines but Gehrig was now on the verge of taking over the spotlight after years of unrivaled run production.

From his first full season (1927) to 1932, Gehrig finished with RBI totals of 175, 142, 126, 174, 184 and 151. Not even the Babe himself could match Gehrig in that category during the 6-year span. Granted, Ruth was on base many times for Gehrig but Ruth also cleared the bases many times, leaving poor Lou with no one to drive in. From one dynamic duo to another, these two Goudey Gehrigs mark a significant point, not only in Lou's career, but also in sportscard history.

### Difficulty:

The #160 Gehrig example is considered the tougher of the two but, like the two Foxx cards from the same set, both pose a real challenge. There seems to be two big condition obstacles here. The first one is toning and discoloration to the edges and borders.

The second obstacle would be a major lack of eye-appeal. For some reason, many of these 1933 Goudey Gehrig cards are found with a very bland look on the front, they just really lack eye-appealing color and focus. Another problem with Goudeys is that these cards were

Photo Courtesy of National Baseball Hall of Fame Library, Cooperstoown, NY

often discarded during the paper drives of World War II, so finding them in any condition is tough in itself.

Finally, "bleeding" might be an issue on the reverse. When the sheets of cards were laid on top of each other, the moist ink would sometimes stick to the reverse of the cards above.

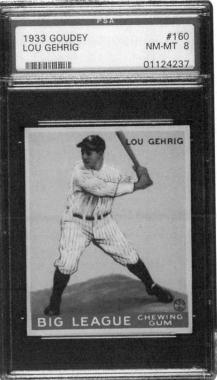

## Comments:

For some reason, these two virtually identical Gehrig cards are continually overlooked in comparison to other Gehrig cards. While these examples do not have the eye-appeal of the 1934 Goudeys or difficulty of the 1933 Delong Gehrig cards, both seem to be underrated at this point. There does seem to be some potential for increased demand with both of these cards, especially the tough #160 Gehrig, which seems grossly overlooked at this point. Remember that there are not many cards available from Gehrig's playing days so the options are limited.

## 1933 Goudey #106 Napoleon Lajoie

### Importance:

One of the hobby's ultimate rarities and most recognizable images, the 1933 Goudey Napoleon Lajoie is a symbol of sportscard collecting. Like the T206 Wagner, the wonderful aspect to this rare card is that it features a Hall of Famer (elected in 1937), further enhancing the card's intrigue. Lajoie was truly one of baseball's elite second baseman.

This 3-time batting champion (1901, 1903 and 1904) and Triple Crown winner (1901) was also a tremendous fielder. In fact, he was considered the best defensive second baseman of his era. He set a 20th century record by batting .422 in 1901 (later to be broken by Rogers Hornsby in 1924 with a .424 mark). With 3,244 hits, he is part of the elite 3,000 Hit Club and his .338 career average ranks high on the all-time list. This is not just Lajoie's best card; it is also considered one of the most valuable cards in the hobby.

### Difficulty:

The toughest aspect of this card is that it is truly scarce in all grades. Not included in the original set, this Lajoie was actually issued in 1934. Collectors could obtain the card through the mail if they were interested in completing their 1933 set but very few took the time to actually do it. The missing Lajoie created a void. As far as condition obstacles are concerned, the Lajoie is subject to the potential problems associated with most Goudeys such as very poor centering and toning, however, the scarcity of the card is what drives the demand.

One interesting aspect to this card is that, considering how elusive this card is, there are a fair amount of high-grade examples. As a result of the mail offer, the Lajoie cards were never placed in packs and the cards usually found a home with hardcore collectors who wanted to complete their set. These collectors were, perhaps, the ones most likely to handle this rarity with care. At the same time, many of these mailed examples were affixed with a paper clip, which left impressions on the surface. This leads many to believe that some Lajoie's were obtained at the factory. Regardless, finding this card at all is a challenge in itself and the difficulty is what fuels the legend.

PSA

1933 GOUDEY #106
NAPOLEON LAJOIE MINT 9
02024708

NAPOLEON (LARRY) LAJOIE

Photo Courtesy of the Tom Candiotti Collection

## 1933 GOUDEY NAPOLEON LAJOIE

## Comments:

When rarities feature a non-star or common player, the card receives limited attention because it loses widespread appeal. That is what makes this card, like the T206 Wagner, so appealing. There's more to the story than mere rarity. The fact that he is a notable Hall of Famer helps create a bigger potential market for the card. In addition, the card itself has become a legend in its own right, a symbol that many collectors are familiar with. They may not know Lajoie's career average, they may not even know who Lajoie is but, I assure you, most collectors recognize the classic image.

# 1933 Goudey Mel Ott (#'s 127 and 207)

## Importance:

This is the first mainstream card of 500 Home Run Club member Mel Ott. While Ott did not fit the description of the prototypical power hitter, he was a small man in size; Ott was a fierce competitor. That desire to compete is found within the image on each of his 1933 Goudey offerings. Both cards feature the mean glare of this unorthodox slugger. With a unique batting stance and uncanny ability to pull the ball, Ott would pound opposing pitchers at his home park, which was The Polo Grounds.

Ott did not possess the marquee value that a Foxx or Ruth had during their careers. When fans think of home run hitters, they think of massive bruisers who can launch the ball into the far reaches of the bleachers. That wasn't Ott. He was able to pile up home runs because of his consistency and hitting technique, much like Hank Aaron did throughout the course of his career.

At the time of his retirement, Ott was the all-time National League leader in RBI's, runs scored and walks. His records were all eventually broken but Ott remains high on the list of career leaders and his 511 homers place him in the most popular club in all of sports. Both Ott cards are keys to the very popular set filled with star power. Ott was inducted into the Hall of Fame in 1951.

## Difficulty:

While the red background, high-number Ott is considered to be the tougher of the two, each card is difficult to find in high-grade. Narrow borders and an inconsistent cutting process help cause these beautiful cards to be off-center most of the time and the color quality varies quite a bit. Also, look for "bleeding" on the reverse as well as toning or discoloration of the edges. When the sheets of cards were laid on top of each other, the moist ink would sometimes stick to the reverse of the cards above causing the bleed. Another problem with Goudeys is that these cards were often discarded during the paper drives of World War II, so finding them in any condition is tough in itself.

Any 1933 Goudey presents a challenge and these Ott examples are no exception.

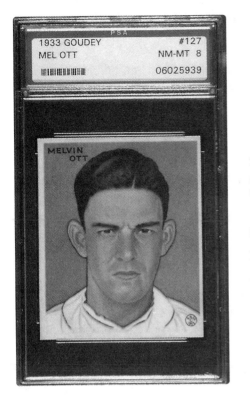

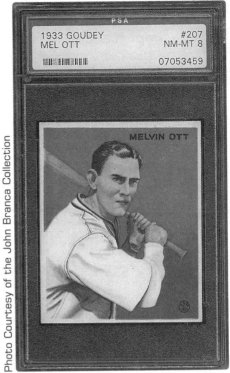

1933 GOUDEY MEL OTT

## Comments:

I will admit that these cards were a borderline choice for this list but, as a member of the most popular club in baseball (500 home runs) and as keys to, quite possibly, the most popular set in the hobby, these two Ott cards should enjoy solid demand in the coming years. In the end, it doesn't really matter to the record books how far you hit them, it only matters how many cleared the wall. In that respect, Ott needed to be recognized but it was the issue that put this card over the top. Keep a close eye on the #207 Ott (red background, w/bat pose). In recent months, that card has started to sell at multiple times the #127 Ott price due to its scarcity and visual appeal.

# 1933 Goudey #230 and #234 Carl Hubbell

## Importance:

These are two key cards of baseball's first left-handed screwball specialist. Carl Hubbell's screwball was tough to hit. How tough? In 1934, during the All-Star Game, Hubbell struck out Babe Ruth, Lou Gehrig, Jimmie Foxx, Al Simmons and Joe Cronin consecutively. Hubbell would also go on to win 253 games, including five straight 20-win seasons from 1933-1937. He was also a two-time league MVP in 1933 (23-12 with a 1.66 ERA) and 1936 (26-6 with a 2.31 ERA). Hubbell's screwball would eventually do him in. He underwent surgery to repair his pitching elbow but was never the same. He was elected to the Hall of Fame in 1947.

## Difficulty:

The Hubbell pitching pose, #230, is seen less frequently than the portrait-style Hubbell (#234). The Goudeys have always been a difficult issue for a multitude of reasons. Toning along the edges and the reverse might be the most common condition obstacle. Those white borders just seem like a magnet for dirt and "age." Another problem with Goudeys is that these cards were often discarded during the paper drives of World War II, so finding them in any condition is tough in itself.

Finally, the issue of color is a significant one. The #234 card has a solid red background and, often, the card is seen with a faded or orange-like tint. If you desire the best, try to locate one with a bold red backdrop instead of the washed out orange. The #230 card has a very light-colored background, which makes it more susceptible to dark print defects. Both Hubbell cards are seldom seen in NM-MT condition. In fact, they are seen less frequently than other star cards like that of Ruth or Ott.

Finally, keep an eye out for "bleeding" on the reverse. When the sheets of cards were laid on top of each other, the moist ink would sometimes stick to the reverse of the cards above.

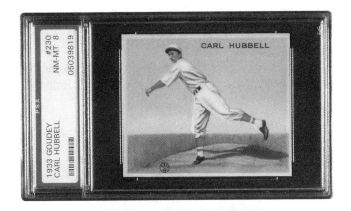

## 1933 GOUDEY CARL HUBBELL

## Comments:

Both cards exhibit those classic images that many collectors are familiar with, especially the portrait of Hubbell. The demand for this particular card is almost purely driven by that great image. Hubbell was a great pitcher, there's no question about it, but that is not why these cards made the list. The classic performance in that All-Star game in 1934 instantly made Hubbell a legend, he will always be remembered for that and the 1933 Goudey set is so popular that this card should enjoy great demand for a long time. Consider this; the overall set is considered one of the most visually appealing sets ever. For these cards to standout from the set, they have to be very special.

## 1933 Goudey Sport Kings #1 Ty Cobb

### Importance:

This is the first card and a key to one of the most popular sets in the hobby. Now, even though this particular card was produced after Cobb's playing days, the card remains very popular. This set provides a variety of stars and eye-appeal like no other set of its day with great athletes from boxers to swimmers. The bright yellow background provides the perfect backdrop for the intense image of Cobb.

As one of only three baseball players included in the set, including Carl Hubbell and Babe Ruth, it shows how dominant Cobb must have been. Many collectors know Cobb for his hitting, a .367 lifetime average and 4,189 career hits, but did you know that Cobb led the league in stolen bases 6 times? As the number one card in the set, the card is a condition rarity.

### Difficulty:

The 1933 Goudey Sport King Cobb, in addition to being the first card in the set and subject to handling abuse, has two major condition obstacles including "bleeding" and toning of the borders and reverse. Something else to look out for is color quality. When this card is found with deep, bold

Image Courtesy of A.K. Miller

color, the card has tremendous eye-appeal. The yellow background becomes a great asset to the card; otherwise, it has a dull appearance and a truly "washed out" look. Finally, as with most Goudey cards, the extremely narrow borders leave little room for error in terms of centering and centering has become increasingly important to collectors.

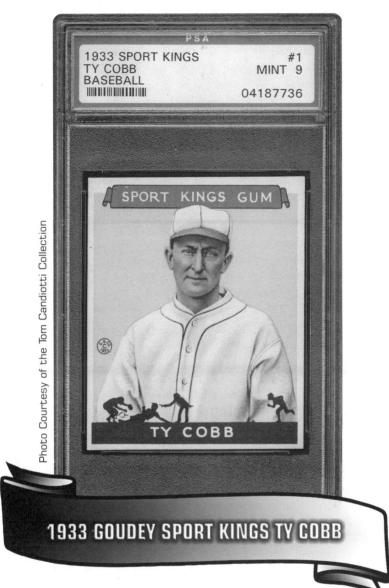

PSA
1933 SPORT KINGS     #1
TY COBB
BASEBALL     MINT 9
04187736

SPORT KINGS GUM

TY COBB

Photo Courtesy of the Tom Candiotti Collection

## 1933 GOUDEY SPORT KINGS TY COBB

**Comments:**

In general, there is a stigma when it comes to cards manufactured after an athlete's playing days, however, that doesn't seem to affect this card or some other great cards like the 1948 Leaf Babe Ruth. Once again, we are reminded that Cobb was actually viewed by many as the premier baseball player during that time period. Cobb was selected as the number one card, not Ruth. Baseball was, during the early part of the 20th Century, centered on strategy, not the 3-run homer and Cobb best exemplified that. This set is one of the most important sets ever produced with its great selection of athletes from different sports and the very appealing design of the cards. It's Ty Cobb and it's the first card in a great set. Sounds good to me.

## 1933 Goudey Sport Kings #2 Babe Ruth

### Importance:

The Babe was chosen as the second card in the set but, in terms of demand, Ruth takes a back seat to no one. Ruth is, without question, the premier card in the set. Ruth is featured on four different cards in the 1933 Goudey baseball set but he is only featured on one here and that makes this card very desirable.

The card is also very tough to find in high-grade. Nothing could be more fitting than "The Babe" in a Sport Kings set. This guy could have been a Hall of Fame pitcher if he wanted too but, as the Sultan of Swat, Ruth was elected as one of the first inductees to the Hall in 1936. It's hard to imagine what it would have been like to watch Ruth in action but, if you combined Greg Maddux, Mark McGwire and Tony Gwynn with a dash of pizzazz, you might get the picture.

### Difficulty:

This card is considered difficult amongst Ruth's listed examples. In fact, this Ruth card is fairly comparable to the 1933 Goudey #149 Ruth (red background) in terms of difficulty. Like most other Goudeys, this card is very susceptible to toning of the borders and edges.

The card is also known for having potential "bleeding" on the reverse as well as a lack of eye-appeal due to poor printing on many examples. When the sheets of cards were laid on top of each other, the moist

Photo Courtesy of National Baseball Hall of Fame Library, Cooperstoown,

ink would sometimes stick to the reverse of the cards above causing the bleed. If the bleeding is not severe, then it should not detract from the aesthetics in a substantial way.

The Cobb example, in this set, is found more often with nice eye-appeal because of the yellow background but the Ruth is often found with a dull look, due to the bland green background color. This is not Ruth's toughest card but it certainly provides a greater challenge than two of his Goudey baseball examples (#144 and #181).

PSA

1933 SPORT KINGS   #2
BABE RUTH       NM-MT  8
BASEBALL
                04277059

SPORT KINGS GUM

BABE RUTH

## 1933 GOUDEY SPORT KINGS BABE RUTH

## Comments:

This is one of the "Babe's" best cards. It's tough in high-grade, the key card in an extremely popular set and the card, in top shape, is one of his best looking examples. After the 1933 Goudey #53 Ruth, this card might be his most popular example. The long-term demand for this one is very promising. After 12 home run, 11 walk, 13 slugging percentage and 8 runs scored titles, it is easy to see why. He almost hit .400 (.393) in 1923. Ruth was the King of Kings and, if you ask me, he should have been the #1 card in the set. Sorry Ty.

## 1934 Goudey #1 Jimmie Foxx

### Importance:

Without question, this is "The Beast's" most important card overall. Foxx was known for his imposing figure at the plate. He would roll up his sleeves on purpose to show off his muscular biceps in hopes of rattling a pitcher's concentration. As the greatest right-handed slugger of his generation, Foxx crushed 534 home runs and was elected to the Hall of Fame in 1951. Foxx also became the first player in history to win three A.L. MVP Awards (1932, 1933, and 1938).

In 1934, Foxx hit .334 with 44 home runs and 130 RBI's, a typical season for the mild mannered Adonis. The 1934 Goudey set, while it missed the inclusion of Ruth, is still a very desirable set. In fact, many argue that these cards are actually more visually appealing than the previous Goudey effort. The set includes Lou Gehrig's most popular cards and they honored Foxx with the #1 slot after his Triple Crown/MVP performance in 1933.

### Difficulty:

It's the #1 card in the set so you know that many of these cards suffered from rubber band constriction. In addition, you have all the common condition obstacles for Goudeys such as "bleeding," toning and discoloration of edges and reverse. With this card in particular, look for nice, bold colors. Many examples are found with a very poor, washed out look. Eye-appeal is drastically altered by the strength of color and eye-appeal is the primary reason collectors are drawn to this set. This card ranks high on the difficulty scale and is currently underrated.

Photo Courtesy of National Baseball Hall of Fame Library, Cooperstoown, NY

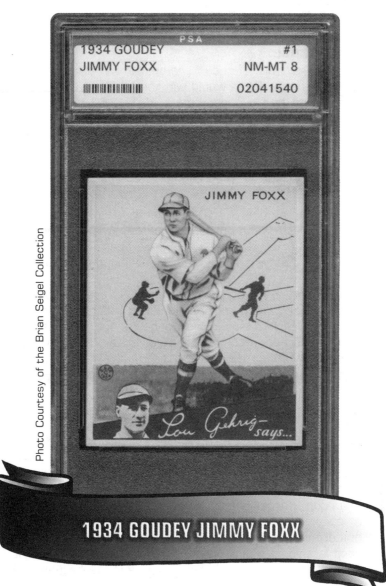

PSA

1934 GOUDEY #1
JIMMY FOXX
NM-MT 8
02041540

## 1934 GOUDEY JIMMY FOXX

## Comments:

As time goes on, Foxx seems to be gaining greater respect in the hobby. Not only does Foxx possess incredible numbers; he also has a compelling story. From his incredible strength to his shocking death (he choked to death on a piece of meat), the story of Foxx draws you in. With all the attention given to other #1 cards like the 1933 Goudey Benny Bengough and the 1952 Topps Andy Pafko, this card seems ridiculously overlooked. Those guys were average to slightly above average players but Foxx was a legend. This 1934 Goudey card is very stunning when it is found in nice shape and the position of the card alone makes it desirable. Add to that the fact that Foxx is one of the top Hall of Famers, and you have a gem.

## 1934 Goudey #6 Dizzy Dean

### Importance:

This is a key card of one of the best and most interesting pitchers of his day. Dean would win the MVP in 1934 by winning 30 games and had a career mark of 150-83 with 154 complete games despite leaving the game at the young age of 30 due to injury. For his efforts, he was elected the Hall of Fame in 1953. Dean was known just as much for his clown-like antics as he was for his gifted right arm when he was part of the St. Louis Cardinals' "Gas House Gang."

His career numbers are not like those of Walter Johnson or Christy Mathewson but Dean's career was cut short by an arm injury. Who knows what could have been for the colorful player but, while he did play, he made a lasting impression.

Well before Yogi Berra would flood the press with his comical comments on the game and life, Dean was practicing his comedy with his bizarre takes. This Goudey is not only one of the most visually attractive cards in the set; it is quite simply one of the most beautiful cards in the entire hobby.

### Difficulty:

The Goudeys have always been a difficult issue for a multitude of reasons. Toning along the edges and the reverse might be the most common condition obstacle. Those white borders just seem like a magnet for dirt and toning. Another problem with Goudeys is that these cards were often discarded during the paper drives of World War II, so finding them in any condition is tough in itself. Also, don't forget potential reverse "bleeding." When the sheets of cards were laid on top of each other, the moist ink would sometimes stick to the reverse of the cards above. This Dean card is seldom seen in high-grade condition. In fact, it is seen less frequently than other star cards like Gehrig from the 1934 Goudey set.

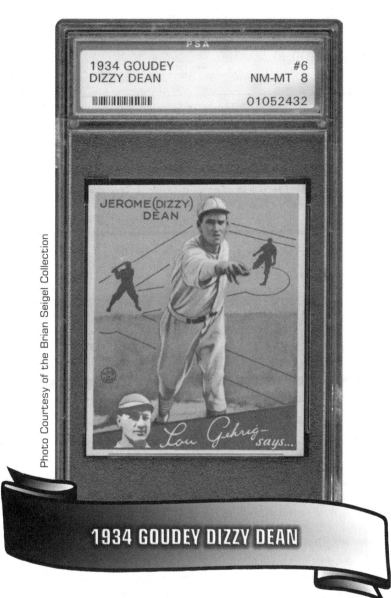

Photo Courtesy of the Brian Seigel Collection

PSA

1934 GOUDEY #6
DIZZY DEAN NM-MT 8

01052432

JEROME (DIZZY)
DEAN

Lou Gehrig says...

**1934 GOUDEY DIZZY DEAN**

## Comments:

Dizzy Dean was a character and an entertainer. Much like "King" Kelly, his reputation was probably as imposing as was his actual accomplishments. Dean's cards always rank high in terms of pure popularity. I chose the 1934 Dean over his 1933 example based on the eye-appeal of the card and the significance of that year. Both of these cards are outstanding and the 1933 issue is part of a more popular set due to the inclusion of Ruth and Gehrig, amongst others, but the deep blue and green colors on the 1934 Goudey Dean give it the visual edge. In 1934, Dean would win 30 games and he remains the last National League pitcher to achieve this feat. This Dean gets the nod.

## 1934 Goudey Lou Gehrig (#'s 37 and 61)

### Importance:

These two specimens are the most popular Gehrig cards in the hobby, with the #37 considered a sportscard classic. Both cards exhibit tremendous color and beautiful artwork on the face. The #37 example is considered the more popular of the two and it features the smiling face of Gehrig against a yellow background. The #61 example is overshadowed by the incredible popularity of the #37 card but it is arguably just as attractive. It features Gehrig from the waist up and holding his weapon with intensity. That weapon would produce a .363 average with 49 homers and 165 RBI's in 1934 and a ticket to the Hall in 1939.

For his efforts, Gehrig won the Triple Crown Award in 1934 but, shockingly, he only finished 5th in the MVP voting. In 1934, Gehrig would put together one of the greatest offensive seasons ever. He even slugged .706 yet no MVP! Ho hum, another Gehrig-like season. At least that's what the voters must have thought.

Each card captures the legend of Gehrig; he was a kind man yet a fierce competitor. In addition, the Gehrig cards are the keys to the set because, this time, the "Babe" was nowhere to be found. The #1 Jimmie Foxx card is also very important but the 1934 Goudey set is Gehrig's stage.

### Difficulty:

Once again, the Goudeys present an array of condition obstacles including toning, "bleed-through" and centering difficulties. The toning on these two Gehrig cards is very, very common so do not be surprised if you have a very tough time locating a copy with at least off-white borders. The existence of minor toning, as long as it is evenly spread, should not be much of a detractor since it is a common trait. "Bleeding" is another obstacle to be wary of. When the sheets of cards were laid on top of each other, the moist ink would sometimes stick to the reverse of the cards above.

The somewhat narrow borders make it difficult to find centered examples. In fact, when was the last time you saw a high-end, centered example? It's probably been awhile and copies that exhibit sharp corners and a centered image do sell for a premium. The #37 Gehrig card has more problems with stray print marks due to the yellow-colored background but both cards are tough.

1934 GOUDEY LOU GEHRIG

## Comments:

These two cards are true classics. They are so visually appealing and tough that, even if Gehrig wasn't the player we have come to know, the cards would be desirable. On the reverse of the #37 card is a quote from Gehrig that reads, "I love the game of baseball and hope to be in there batting them out for many years to come, fortune has been kind to me..." Just a few years later, Gehrig would be stricken with ALS and soon thereafter lose his life. This Goudey pair will always be popular, as popular as the man they feature, a man that was taken from us much too soon. The Iron Horse is a keeper and an American hero.

## 1934 Goudey #62 Hank Greenberg

### Importance:

This is one of the greatest sluggers in baseball history on his most attractive card. Greenberg had some incredible seasons for the Detroit Tigers and, despite missing playing time (nearly four years) due to military service, he left a permanent mark on the game. With career highs of 183 RBI's in 1937 and 58 home runs in 1938, Greenberg was a true slugger during an era that featured few comparable power hitters or run producers. Only Jimmie Foxx and Lou Gehrig could compete with Greenberg's towering drives and ability to hit with men on base.

Greenberg would also win two MVP's along the way, one in 1935 and another in 1940. In only 9 full seasons, Greenberg amassed 331 homers and drove in 1,271 RBI's. For his efforts, Greenberg was inducted into the Hall of Fame in 1956.

Greenberg, much like Jimmie Foxx, has an almost "cult-like" following. He may not be as popular as Babe Ruth or Mickey Mantle but his fans are loyal. With the recent release of a Greenberg documentary, his accomplishments should start reaching the masses. The 1934 Goudey set is very popular and this Greenberg example is one of the keys and, arguably, his most attractive card.

### Difficulty:

The 1934 Goudey cards are susceptible to edge toning, "bleeding" on the reverse and centering difficulties. The toning on all Goudey cards is very, very common so do not be surprised if you have a very tough time locating a copy with at least off-white borders. The existence of minor toning, as long as it is evenly spread, should not be much of a detractor since that is a common trait. Also, look out for "bleeding" on the reverse. When the sheets of cards were laid on top of each other, the moist ink would sometimes stick to the reverse of the cards above. Color doesn't seem to be a problem with this card but make sure that you seek out examples with bold color because, without it, the card will have serious eye-appeal problems due to a "washed-out" appearance.

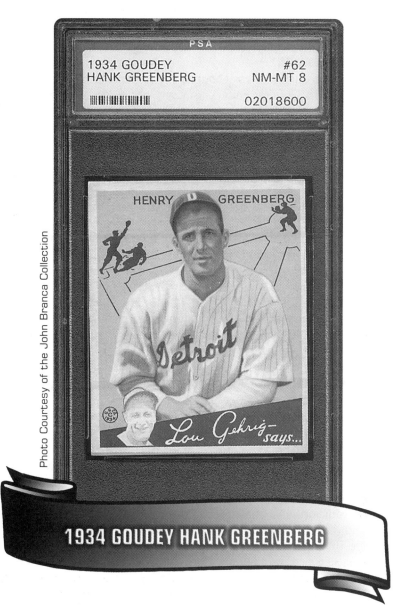

Photo Courtesy of the John Branca Collection

PSA

1934 GOUDEY
HANK GREENBERG

#62

NM-MT 8

02018600

**1934 GOUDEY HANK GREENBERG**

## Comments:

Just try to imagine the fan base Greenberg would have if he played for the New York Yankees. We can contemplate the impact that wearing pinstripes would have with many players like Stan Musial or Hank Aaron but, with Greenberg, it was almost a reality. The Bronx native was offered a contract from the Bronx Bombers but he rejected it because they wanted Greenberg to play somewhere other than first base. Why? They had this other guy named Gehrig. Greenberg went on to make history in Detroit. With the overall popularity of the set and the great eye-appeal, this card should enjoy solid demand for years to come.

## 1934-36 Diamond Stars #1 Lefty Grove

### Importance:

The first card in a very tough, yet undervalued pre-war set. Like the 1934 Goudey Foxx, this card has a lot going for it because it's not only the first card in the set but it also features a great player.

Lefty Grove was a dominant pitcher in his day. Many baseball experts feel that Grove may have been not only the best left-handed pitcher ever, but the best pitcher period. In fact, Grove has the highest winning percentage amongst 300-game winners (.680 with a 300-141 record). From 1927-1933, Grove would win 20 or more games in each and every season, including an astonishing year when he went 31-4 with a 2.06 ERA.

Grove will be remembered primarily as the ace of the Philadelphia Athletics, though he did have a few very productive seasons for the Boston Red Sox. He was inducted into the Hall of Fame in 1947. If this set included a Babe Ruth or Lou Gehrig card, the Grove would probably be looked at in an entirely different light.

### Difficulty:

This card is extremely tough not only because it's the first card in the set but also because of the inherent problems associated with all Diamond Stars. These cards are simply found with a "dirty" look more times than not. The borders always seem to have a gray or toned look.

In addition, the cards generally have centering problems. After the rubber bands got through with Mr. Grove, it is hard to imagine finding a high-end copy. In fact, while many of the cards on this list are very tough, I have not personally seen this particular card offered publicly in NM-MT condition or better in years.

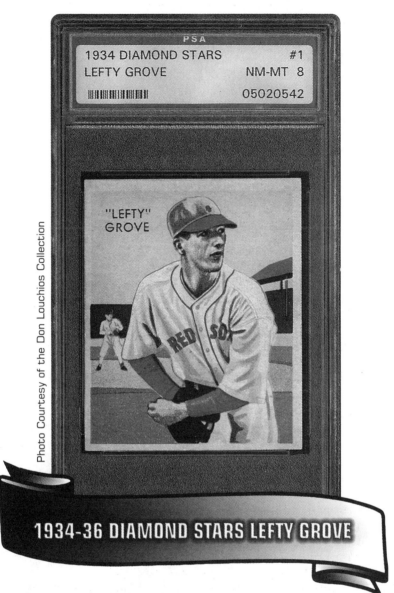

**1934 DIAMOND STARS** #1
**LEFTY GROVE** NM-MT 8
05020542

"LEFTY" GROVE

RED SOX

## 1934-36 DIAMOND STARS LEFTY GROVE

## Comments:

Again, like the 1934 Goudey Foxx, this card should enjoy a great deal of future demand considering the rarity of the card and the stature of Grove as a player. When fans talk about the greatest pitchers in baseball history, you often hear names like Johnson, Mathewson, Koufax, etc. but Grove is hardly an afterthought. The 1933 Goudey Benny Bengough and 1952 Topps Andy Pafko steal the #1 card spotlight but Grove was a far better player. The only real detractor for this card is the fact that the set, while very interesting and colorful, never really caught fire like the Goudeys or Play Balls of the pre-war era. The outlook is still great for Lefty.

# 1938 Goudey Joe DiMaggio (#'s 250 and 274)

## Importance:

The official rookie card of "Joltin Joe." Joe DiMaggio ranks right up there with Mantle, Ruth and Gehrig as one of the most cherished Yankee legends. What could be more representative than a rookie card of the American icon? The difficulty and set popularity have propelled this card to new heights in the last two years.

While there was a 1937 O-Pee-Chee (Canadian) example a year earlier, these two Goudey variations are the cards that the overwhelming majority of collectors seek out. The 1938 Goudeys are considered classics because of their unique designs and assortment of stars. As you might imagine, these two cards are the keys to the set.

In 1938, DiMaggio had a typical DiMaggio-like season by hitting .324 with 32 homers and 140 RBI's. DiMaggio was more than just a baseball superstar, he was an American icon. These two Goudey examples are only amongst a handful of mainstream issues to feature the Yankee great during his playing days.

## Difficulty:

The 1938 Goudeys are extremely difficult and are just starting to get the respect they deserve in the market. The cards are very susceptible to print defects and centering or tilt problems but the biggest problem seems to be ton-

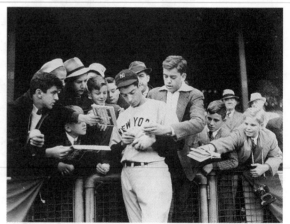

Photo Courtesy of National Baseball Hall of Fame Library, Cooperstown, NY

ing. The cards have a white background and white borders surround the image so, in other words, there is no place to hide the toning. It can really be an eyesore. High-grade examples are scarce with many copies exhibiting an almost yellow/brown color along the edges. The #274 or cartoon DiMaggio has always been considered slightly tougher than the #250 card but both are difficult.

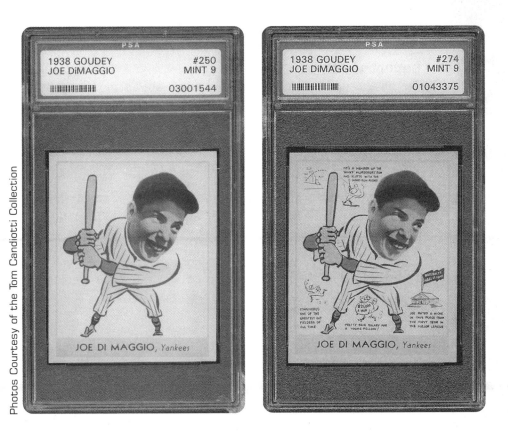

1938 GOUDEY JOE DIMAGGIO

## Comments:

With the nice selection of stars in the set, coupled with the fact that the set is small enough to viably complete, these two DiMaggio cards have a lot going for them. In many ways, the perception of these cards is similar to the 1939 Play Ball Ted Williams rookie. Many collectors actually prefer the 1941 Play Ball Williams to his actual rookie card because Ted's rookie lacks color and is not quite as difficult as the 1941 example. While it is true that, based on pure popularity, the 1941 Play Ball DiMaggio is arguably a more desirable card, the 1938 Goudeys are tougher (unlike the 1939 Play Ball Williams in comparison to the 1941 example) and both are considered his true rookie cards.

## 1938 Goudey Bob Feller (#'s 264 and 288)

### Importance:

This is a tough rookie card of one of baseball's most legendary pitchers. If Bob Feller had not missed nearly four full seasons due to military service, who knows what his career numbers would look like. Feller had a fastball that went unmatched in his day. With 266 victories, a 3.25 ERA, over 2,500 strikeouts and 3 no-hitters, Feller was a dominant force on the mound.

In 1938, Feller's first full season on the hill and at the age of 19, he posted a 17-11 record with a league-high 240 strikeouts. To have such great success at such a young age is truly amazing, fans seem to embrace the youthful stars in sport. He would lead the league in that category 6 more times in his career with a high of 348 in 1946. Both 1938 Goudey examples are considered keys to the set and the set is considered one of the most challenging in the hobby.

### Difficulty:

The 1938 Goudeys are extremely difficult and are just starting to get the respect they deserve in the market. The cards are very susceptible to print defects and centering or tilt problems but the biggest problem seems to be toning. The cards have a white background and white borders surround the image so, in other words, there is no place to hide the toning. It can really reduce the eye-appeal. High-grade examples are scarce. The #288 or cartoon variation Feller has always been considered slightly tougher than the #264 card but both are difficult.

Photo Courtesy of the John Branca Collection

1938 GOUDEY BOB FELLER

## Comments:

Bob Feller was a classic power pitcher and this card has a lot of potential. He does not possess the overall career numbers that a Ryan or Clemens have but his story is compelling. There are a few other Feller cards on this list but this is his only rookie card. The 1948 Leaf Feller might be a bit tougher to find in high-grade but this card has more personality, better eye-appeal and a more interesting design. This set has always been popular and collectors are realizing how tough this card really is. It just always seems to have condition problems. Find a high-grade example and cherish it.

## 1939 Play Ball #26 Joe DiMaggio

### Importance:

This is the first Play Ball card of "Joltin Joe." This DiMaggio card is one of two major keys to the 1939 Play Ball set. The other major key would be the Ted Williams rookie card. His 1941 Play Ball card receives much higher demand because of the presence of color amongst other things but this is his first Play Ball card and that is significant. This DiMaggio card is one of those cards that is immediately recognizable to even the novice collectors. It has a classic quality about it; the image is simply memorable.

In 1939, DiMaggio would continue to excel at the plate and in the field. He would lead the league in hitting with a .381 batting average, smack 30 homers and drive in 126 runs (his 4th consecutive season with 100 RBI's or more). It would result in the first of three MVP Awards for Joe and, despite missing three years to the service; his career track record was more than worthy of Hall of Fame induction (1955).

### Difficulty:

This DiMaggio card is not extremely difficult to find in high-grade but it's not exactly easy to find either. Condition obstacles include poor centering and stray print marks across the face. With the basic black and white design, print marks are easily visible causing eye-appeal problems. Also, beware of toning along the edges. Finally, bleeding on the reverse is very common. Slight bleeding, as long as it's not an eyesore, is acceptable under high-grade standards but certainly a defect you should try to avoid if possible.

Photo Courtesy of National Baseball Hall of Fame Library, Cooperstoown, NY

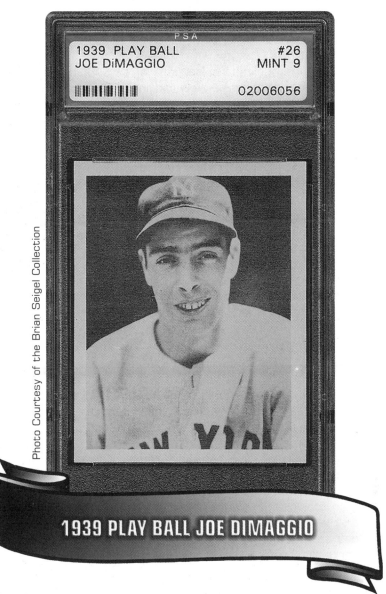

Photo Courtesy of the Brian Seigel Collection

1939 PLAY BALL JOE DIMAGGIO

## Comments:

The reality is that this DiMaggio card is not one of his more attractive examples but it still remains a classic. Much has been said of DiMaggio's private life over the years, some positive and some negative but no one will dispute his grace, hustle or performance on the field. The greatest center fielder of his era, maybe ever, DiMaggio's sportscards rank high on the list. This card is a great portrait of an all-time great approaching the prime of his career. The image is unmistakable.

## 1939 Play Ball #92 Ted Williams

### Importance:

The only recognized rookie card of the "Splendid Splinter." A very young Williams is pictured in full swing on the front. It would be that classic swing that helped make Williams one of the greatest hitters to ever play the game. He wanted to be known as the greatest hitter who ever lived. Are you going to argue with him?

If Ted Williams had not missed roughly five seasons in the service during his prime, his numbers would be absolutely astronomical. Williams finished with a .344 batting average (he is also the last man to hit .400 in a season with a .406 mark in 1941), the highest on-base average of all-time at .483, the second highest slugging average at .634 and he hit 521 career homers. His numbers have to be taken in context; those 521 homers could have easily been near 700 without the lost time. This is a classic card and the key to the 1939 Play Ball set.

### Difficulty:

Like the DiMaggio card from the same set, this Williams example is not incredibly difficult but it does have some condition obstacles. Centering might be the biggest problem for this card. The card is usually found off-center one way or the other. This card also suffers from a bland look most of the time. It's hard to imagine a black and white card with a lot of eye-appeal but, if you are patient, you can find examples that have much better focus than others do.

Also, look out for black print spots on the front. Finally, bleeding on the reverse is very common. Slight bleeding, as long as it's not an eyesore, is acceptable under high-grade standards but certainly a defect you should try to avoid if possible.

Photo Courtesy of the Don Louchios Collection

PSA

1939 PLAY BALL     #92
TED WILLIAMS

MINT 9

08142787

**1939 PLAY BALL TED WILLIAMS**

## Comments:

While this card may not be Ted's best looking card or most popular one, it is still his only rookie card and that carries a lot of weight. The classic swing on the front of the card is an image that will remain a classic for years to come. Despite the lack of color, this card remains popular. It's the rookie card of, arguably, the best hitter who ever lived. Williams hit for an average higher than modern batting champs Tony Gwynn and Wade Boggs but also powered the ball over the fence at a faster rate than guys like Mickey Mantle and Mike Schmidt. His hitting legacy is nearly unbelievable.

## 1940 Play Ball #1 Joe DiMaggio

### Importance:

It's the first card in a set loaded with Hall of Famers and it happens to feature Joe DiMaggio. The 1940 Play Ball set has never been considered one of the most visually appealing sets ever produced but the set includes some very important cards and this is one of them.

This card, along with the Joe Jackson and Ted Williams cards, are the keys to the set. This time, unlike the 1939 issue, it is DiMaggio showing off his classic swing instead of Williams. The image is another classic, one that would be used a year later on DiMaggio's most popular card.

In 1940, DiMaggio would have another stellar season for the Yankees. He led the league with a .352 batting average, drilled 31 homers and drove in 133 RBI's. It was the 5th consecutive season that DiMaggio reached 100 RBI's and the 4th consecutive year he would reach 30 homers.

### Difficulty:

This card is not only tough because it's the first card in the set, it also has the typical problems associated with the issue. Of course, I am sure plenty of rubber bands had their way with poor Joe throughout the years as collectors inflicted punishment on those poor number one cards placed at the top of the stack.

The one other condition obstacle that seems to rise above the rest is toning. This card can be found with varying degrees of toning on along the edges and it can really hinder the eye-appeal. In addition, be aware of centering difficulties. Unlike the 1939 Play Balls, which have enormous borders, these 1940 Play Balls have small ones. This is a very tough card overall.

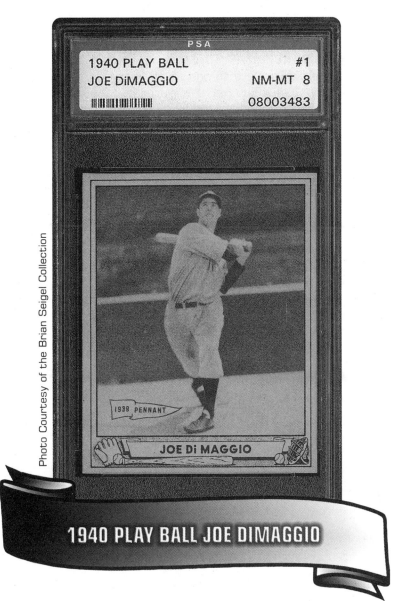

PSA

1940 PLAY BALL #1
JOE DiMAGGIO NM-MT 8
08003483

Photo Courtesy of the Brian Seigel Collection

1939 PENNANT

JOE Di MAGGIO

1940 PLAY BALL JOE DIMAGGIO

## Comments:

Perhaps DiMaggio's greatest achievement as a hitter is the fact that he only struck out 369 times in his whole career while hitting 361 homers. In other words, this guy almost homered more often than striking out. Amazing! Like the 1934 Goudey Foxx and 1934-1936 Diamond Star Grove, this #1 card is a treasured specimen. Like the 1939 Play Ball set, the 1940 Play Ball set is not at the top of most collector want lists but this set, unlike the 1939 issue, has more star power. If Benny Bengough and Andy Pafko #1 cards continue to command great demand in the market, then this card should continue to attract attention.

## 1940 Play Ball #225 Shoeless Joe Jackson

### Importance:

This is a final tribute to one of the game's most intriguing players. The 1940 Play Ball set features several post-playing days cards of Hall of Famers and this Jackson, though technically not a Hall of Famer, is one of three major keys to the set. It's amazing that this card is considered as valuable as it is today.

In the same set, you have a 2nd year card of Ted Williams, perhaps the greatest hitter who ever lived, and a #1 card of Joe DiMaggio who was an international celebrity. Both were still playing at the time but Jackson was long banned from the game yet his card is still, arguably, the most valuable in the set.

In Jackson's first full season, he hit .408. In his last full season, he hit .382. It's too bad baseball fans were deprived of seeing what Joe could do over the course of his entire career but the "Black Sox" scandal of 1919 resulted in a lifetime ban from the game. It's still not clear what role Jackson played in the whole mess but the ban remains.

### Difficulty:

Very few high-grade Jackson examples ever turn up on the open market. The one condition obstacle that seems to rise above the rest is toning. This card can be found with varying degrees of toning along the edges and it can really hinder the eye-appeal. In addition, be aware of centering difficulties because, more often than not, this card is off the mark side to side. Unlike the 1939 Play Balls, which have enormous borders, these 1940 Play Balls have small ones. This is a very tough card overall.

"SHOELESS JOE" JACKSON

## 1940 PLAY BALL SHOELESS JOE JACKSON

**Comments:**

The 1940 Play Ball set is not the most attractive set in the hobby but, with Jackson, you have few choices. Jackson has a very loyal following and his place in history, for good and bad reasons, is solid. Out of all the Jackson cards on the list, this one is probably the least desirable but it still made the list. This is an affordable alternative to the Cracker Jack examples and more mainstream than his true rookie card, which is virtually impossible to find in any condition. As a matter of fact, the so-called Jackson rookie (E-90-1) is so obscure that most collectors, even advanced ones, don't even know what it looks like.

# 1941 Play Ball #14 Ted Williams

## Importance:

Arguably, Ted's most popular card due to its beauty and his memorable 1941 season. Why was the 1941 season memorable? Williams went on to hit .406 for the season! Going into the last day of the season, Williams could have taken himself out of the lineup and claimed a .400 average exactly. Instead, Williams insisted on playing in the doubleheader. It was a major risk but he ended up going 6 for 8 and actually raised his average to .406! He would also add 37 homers, 120 RBI's, 145 walks and a .551 OBP. Williams would unfortunately finish second in the MVP voting to another guy named DiMaggio but Williams remains the last man to hit .400.

Over the years, this card has actually outperformed the 1939 rookie and the 1940 Play Ball Williams, both black and white issues lacking much eye-appeal, due to the use of color and significance of the year.

## Difficulty:

The 1941 Play Balls are definitely subject to toning and centering difficulties. The design is much like the 1940 Play Balls except, this time, the cards included the use of color. The borders, however, remain narrow, which causes the centering to be all over the place. Finally, one condition problem that is unique to the 1941 Play Balls is the variance in color quality. Some Williams examples are found with a bright look while others have a very "washed out" appearance.

Look for copies with a very deep peach/orange color in the background. Others, usually the majority, have very faint color. If you find an example that has nice color, you will instantly appreciate the difference. While not quite as difficult as his 1940 Play Ball example, the 1941 Play Ball Williams does present a solid challenge in Near Mint condition or better.

Photo Courtesy of the Tom Candiotti Collection

PSA

1941 PLAY BALL        #14
TED WILLIAMS

MINT 9

07036531

"TED" WILLIAMS

1941 PLAY BALL TED WILLIAMS

## Comments:

There are few true classics cards in the hobby. A classic card is one of those treasures that stands for something more than just a recap of the prior season. It might not be quite the equivalent to a 1952 Topps Mantle or a T206 Wagner in terms of "classic" power but the 1941 Play Ball Williams is one of the true classics and, arguably, his best card overall. This is just a great card overall and, if I were ranking the cards by popularity alone, it would be high on the list. It resides in a popular set, the set is very attractive, it's considered a tough card, it features the legendary Ted Williams and 1941 was a memorable year for a multitude of reasons. Need I say more?

## 1941 Play Ball #54 Pee Wee Reese

### Importance:

The only recognized rookie card of popular Hall of Fame short-stop Pee Wee Reese. Reese wasn't the fastest or most power-ful player on the field but he was an excellent defensive player and a leader in the clubhouse for the popular Brooklyn Dodgers. In fact, despite lackluster offensive numbers, Reese would finish in the top 10 (for the MVP voting) 8 times and was elected to the Hall of Fame in 1984. It took a little while but Pee Wee got there. His personable nature just adds to the appeal of his collectibles.

By the way, his nickname (Pee Wee) had nothing to do with his physical size. It was given to him because Reese was a very talented marbles player when he was a youngster. The name stuck with him forever. What was his real first name? Harold. This card is a key in a set filled with stars.

### Difficulty:

This particular card is rarely offered. Just check your auction catalogues and the Internet, the Reese rookie is seldom seen for sale, especially in high-grade. The difficulty is very deceptive. All 1941 Play Balls are definitely subject to toning and centering difficulties. The design is much like the 1940 Play Balls except, this time, they were produced in color. The borders, however, remain narrow, which causes the centering to be all over the place.

Finally, one condition problem that is unique to the 1941 Play Balls is the variance in color quality. Some Reese examples are found with a bright look while others have a very "washed out" appearance. If you find an example that has nice color, you will instantly appreciate the difference. The background, if bold, can really help the image of Reese jump off the cardboard.

PSA

1941 PLAY BALL      #54
PEE WEE REESE     MINT 9

08016746

"PEE WEE" REESE

## 1941 PLAY BALL PEE WEE REESE

## Comments:

Reese was a staple with the Brooklyn Dodgers during their heyday. He was the captain of the infield and was able to rally his troops around Jackie Robinson after a less than warm reception. He was also so likable that he was hired as the head of player recruitment at the H&B bat factory after his major league career came to an end. This card is certainly one of the keys and, while it is not as valuable as the DiMaggio or Williams cards, it is the most significant rookie in the set. The first two attempts by Play Ball pale in comparison to this colorful set. Reese picked a good time to make his debut.

# 1941 Play Ball #71 Joe DiMaggio

## Importance:

The most desirable DiMaggio card in the hobby and the key to the 1941 Play Ball set. There is plenty of star power in the 1941 Play Ball set but this card is the most valuable. It was during the 1941 season when DiMaggio would set a major league record by hitting safely in 56 consecutive games.

That same year, DiMaggio would also go on to win the American League MVP Award after finishing with a .357 batting average, 30 homers and a league-leading 125 RBI's, denying that sweet swinging lefty from Boston. It would be one of three times the "Yankee Clipper" would come away with A.L. MVP. The 1940 Play Ball DiMaggio used the same classic image but, with the addition of color, the 1941 example stands out.

This card is a classic, maybe even more so than the Ted Williams card from the same set. DiMaggio's great swing is pictured and how fitting considering that his unbelievable consecutive-game hitting streak was accomplished that very same year.

## Difficulty:

While the DiMaggio example is susceptible to the usual condition obstacles associated with other 1941 Play Balls like centering difficulties, toning seems to be the biggest one. For example, I have seen many more DiMaggio examples with toning problems than Ted Williams cards. One problem that this card shares with the Williams card is the variance in color quality. Finding examples with a "washed out" look is a common occurrence. Look for examples that exhibit deep, purple color in the background.

Photo Courtesy of National Baseball Hall of Fame Library, Cooperstoown, NY

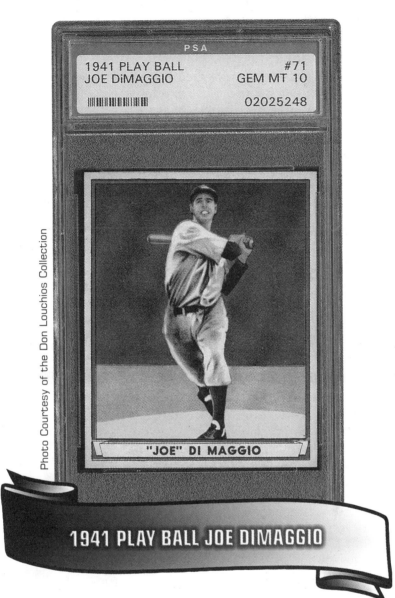

**1941 PLAY BALL JOE DiMAGGIO**

## Comments:

What the hitting streak symbolized for DiMaggio was more than just a mere hitting record, it symbolized the way DiMaggio played the game his entire career. He was simply consistent. In 13 seasons with the Yankees, he made 13 All-Star Teams. DiMaggio drove in 100 or more runs in all but two seasons where he had 500 at bats or more. In the two that DiMaggio failed to reach 100 RBI's, he drove in 95 and 97 respectively. DiMaggio was a constant for the Yankees, the reason they would enjoy so many trips to the postseason during his reign as the best center fielder in baseball. This card would rank very high if the list was based on overall desirability and it should always enjoy great demand.

## 1948 Bowman #6 Yogi Berra

### Importance:

The only recognized rookie card of the popular New York Yankee catcher. Yogi Berra did not exactly fit the mold of a great athlete but you cannot argue with his accomplishments. Winner of three MVP awards, Berra helped lead the New York Yankees to numerous World Series appearances. Berra, as a member of the Yankees, made it to the World Series 14 times and won the title in 10 of those appearances. It's no wonder that (at the time of publication) Berra remains the all-time leader in Series hits and games.

Berra's combination of popularity, offensive prowess, World Series records, leadership and position make him an easy choice. The 1948 Bowman set has a few key Hall of Famer rookie cards and this card is certainly one of the keys to the set.

### Difficulty:

The 1948 Bowmans suffer from two major condition obstacles, centering difficulties and print defects. The black and white design creates a haven for black print spots to clutter the image. In addition, look for toning along the edges. Due to the basic design, toned borders are very noticeable. These are not as tough as the 1948 Leafs but they are still tough in their own right.

Photo Courtesy of National Baseball Hall of Fame Library, Cooperstoown, NY

Photo Courtesy of the John Branca Collection

PSA

1948 BOWMAN          #6
YOGI BERRA          MINT 9

09093401

**1948 BOWMAN YOGI BERRA**

## Comments:

Yogi Berra has a very loyal following amongst collectors. His cartoon-like image and great numbers give collectors two great reasons to seek out his cards. Add to that the fact he was a Yankee during a time when they were dominating the competition and you have a very popular player. The 1948 Bowmans are not the prettiest cards, due to their plain design, but you can't go wrong with a Yogi rookie. In 1948, Berra would play in 100 games for the first time in his career. After hitting .305 and driving in 98 runs that year, Berra would find himself in the starting lineup for over a decade.

## 1948 Bowman #36 Stan Musial

### Importance:

One of only two recognized rookie cards of "Stan the Man." This card, along with the Yogi Berra rookie, is a major key to the 1948 Bowman set. If Stan Musial were a New York Yankee, his cards might be worth double or triple what they are worth today.

In 1948, 7 years after his Major League debut, Musial hit .376 with 39 homers and 131 RBI's. The batting average and RBI totals led the league but he also led the league in runs scored (135), hits (230), doubles (46), triples (18), OBP (.450) and slugging percentage (.702). Most were career bests for Musial in a career that featured one great year after another.

This card is very comparable to the 1939 Play Ball Ted Williams card in that neither of the cards are really considered very visually attractive but, at the same time, you can't deny that they are both key rookie cards. He ranks right up there with the likes of Ted Williams when it comes to pure hitting ability; this card is simple and classic.

### Difficulty:

Like the Berra card, this 1948 Bowman Musial card is very susceptible to centering problems and print defects. The card features a headshot of Musial so beware of print marks that get close to his face; they can create a major eyesore. Keep in mind that border toning and toning on the reverse may also be condition obstacles and are very common for the issue. Rough-cuts may also be present but, unless they are severe, they are generally not considered a detractor.

Photo Courtesy of the John Branca Collection

1948 BOWMAN STAN MUSIAL

## Comments:

Musial is one of those players who seems to be getting more and more respect as time goes on. When collectors start to realize the importance of his accomplishments, his cards are sure to enjoy a surge in demand. The Leaf Musial has been getting more attention in recent years because the overall set is superior in difficulty and star power to the Bowman issue but this card is considered more mainstream. This signified the beginning for Bowman and Musial was the first of many key rookie cards to dominate baseball cards sets from the late-40's to the mid-50's.

# 1948-49 Leaf #1 Joe DiMaggio

## Importance:

The first card in a very tough and popular set which happens to be Joe DiMaggio's last major issue. The 1948 Leaf set is one of the most popular sets in the hobby due to its difficulty and inclusion of so many great players. You have key cards of Babe Ruth, Satchel Paige, Ted Williams, Bob Feller and rookie cards of Jackie Robinson and Stan Musial to name a few. The DiMaggio example also happens to be one of the more attractive cards in the set with a beautiful lime-green background.

The 1948 and 1949 seasons were both productive for DiMaggio. In 1948, he would hit .320, while leading the league with 39 homers and 155 RBI's in only 153 games. In 1949, DiMaggio would unfortunately miss about half the season but he came back to hit .346 with 14 homers and 67 RBI's in only 76 games.

Like his 1940 Play Ball issue (also a number one card), but to an even higher degree, this card should enjoy great demand in the future as the set continues to get more attention. DiMaggio was always consistent when he played and this card is of extreme importance.

## Difficulty:

If you combine the fact that this card is the first card (the first cards in each set were usually subject to overhandling and rubber band damage) in a set that is considered to be one of the toughest sets in the hobby, you have a card of extreme difficulty. Also, this card is rarely found centered. In addition, even if you find one that is nicely centered, you have to contend with focus, print, paper and toning problems.

The quality of the image, whether it's the focus or color, varies so much on this card which makes it imperative that you see as many examples as you can to make an informed decision. In addition, most Leaf cards have a very dull appearance and lack clarity. This card would rank high on the list of pure difficulty.

PSA
1948 LEAF          #1
JOE DI MAGGIO      NM-MT 8
05012425

JOE DI MAGGIO

**1948-49 LEAF JOE DIMAGGIO**

## Comments:

With all the positive attributes of this card, it would be hard to overstate the importance of this key. Once again, you have to look at the demand for non-star, number one cards to realize the importance of this DiMaggio example. Other key number one cards include the 1933 Goudey Benny Bengough, the 1934 Goudey Jimmie Foxx, the 1934-36 Diamond Stars Lefty Grove, and the 1952 Topps Andy Pafko. All of the above mentioned cards are important but this number one card is, arguably, the most appealing overall. When you match an icon with a set of this magnitude, this number one card just might be the most interesting in the hobby.

# 1948-49 Leaf #3 Babe Ruth

## Importance:

This is the last major card featuring the "Sultan of Swat." All right, so this card was produced after Ruth's playing days and, in fact, very close to the time of Ruth's death. The interesting thing is that collectors do not treat this card like a post-career commemorative issue. It is a key card in a very tough and popular set.

The image of Ruth is a classic. A writer once compared Ruth's face to a catcher's mitt. This card captures Ruth's unmistakable face, a face that actually helps increase his legend. Have you ever seen a face that even remotely resembles Ruth's?

How great was Ruth? Take this for example. Did you know that Ruth, on two separate occasions (1920 and 1927), belted more home runs by himself than each individual team in the entire American League did? There just are not enough words to sum up the pure domination that Ruth displayed.

## Difficulty:

This card, like other 1948 Leafs, is a tough one. This card is constantly found off-center with incredible variations in eye-appeal. The color, print and focus quality are very inconsistent on this issue. You can have two 1948 Leaf Ruth cards right next to each other and

Photo Courtesy of National Baseball Hall of Fame Library, Cooperstoown, NY

they won't even look like the same card.

Some examples have a bold red background while other have a light orange one, the eye-appeal on this card can really vary. Keep in mind that the overwhelming majority of these Leaf cards have a very dull appearance and lack clarity from the above-mentioned printing dilemmas.

1948-49 LEAF BABE RUTH

## Comments:

This card is not Ruth's most appealing card but, nevertheless, it is a key card in a great set. The image on this card is one that many collectors can relate to; it's an image that they are familiar with. For this reason, along with the difficulty and popularity of the card, the fact that it was produced after his playing days doesn't seem to be much of a detractor. When you are as great as Ruth, I guess it doesn't really matter. It's definitely an affordable alternative to a Goudey example.

## 1948-49 Leaf #4 Stan Musial

### Importance:

This is one of two recognized rookie cards of "Stan the Man." This Musial rookie card, as opposed to the 1948 Bowman example, was produced in color. The 1948 Leaf Stan Musial card is one of a few key rookies to the popular 1948 Leaf set and it's more visually attractive than the 1948 Bowman Musial. With well over 3,000 hits (3,630) and nearly 500 home runs (475), Musial is considered one of the most complete hitters of all-time.

In fact, Musial was so consistent at the plate that he finished with the exact same number of hits at home as he did on the road, 1,815. He was elected to the Hall of Fame in 1969 after playing his entire career with the St. Louis Cardinals. In my opinion, this is his best rookie card.

### Difficulty:

This card suffers from the typical condition problems associated with 1948 Leafs with the most common problem being poor centering. The examples with strong color seem to really jump out at you if you are lucky enough to find one. Another major problem, with all 1948 Leafs, is the fact that these cards are produced on ridiculously poor paper. Add to that the fact that these cards were subject to a crude cutting process and you have the problem of finding sharp examples. In addition, most Leaf cards have a very dull appearance and lack clarity. This is quite possibly Musial's toughest card.

Photo Courtesy of National Baseball Hall of Fame Library, Cooperstoown, NY

Photo Courtesy of the Tom Candiotti Collection

PSA

1948 LEAF #4
STAN MUSIAL MINT 9
01022203

STAN MUSIAL

1948-49 LEAF STAN MUSIAL

## Comments:

Stan Musial cards are growing in popularity as people realize how good he was. The St. Louis Cardinals have a rich history with the likes of Bob Gibson, Dizzy Dean and Mark McGwire but Musial is the most legendary figure in the club's history. Musial won three MVP's, and, in addition to his startling home run and hit totals, finished with 1,951 RBI's, 1,949 runs scored, 725 doubles, 177 triples, a .331 batting average and a .559 slugging percentage (higher than either Mantle or Mays). This card seems to be very underappreciated in comparison to other key rookie cards from his era. Keep a close eye on this one; collectors are starting to wake up.

## 1948-49 Leaf #8 Satchel Paige

### Importance:

This is, arguably, the toughest post-war card in the entire hobby. Satchel Paige was a legend of both the Negro Leagues and the Major Leagues. Paige may not be as popular as Mickey Mantle or Ted Williams but he has a very strong following. Unfortunately, due to a time of blatant racism, fans were deprived of watching this legend face major league hitters in his prime.

In 1948, at the age of 42, Satchel only started 7 games but he won 6 of them to go along with his 2.48 ERA. It was his first season in the Major Leagues but he was already older than some fathers of Major League players. We can only imagine what he could have accomplished if he was given a chance but poor Satchel had to wait for Jackie Robinson to break the color barrier before he could show fans his stuff. In a set filled with major stars like Ruth, DiMaggio, Williams and Robinson, the Paige is considered the most valuable by a very large margin. This short printed rarity is one of major importance.

### Difficulty:

This card is, without question, the toughest card to find in high-grade from the 1948 Leaf set. First of all, it's a short print so it's hard to find it in any condition let alone high-grade. Second, the 1948 Leafs are subject to just about every type of condition obstacle including poor paper, centering, focus, print and color quality.

The two big problems with this card seem to be print and focus. In addition, most Leaf cards have a very dull appearance and lack clarity. The couple of high-grade examples that have surfaced have sold for astronomical prices; this card is a major condition rarity.

1948-49 LEAF SATCHEL PAIGE

## Comments:

I can't say enough about how tough this card is. It is unfortunate that fans were only able to see Satchel pitch after his prime but there are so many great stories about the ability of this man to throw a baseball that it's uncanny. When he did pitch, he packed the ballpark with fans. Those who faced him have the ultimate respect for his talents and he did return that respect. After Babe Ruth crushed a home run off Satchel during an exhibition, Satchel met Ruth at the plate to shake his hand. Those who collect his cards realize how significant Paige is to the history of the game. His legendary status coupled with the difficulty of this card make this one a true centerpiece.

## 1948-49 Leaf #32 Warren Spahn

### Importance:

This is one of only two recognized rookie cards of baseball's all-time winning lefty. That's right; Warren Spahn has more victories than any other left-handed pitcher in baseball history with 363 wins. Koufax and Carlton threw harder and Grove may have been more dominating but Spahn was the most durable of the bunch. Spahn won 20 or more games 13 times in his career and compiled his huge career total despite not winning a game until he was 25 years of age.

In 1973, he was elected to the Hall of Fame after 21 years on the mound with a career ERA of 3.09. Spahn does have another rookie card that appears in the 1948 Bowman set but this Leaf issue is tougher and more popular than the Bowman Spahn rookie card. This Leaf Spahn is one of a few key rookie cards, along with legends Jackie Robinson and Stan Musial, in this fascinating set. At some point, people will start to ask, "Why isn't Spahn's Leaf rookie worth more if he was such a good pitcher?"

### Difficulty:

The Spahn Leaf rookie card is tough as is every card in this difficult set. The Spahn card is often found with a dark, bland look to it. Part of the reason is due to toning along the edges and it is also partly due to the colors chosen for this card. If you can find a Spahn example with nice clean borders, it can really change the eye-appeal for this issue. The crude cutting process, poor paper quality and commonly found print defects just add to the misery. In addition, most Leaf cards have a very dull appearance and lack clarity. All these Leafs are tough. When was the last time you saw a blazing 1948 Leaf Spahn rookie?

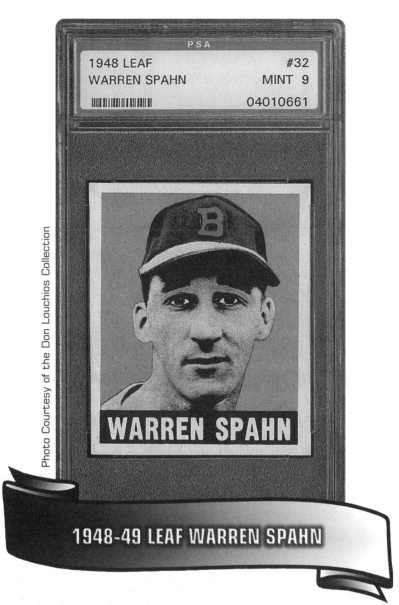

PSA

1948 LEAF          #32

WARREN SPAHN     MINT 9

04010661

**WARREN SPAHN**

**1948-49 LEAF WARREN SPAHN**

## Comments:

Warren Spahn did not receive the attention that Sandy Koufax or Steve Carlton did but the fact remains that Spahn is the all-time leader in victories for a southpaw. Spahn will probably gain respect because, as we look to the future, all collectors will see are Spahn's great numbers. I chose the Leaf Spahn over his Bowman rookie, another great card, because the Leaf example has more going for it. It's tougher, more colorful and part of a much better set overall. The Leaf Spahn rookie may be a "sleeper" and it certainly seems underrated at this point. As a key rookie card in a very popular set, this card should always enjoy solid demand.

## 1948-49 Leaf #76 Ted Williams

### Importance:

This is a key card of Ted Williams in a very popular set. The 1948 Leaf Williams is the first mainstream post-war card featuring the "Splendid Splinter." The card is considered one of Ted's most visually appealing cards as it features that magical swing that helped make him a legend. This card, along with the likes of Joe DiMaggio and Jackie Robinson, are keys to this wonderful set. In 1948 and 1949, Williams enjoyed typical "Splendid Splinter" seasons.

In 1948, Williams hit a league-high .369 with 25 homers and 127 RBI's but he would outdo himself one year later with a .343 average, 43 homers and 159 RBI's (both league bests). He would be awarded the league's MVP Award for his tremendous 1949 season.

### Difficulty:

This card, as part of the 1948 Leaf set, is very tough. This card is commonly found with toning along the edges and reverse of the card. The toning can be a major detractor when it comes to visual appeal but, unfortunately, that isn't the only problem. Centering, print defects and color quality all help make this card a real challenge in high-grade. In addition, most Leaf cards have a very dull appearance and lack clarity. When you can find an example that has a rich orange/red background along with white borders, the card really jumps out at you. This is one of Ted's tougher cards.

Photo Courtesy of National Baseball Hall of Fame Library, Cooperstoown, NY

PSA

1948 LEAF #76
TED WILLIAMS MINT 9

03022540

**TED WILLIAMS**

**1948-49 LEAF TED WILLIAMS**

## Comments:

The 1948 Leaf Williams is a great card for a number of reasons. It's tough, in a popular set, attractive and it features one of the game's greatest hitters during the midway point of his career. Just think of his career numbers: .344 average, 521 homers, 1,798 runs, 1,839 RBI's, 2,019 walks, a .634 slugging average and a .483 on-base average. Williams did it all after missing nearly 5 seasons to military service. The 1948 Leaf set has so much star power that the demand for each key card should remain strong. This card has a very bright future.

## 1948-49 Leaf #79 Jackie Robinson

### Importance:

This is the only true rookie card of baseball's first African-American representative. You can't say enough about the importance of this man. He not only broke the color barrier in baseball; he became a legend in American history. He endured racist taunts and hate mail long before the likes of Hank Aaron and Ken Griffey Jr. would step on the field. If it weren't for Robinson's sacrifice, baseball fans would not have the privilege of watching the great African-American players who grace the field today.

In 1949, Robinson would have his finest year by hitting .342 (a league-high) with 124 RBI's, 122 runs scored and a league-leading 37 stolen bases. This Leaf rookie card is a classic and it would rank very high on the list of pure importance.

### Difficulty:

This card is susceptible to numerous condition problems and perhaps more problems than the average card in this very tough set. 1948 Leaf collectors are aware of the poor paper quality, crude cutting process, toning and centering problems but this Robinson card has even more problems.

One of this card's biggest problems is the stray print marks that affect the image. The background on this card is a very light yellow color so dark print marks really damage the eye-appeal of the card. In many cases, it's simply unavoidable so just make sure the print marks don't take away too much from the visual appeal of the card. In addition, most Leaf cards have a very dull appearance (the Robinson usually exhibits a faint, yellow color) and lack clarity. When was the last time you saw a truly focused copy? This is a very tough card overall.

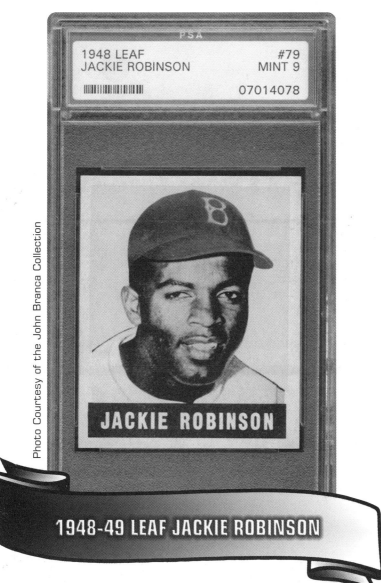

PSA

1948 LEAF          #79
JACKIE ROBINSON    MINT 9

07014078

JACKIE ROBINSON

## 1948-49 LEAF JACKIE ROBINSON

## Comments:

This is just a great card for so many reasons. Robinson was a great player, a great human being, it's a tough card, a popular card, a key card to the set, a rookie card and it signifies progress during a key time in our country's history. It is unfortunate that Jackie had to wait so long (he was 28 years old when he made his debut) but Paige and Campanella suffered the same fate. Their sacrifice helped create opportunity for many of the great stars of today. We cannot forget that and, hopefully, the players can fully appreciate what Jackie meant, and still means to the game. This card may not be Robinson's most attractive looking card, but it marks the beginning of a new era in the game.

## 1948-49 Leaf #93 Bob Feller

### Importance:

This is one of "Rapid Robert's" earliest cards and perhaps his toughest. Bob Feller was the premier power pitcher of his day and, ultimately, a Hall of Famer in 1962. Have you ever seen that film where, on the first try, Feller fires a baseball through a small hole when challenging a motorcycle to a speed contest? The hole was only a fraction larger than the ball itself, Feller didn't even warm up and the motorcycle had a head start, it was amazing!

In 1948 and 1949, Feller would win 19 and 15 games respectively while leading the league in strikeouts in 1948. While they were not Feller's best two years, they were productive and he just came off back-to-back 20 win seasons in 1946-47. This Leaf Feller card is certainly one of the toughest and most desirable cards in the set, only a few cards are more desirable than this one

One interesting aspect to this card is that it really is, arguably, Feller's least visually attractive card, however, the set popularity and difficulty of the card helped vault it onto the list. This card just doesn't come up for sale very often in high-grade; the demand is strong.

### Difficulty:

This card is painfully difficult. When was the last time you saw a high-grade example? It's probably been awhile and that is most likely due to the fact that this card was short printed like the Satchel Paige Leaf card. This card is susceptible to all the condition obstacles associated with 1948 Leafs but there are two major problems with this card, print quality and centering. This card is almost always seen out of focus and with print marks all over the yellow background. In addition, try to find one centered. It's almost impossible. This card would rank very high on the list of pure difficulty.

1948-49 LEAF BOB FELLER

## Comments:

Bob Feller has a very loyal following and this is one of his most important cards. Collectors are drawn to the power pitchers much like they are drawn to the power hitters. Fans like to see something out of the ordinary, something that leaves them in awe. Feller could fire a baseball with incredible velocity. The 20th Century started with Walter Johnson and ended with Nolan Ryan but Feller was the dominant right hander in between and this card, which is certainly his toughest mainstream card, captures Feller in his prime.

## 1949 Bowman #84 Roy Campanella

### Importance:

This is the only recognized rookie card of the legendary catcher and a key to the set. Roy Campanella was simply one of the best catchers in baseball history. In 1949, Campanella played his first full season and, after hitting .287 with 22 homers, the Dodgers decided to make him a regular for years to come. He won three MVP awards for leading his Brooklyn Dodger team to several pennant-winning seasons during the 1950's.

Campanella's 142 RBI's in 1953 remains a record for catchers and his rocket arm was a menace to those on the bases. Unfortunately for Campanella and baseball fans, he entered the major leagues after already playing several seasons in the Negro Leagues and his career was further cut short by hand injuries and a car crash that left "Campy" paralyzed for life.

### Difficulty:

The 1949 Bowmans have trouble with centering due to the design of the cards. The cards are smaller in size than most other post-war cards and the borders are very narrow so many of these are found off-center, there is little room for error. You may find examples with toned borders. If the borders are white, it really helps to provide an attractive frame on the card.

Reverse staining is also very common on all early Bowman issues whether it be from wax or gum, and this can downgrade a card

Photo Courtesy of Troy Kinunen

significantly based on the severity. Finally, look for a bold-colored background. With the Campy, it should have a nice orange/red color behind his face. Sometimes, the color can be faint and unattractive.

1949 BOWMAN ROY CAMPANELLA

## Comments:

Who knows what Campanella could have accomplished if he had the chance. Despite being limited by racism and injuries, Campanella proved to be one of the finest catchers in baseball history. This card is significant in that it represents a time of change and improvement to the game itself. Jackie Robinson wasn't the only African-American who had to endure the pain of breaking the color barrier and Campanella, arguably, had a better career. Roy did have better looking cards produced in his career but this is his only true rookie card and, like the 1939 Play Ball Williams or 1948 Bowman Musial, the importance of the card is undeniable.

## 1949 Bowman #224 Satchel Paige

### Importance:

This is a key card of the most recognizable pitcher in Negro League history. Satchel Paige was deprived of a major league career for most of his playing days but he eventually signed with Cleveland in 1948. While his major league career was brief, Paige was able to show fans and players a glimpse of what could have been with some legendary performances.

In 1949, well past the age of 40, Paige finished the season with a 3.04 ERA, 4 wins and 5 saves. Paige even made an appearance at the age of 59 in 1965, he could do almost anything. Despite a brief career in MLB, he was elected to the Hall of Fame in 1971. This card is one of the few keys to a set that includes the Roy Campanella and Duke Snider rookie cards as well.

There are endless stories about this great pitcher and all of them are interesting. How many pitchers can say that they faced Babe Ruth and Josh Gibson of the 1920's and 1930's yet also faced star players of the 1950's? The answer is Satchel.

### Difficulty:

The 1949 Bowmans have trouble with centering due to the design of the cards. The cards are smaller in size than most other post-war cards and the borders are very narrow so many of these are found off-center, there is little room for error. You may find examples with toned borders. If the borders are white, it really helps to provide an attractive frame on the card.

Reverse staining is also very common on all early Bowman issues. Whether it be from wax or gum, this can downgrade a card significantly based on the severity. Finally, look for a bold-colored background. With Paige, you want a bold blue/green background. Sometimes, the color can be faint and unattractive.

PSA

1949 BOWMAN
SATCHELL PAIGE
#224
MINT 9
06012329

LEROY "Satchell" PAIGE

1949 BOWMAN SATCHEL PAIGE

## Comments:

This card is one of only three mainstream Paige cards in existence and two of the three made the list. This Paige was chosen over the 1953 Topps Paige for a few reasons. The 1953 Topps Paige, a great card in its own right, was Satchel's first Topps card but this Bowman beauty was produced four years earlier, it is a major key and, while it is not nearly as significant as his 1948-49 Leaf example, many collectors view this Bowman Paige as a rookie card. In fact, this Bowman Paige does have an edge on the Leaf in terms of visual appeal.

## 1949 Bowman #226 Duke Snider

### Importance:

This is the only recognized rookie card of one of baseball's most popular figures from the 1950's. There was Mickey, Willie and the Duke, three great center fielders, all playing in New York. Snider was often overshadowed by Mantle and Mays but Snider remains one of baseball's most popular personalities. Snider led the Brooklyn Dodgers at the plate for several years as their most feared hitter.

In 1949, Snider hit .292 with 23 homers and 92 RBI's in his first full season. He would continue to be the Dodgers' regular center fielder for over a decade. This rookie card is one of the keys to the set, which is far more attractive than Bowman's previous offering.

Snider, like Mantle, had a lot of potential contenders for inclusion on this list but including his only recognized rookie card was automatic. It's true that some of Duke's later Bowman and Topps examples have superior eye-appeal, after card companies started to use more and more color in the manufacturing process, but this card is, arguably, his most important.

### Difficulty:

The 1949 Bowmans have trouble with centering due to the design of the cards. The cards are smaller in size than most other post-war cards and the borders are very narrow so many of these are found off-center, there is little room for error. You may find examples with toned borders. If the borders are white, it really helps to provide an attractive frame on the card. Reverse staining is also very common on all early Bowman issues.

Whether it be from wax or gum, this can downgrade a card significantly based on the severity. Finally, look for a bold-colored background. For Duke, you want to look for a nice yellow/green backdrop behind his face. Sometimes, the color can be faint and unattractive.

1949 BOWMAN DUKE SNIDER

## Comments:

Duke Snider is a fan favorite and this is his official rookie card. The Dodgers, like the New York Yankees, have a rich history filled with legendary stars and Snider is a key figure along with Jackie Robinson, Pee Wee Reese, Sandy Koufax and Roy Campanella. This card may not be the toughest one on the list and Snider may not be quite as popular as Mantle but this card should enjoy solid demand in the future. The Duke is a mainstay.

# 1950 Bowman #98 Ted Williams

## Importance:

This is the first Bowman card to feature the "Splendid Splinter." In 1950, Bowman decided to add a great slugger named Ted Williams to their set. It was a good decision. This card, along with the Jackie Robinson card, are the keys to the set. Once again, Bowman outdid themselves in terms of design. Their 1950 offering was clearly more attractive than their previous two of-ferings. These cards look somewhat similar to the beautiful Goudeys of 1933, like little pieces of artwork.

This classic image, which would be reused for Bowman's 1951 Williams card, features the sweet-swinging lefty with a blue sky in the background. In 1950, Williams would hit .317 with 28 homers and 97 RBI's, not typical numbers for "Teddy Ballgame." Oh, I forgot to mention that he did that in a mere 89 games! As Bowman's very first effort to capture Williams, this is a very important card.

## Difficulty:

Centering is the biggest condition obstacle here as these cards are small with very narrow borders. It is very difficult to find these cards cut perfectly centered off the sheet. Border ton-ing and color quality can also be problems. This card is com-monly found with very faint color that, in turn, deprives the card of eye-appeal. This Williams card is famous for having a faint print line that travels from his cap downward to the roof of the stadium in the background. Since this defect is typical for the card, it will not detract from the overall grade.

Reverse staining is also very common on all early Bowman is-sues, whether it be from wax or gum, and this can downgrade a card significantly based on the severity. The last obstacle to look for is the cut itself. These Bowmans will sometimes have a very rough-cut and sometimes a smooth one. Rough-cuts are not necessarily a bad thing just make sure that the cut doesn't affect the eye-appeal or the corners too severely.

Photo Courtesy of the Don Louchios Collection

1950 BOWMAN TED WILLIAMS

## Comments:

You can never go wrong with Ted Williams and this is his first Bowman issue. The card is attractive and one of two major keys to the 1950 Bowman set. Williams is one of those players who reached another level of stardom, a level that only players like Mantle and Ruth achieved. If you can find this card centered and sharp, you really have something. This is not Ted's toughest or most valuable card but it's important nonetheless. The 1950 Bowman set lacks the star power that other sets have (Mantle and Mays would join the fun the very next year) but that makes this card affordable in comparison to some of his other issues.

## 1951 Bowman #1 Whitey Ford

### Importance:

This is the first card in a very popular set and it happens to be a rookie card of one of the most beloved New York Yankee pitchers of all-time. This card has a lot going for it including Ford's smile on the front which captures the joy of playing for the Yankees during a time when they always seemed to win. Whitey Ford was a dominant pitcher on many Yankee championship teams in the 1950's and 1960's.

In fact, this Hall of Famer still holds the record for the highest career winning percentage (.690) among 200-game winners. Ford used a variety of pitches and great control to baffle opposing batters. His career 2.71 ERA in World Series play gave him the reputation of being a "Big Game" pitcher, Ford came through when it mattered most. He was inducted into the Hall of Fame in 1974.

Whitey made his debut in 1950 and, after being called up halfway through the season, compiled a 9-1 record with a 2.81 ERA. Ford would miss the next two years after serving in the military but came back as one of New York's starters in 1953. This card is one of several keys to the 1951 Bowman set that includes rookie cards of Willie Mays and Mickey Mantle as well.

### Difficulty:

In addition to being the first card in the set and, in turn, being a target for the rubber bands of collectors, this card has problems with centering and picture quality. More often than not, you see this card with a faint appearance on the front. Whether the image is slightly out of focus or the color is faint, the card is in need of pizzazz more often than not. Reverse staining is also very common on all early Bowman issues. Whether it be from wax or gum, this can downgrade a card significantly based on the severity. This card is a real condition rarity for the 1951 Bowman set.

Photo Courtesy of the John Branca Collection

PSA

1951 BOWMAN #1
WHITEY FORD MINT 9

07053831

ED "WHITEY" FORD

## 1951 BOWMAN WHITEY FORD

## Comments:

With the loyal New York Yankee collector base out there, this card enjoys tremendous popularity. The Yankees just have a rich history like no other franchise in the game and Ford is a very significant figure in that history. He was the ace of the staff when Mantle was blasting home runs and Berra was behind the plate. The bottom line is that this is a rookie card that features a Yankee great and it's the first card in a tremendous set, the ultimate trio. What more could you ask for?

# 1951 Bowman #253 Mickey Mantle

## Importance:

This is the only recognized rookie card of "The Mick." Mickey Mantle is quite simply the most widely collected baseball player on the planet. He was the hero of choice for youngsters around the globe during the 1950's and 1960's. The pressure on him was immense as he inherited center field from Joe DiMaggio, one of the most beloved Yankees of all-time.

In 1951, Mantle would make his debut for the Yanks. Even though he only played part-time and hit a mere 13 homers, most of those homers were of the tape measure variety. Management immediately recognized the potential this young man possessed and Mantle would patrol the center field grass for years to come. Despite terrible injuries that robbed him of his speed, Mantle went on to be one of the most devastating sluggers in baseball history. This card is the key to a very popular set and the classic pose is a memorable one. This is one of the most important cards on the list.

## Difficulty:

Centering, centering, centering. If there was one major condition obstacle to this card, it has to be centering. Very few examples are found well centered. When you do find one, it never seems to be sharp so finding one in high-grade poses a real challenge. Black print marks can also be an eyesore if they get too close to Mickey's face. The light-blue background makes it hard to miss any print marks so watch out.

Speaking of color, many collectors focus on the hat area, looking for bold color in addition to a focused image of Mantle's face. In addition, many of these examples are often found with a rough-cut. Rough-cuts are not usually considered a detractor but some collectors cringe at severe, jagged edges. Reverse staining is also very common on all early Bowman issues. Whether it stem from wax or gum, this can downgrade a card significantly based on the severity. This is widely considered to be tougher than his 1952 Topps example, which usually steals the spotlight.

1951 BOWMAN MICKEY MANTLE

## Comments:

You can't say enough about Mickey Mantle. He was a hero as a player and a hero towards the end of his short life when he accepted responsibility for his drinking problems. Mantle wasn't a perfect human being but that is part of why he attracted so many fans. He had flaws as a person which made him human but his play on the field was like that of no average man. His only official rookie card is tough and popular, leaving its owner with a true hobby treasure. It remains to be seen how well this Bowman example will perform in terms of demand against his, admittedly, more popular 1952 Topps card over the years. The Topps Mantle certainly has the edge in popularity but, once again, this is his only true rookie card. Case closed.

## 1951 Bowman #305 Willie Mays

### Importance:

This is the only recognized rookie card featuring Willie Mays. The "Say Hey Kid" was, perhaps, the best all-around player that the game of baseball has ever seen. He hit 660 home runs, had great speed, was terrific defensively and he did it all with a natural grace unmatched during his era. He could crush like Mantle and Aaron but throw and field like Clemente. His all-around talent was amazing.

In 1951, he started his career in a horrific slump but broke out of it with a home run blast off of fellow Hall of Famer Warren Spahn. Mays finished the year with a .274 average and 20 homers, giving fans just a glimpse of what was to come. This card is only second to the Mantle rookie when it comes to the 1951 Bowman set and it might actually be tougher. This is clearly one of the most significant rookie cards in the hobby.

### Difficulty:

This card is very, very tough. Like the Mantle rookie card, this Mays example has to battle poor centering due to its narrow borders. The horizontal design seems to only increase the appearance of bad centering and very few sharp examples are ever found centered. Another obstacle to look for is the lack of eye-appeal or bland color. A nice showing of gloss, along with bold color, can really help this card's appearance.

Photo Courtesy of Troy Kinunen

Reverse staining is also very common on all early Bowman issues whether it be from wax or gum, and this can downgrade a card significantly based on the severity. This is one of Willie's tougher (if not the toughest) cards.

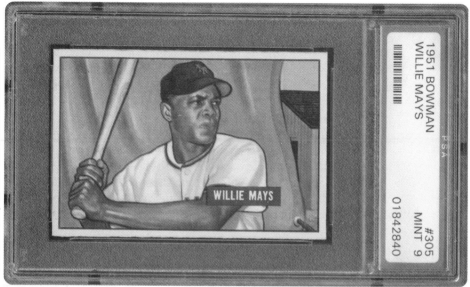

Photo Courtesy of the John Branca Collection

1951 BOWMAN
WILLIE MAYS

PSA

#305
MINT 9

01842840

WILLIE MAYS

## 1951 BOWMAN WILLIE MAYS

## Comments:

How can you go wrong with a tough rookie card of baseball's best all-around player? It's the only official rookie card for Mays, it's tough and it's the second most valuable card in a very popular set. Unlike the comparison between the 1951 Bowman and 1952 Topps Mantle, this Bowman Mays has a clear edge. For whatever reason, collectors have not been drawn to the 1952 Topps Mays like they are to the Mantle, so the Bowman rookie card, in Willie's case, gets most of the attention. Mays cards, in general, have been steadily gaining in popularity over the years. For too many years, Mantle overshadowed Mays but Mays is gaining more respect as time goes on. There is simply fabulous, ongoing demand for this great rookie card.

# 1952 Bowman #1 Yogi Berra

## Importance:

This is the first card in the 1952 Bowman set and it features fan favorite and 1951 A.L. MVP Yogi Berra. The 1952 Bowman set, while not as popular as the previous Bowman issue, is filled with a nice selection of star cards and it features great artwork. The first slot in the set was given to a man who didn't look like much of an athlete but boy could he play. Berra was the field general for the most dominating team in Yankee history and he was a great run producer at the plate.

In 1952, Berra hit .273 with 30 homers (a career high for Berra) and driving in 98 runs after winning the A.L. MVP in 1951. His home run and RBI marks were actually better in 1952. He might be the most quoted baseball player in history and his saying, "It ain't over till it's over," might be the most popular saying in sports. As the first card in a quality set, this card is very important.

## Difficulty:

As the first card in the set, it also has its share of condition obstacles. I am sure this card was often strangled by collectors who chose rubber bands to hold Yogi hostage. Also, the 1952 Bowmans, maybe even more so than the 1951 Bowmans, are commonly found with toning along the edges. Toned edges can make for a real eyesore if the toning is severe and they are very commonly found on cards from the first series of this set. With narrow borders, this card can give you trouble if you are looking for a centered copy.

Reverse staining is also very common on all early Bowman issues. Whether it stem from wax or gum, this can downgrade a card significantly based on the severity. Remember that rough-cuts are not necessarily a bad thing; just make sure it's not so severe as to ruin the eye-appeal of the card. Beauty is In the eye of the beholder.

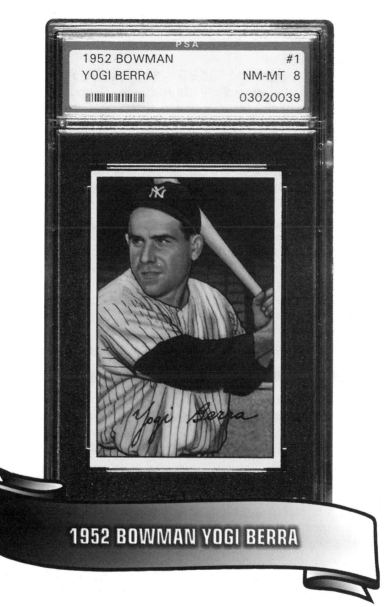

1952 BOWMAN      #1
YOGI BERRA      NM-MT 8
03020039

**1952 BOWMAN YOGI BERRA**

## Comments:

Yogi Berra, much like Whitey Ford, has a following that is much stronger than one would think. As an individual, he was one of the greatest catchers in baseball history and won the MVP award on three separate occasions. As a Yankee, he is elevated to legendary status and part of a major dynasty. Also, like Ford's 1951 Bowman card, this Bowman Berra has an assortment of positive characteristics going for it. The importance of this number one card is, perhaps, elevated considering that the 1952 Bowman set lacks any major rookie card so the focus turns to the stars and Berra was one of the brightest.

# 1952 Bowman #101 Mickey Mantle

## Importance:

This is the key to the 1952 Bowman set and a wonderful piece of artwork. This example, while not nearly as popular as his 1952 Topps issue, is a great example of the beauty of vintage 1950's cards. Forget about laser printed, gold foil cards of today, I'll take the great images provided by artists during vintage times. The card shows a young, extremely confident Mantle with his arms crossed. Early in his career, Mantle's confidence was actually in doubt but once he found his powerful swing, it was all over for opposing pitchers.

In 1952, Mantle gained a little more experience and it showed at the plate after hitting .311 with 23 home runs and 94 runs scored. Mantle would end up scoring 100 or more runs for the next 9 straight years en route to Hall of Fame induction in 1974. This card really captures Mantle's presence.

## Difficulty:

The 1952 Bowmans, maybe even more so than the 1951 Bowmans, are commonly found with toning along the edges. Toned edges can make for a real eyesore if the toning is severe. With narrow borders, this card can give you trouble if you are looking for a centered copy. Reverse staining is also very common on all early Bowman issues. Whether it be from wax or gum, this can downgrade a card significantly based on the severity.

This card is not one of the toughest Mickey Mantle cards on the list but it's one of those cards that is hard to find with all the right qualities together. If it's sharp, it's usually off-center. If it's centered, it's usually soft or has faint color. I think you get the picture.

Photo Courtesy of the John Branca Collection

PSA

1952 BOWMAN      #101
MICKEY MANTLE     MINT 9

03537908

**1952 BOWMAN MICKEY MANTLE**

## Comments:

To this day, I don't understand why this card is so dramatically overlooked in comparison to his 1952 Topps card. That is not to say that the 1952 Topps card shouldn't enjoy higher demand, it should for many reasons but the gap is too wide in my opinion. The 1952 Bowman set will never be as popular as the Topps issue but it is no slouch. There are many great cards in the set; there's even a Musial card that wasn't included in the Topps set. This card would not rank extremely high on the list in terms of pure difficulty but it's still a very significant card in the hobby.

## 1952 Bowman #196 Stan Musial

### Importance:

This is one of the most beautiful cards in the entire hobby and it features legendary hitter Stan Musial. This card would be popular regardless of Stan's performance, it's that appealing. The fact that Musial became one of baseball's greatest hitters turns the card from an artful wonder into a classic. The card, certainly one of the keys to the set, exhibits a great combination of colors and a razor sharp image of "Stan the Man."

In 1952, Musial hit .336 with a .538 slugging average, 105 runs and 194 hits, all league-highs. He would continue to pile up hits year in and year out en route to his Hall of Fame admission in 1969. Did you know that Musial collected the exact same amount of hits on the road as he did at home with 1815? How's that for consistency. This card captures Musial at his best, in his batting stance.

This card, while not his rookie, might be his most popular example. There are other Musial cards that may be more valuable, including his 1953 Bowman example, however, this has a classic feel to it and may be one of the best looking cards ever issued.

### Difficulty:

This card is not one of the tougher vintage cards on this list but this card is much tougher than any modern creation. Due to a "find," you can acquire this card without major problems, but centering is another issue. Many of these cards are not found well-centered, leaving many examples shy of what would be tolerable for "Mint" status.

Reverse staining is also very common on all early Bowman issues. Whether it be from wax or gum, this can downgrade a card significantly based on the severity. Also, look for extra bold color on this one because, when you find one, the eye-appeal is amazing. Not a very tough card, but it doesn't need to be to make the list.

PSA

| 1952 BOWMAN | #196 |
| STAN MUSIAL | MINT 9 |
| | 05322035 |

## 1952 BOWMAN STAN MUSIAL

## Comments:

Stan Musial continues to gain popularity years after his retirement. His wonderful personality at shows has helped his cause because he's not only a baseball legend; he's also a great guy, much like Harmon Killebrew. Remember that popularity can often enhance sportscard desirability beyond a player's performance level or career accomplishments. Some of the greatest players in the game don't have a great collector following but Musial has a very loyal following and it's growing. This Musial card is simply one of the most visually appealing cards of the era.

# 1952 Bowman #218 Willie Mays

## Importance:

This is a deceptively difficult early Mays card and a key to the set. Like the Mantle card from the same set, this card puzzles me. If you think about it, it should be worth a lot more than it currently is. It's only the second Bowman issue available for Mays and it is, by far, tougher than the 1952 Topps issue yet it sells for much less. Mays was a victim of the times. Racism ate at his soul and eventually turned a cheerful young man into a bitter, machine-like performer. You can talk about Mantle, Aaron or Clemente, but it is Mays who has the best overall statistics of the group.

Of all the great skills Mays possessed, the most impressive might be his combination of power and speed. Until Mays came along, not too many others had the ability to steal a base and hit a home run with regularity. In 1955, Mays became the first player in National League history to hit 50 or more homers and steal 20 or more bases in a single year. If he played in a different park, he may have challenged Ruth before Aaron did. Power and speed on the field, eye-appeal and difficulty on the cardboard, winning combinations all around.

## Difficulty:

As part of the tough high-number series, this Mays card is tougher than most collectors realize. It's not quite a short print but it is far less common than the regular star cards from the same set. The 1952 Bowmans, maybe even more so than the 1951 Bowmans, are commonly found with toning along the edges. Toned edges can make be a real problem if the toning is severe. With narrow borders, this card can give you trouble if you are looking for a centered copy and this Mays is often found way off-centered.

Reverse staining is also very common on all early Bowman issues. Whether it be from wax or gum, this can downgrade a card significantly based on the severity. Also, look for nice print quality on this one. The Mays isn't the most eye-appealing card but, when focused, it can be attractive.

| PSA | |
|---|---|
| 1952 BOWMAN | #218 |
| WILLIE MAYS | NM-MT 8 |
| | 06019811 |

## 1952 BOWMAN WILLIE MAYS

## Comments:

While Mays might still be one of the most underrated players in baseball history, it is actually a blessing for collectors. There seems to be a window of opportunity to acquire Mays cards at reasonable levels in comparison to other legends of the game. This guy won batting, home run, stolen base and fielding titles. He won the MVP (twice), the Rookie of the Year, numerous Gold Gloves and played in 24 All-Star games. Nobody in the game has ever been so successful in so many facets of the game. Knowing how tough this card is, try to rationalize why it's so overlooked in comparison to other cards. It doesn't make any sense. It's not like the card is unattractive, it's a nice looking card, it's tough and it's Willie Mays. What's wrong with this picture?

## 1952 Topps #1 Andy Pafko

### Importance:

This is the most important #1 card in the post-war era. You might be wondering who Andy Pafko is. Well, Pafko did not have a very distinguished career, although he did manage to club 213 homers and bat .285 along the way. Pafko was given the honor of being the very first card in the most popular post-war set of all-time, the 1952 Topps issue.

We all have heard the stories about rubber bands destroying number one cards as youngsters across the country placed these lethal wraps around the edges of cards. The first card in each stack was always the one to take the brunt of the abuse and poor Pafko took a lot over the years. This is simply the most sought after non-star card in the hobby due to its number one spot and inclusion in the most popular post-war set.

### Difficulty:

As the first card in the set, you already have an idea of what this card means to the 1952 Topps set builder. The Pafko card took major abuse from overhandling and rubber bands, always residing at the top of the stack. It's simply the most challenging card in the entire set with centering being the biggest inherent condition problem. In fact, there is a very low population of these cards in Near Mint or better condition, with NM-MT 8's few and far betweeen.

A few years back, a collector stumbled across an unopened pack of 1952 Topps cards and decided to open it. With only five cards inserted into each pack, the chances of pulling a Pafko were incredibly slim. After removing the first two cards in the pack, there it was, a beautiful Pafko. That exact card would eventually grade as a Gem Mint 10 by PSA and sell for $83,870. Till this day, no other example has reached a MINT 9 status let alone a Gem Mint 10. There is still only a handful of PSA 8's in circulation, not nearly enough to satisfy the collecting public. This is an extraordinarily tough card, one of the toughest on the list in high-grade.

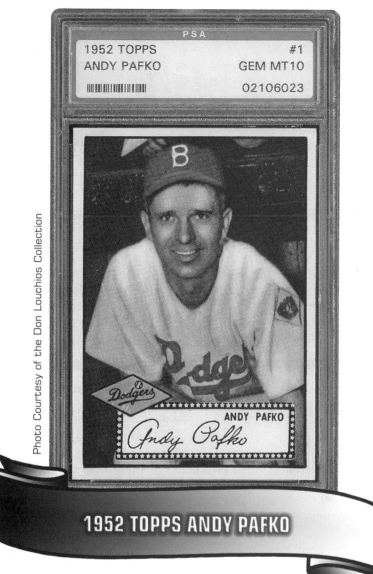

PSA

1952 TOPPS                                    #1

ANDY PAFKO                           GEM MT10

                                     02106023

1952 TOPPS ANDY PAFKO

## Comments:

You may have noticed that I chose not to include any other non-star rarities on this list (with the exception of the Jim Lansford example in the football section) and I still defend that approach vehemently. I believe, in most cases, once you get past the small group of collectors who want the non-star rarity or even the star obscurity, the demand falls quickly in the general market. This Pafko is different. The 1952 Topps set is so popular and this card is so tough, that I simply could not ignore it. With the set in such high demand and being unquestionably significant as a symbol of the hobby, the Pafko, despite his non-star status, should remain a focal point for future generations of collectors. If you want a high-grade 1952 Topps set, you have to own this card.

## 1952 Topps #191 Yogi Berra

**Importance:**

This is the second Topps issue (his first was the 1951 Topps Red Back) to feature Yogi and a key to the set. Yogi Berra is a study in contrast. He was a clown but a leader. He made illogical statements but he was brilliant. He looked like a non-athlete but he was the best catcher in the game. Forget about his name, what he looks like and especially what he sounds like, Yogi Berra is what all catchers strive to be. This Hall of Famer (elected in 1972) called a great game and mashed at the plate, you couldn't ask more from a backstop.

The New York Yankees had a lot of talent when Berra was catching for them but it was Berra who was named MVP on three different occasions. He was also the only catcher to call a perfect game in the World Series and he played for 10 World Series Championship teams. This leader is a very important figure, not only Yankee history, but baseball history as well. Yogi was a winner.

**Difficulty:**

Hey, I heard that there was a "find" of these cards several years ago so they must be easy to find in high-grade, right? Wrong. While these cards were the subject of two different "finds" years ago, most of the cards from each "find" were off-center with many of them severely off-center. These cards are not easy at all. Centering and tilts, as indicated by cards removed from the "find," are probably the most common problems with diamond cuts being extremely common (diamond cuts are found where the image and the border/frame seem to be misaligned, causing a tilt or angled appearance).

After that, the borders seem to really range in appearance. Look for examples that have bright, white borders. The examples from the "find" usually have them. Finally, beware of paper wrinkles on the reverse. They are not quite creases (they don't go through the cardboard) but they will downgrade a card significantly and they are hard to see with the naked eye.

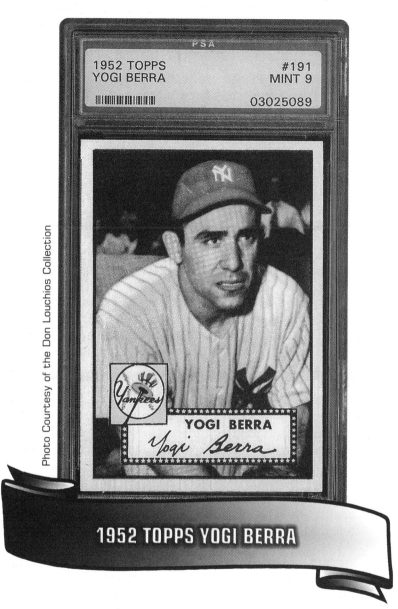

PSA

1952 TOPPS #191
YOGI BERRA

MINT 9

03025089

YOGI BERRA

1952 TOPPS YOGI BERRA

## Comments:

Yogi Berra was the backbone of the Yankees before Mantle became the superstar who dominated in the 1950's and early 1960's. Berra also won just as many MVP's as "The Mick." Add to that the fact that this card is very tough to find in top grades and you have a great overall card. This is a key for many reasons. The 1952 Topps set, as a whole, will always enjoy great demand as an attractive beauty and the first full-sized set issued by Topps. One hundred years from now, all someone will have to say is "Yogi" and people will immediately know whom they are talking about.

## 1952 Topps #261 Willie Mays

### Importance:

This is the first Topps card featuring Hall of Fame legend Willie Mays. While this card is not his rookie, it is one of Willie's best cards. This card is part of the widely collected 1952 Topps set and it is certainly one of the major keys. The image captures an intense Mays who was, perhaps, the best center fielder and overall player the game has ever seen. Who will forget his incredible over the shoulder catch of Vic Wertz's 450ft drive in the World Series?

It has been argued that if Mays did not hit in windy Candlestick Park late in his career, he would have been the all-time leader in home runs. Regardless, his accomplishments are astounding. This two-time NL MVP was inducted to the Hall of Fame in 1979.

There was no player, during that era, who was better than Willie Mays. He possessed a showman quality and a love of the game that could not be matched. Mays was perhaps the best pure entertainer since Babe Ruth and, like Ruth, it wasn't just flamboyant style. It was the ability to do what the other players couldn't do; they were both ahead of their time. This card has been overlooked for too long.

### Difficulty:

This card is not the most difficult Mays card on the list but it still has its problems. The biggest problem with this card seems to be the presence of tilts or diamond cuts (diamond cuts are found where the image and the border/frame seem to be misaligned, causing a tilt or angled appearance). As a result, it is difficult to find a centered copy.

In addition, this card can really vary in eye-appeal. Look for a bright example with clean borders and a sharp image. This card can be very bland without it. There were two major "finds" of 1952 Topps cards years ago and, in those "finds," there were many Mays cards found. That doesn't mean they were all high-grade, the card is still not that easy.

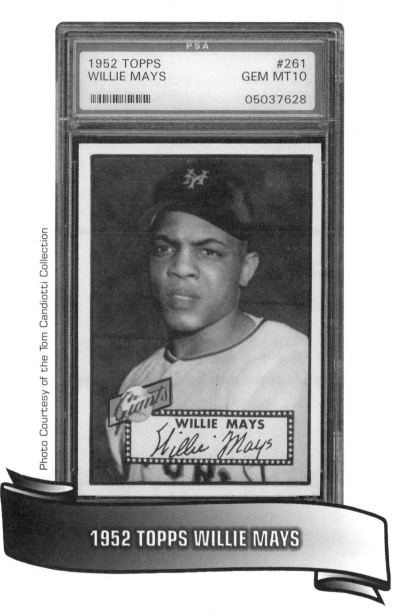

Photo Courtesy of the Tom Candiotti Collection

PSA
1952 TOPPS          #261
WILLIE MAYS

GEM MT10

05037628

1952 TOPPS WILLIE MAYS

## Comments:

In my opinion, regardless of the two "finds," this card might be one of the most overlooked cards today. The Mantle card, from the same set, is treated like royalty despite the fact that, like Mays, Mantle's true rookie card resides in the 1951 Bowman set. Over time, Mays will be recognized for the player that he was and his 1952 Topps card will be more closely aligned with the Mantle in terms of demand. The 1950's was a magical time in the game. There were so many great stars and New York was the home for many of them. Mays was the best.

# 1952 Topps #311 Mickey Mantle

## Importance:

This is, perhaps, the most recognizable sportscard in the entire hobby and it's Mickey Mantle's most desirable card. This is one of those cards that symbolizes baseball card collecting. The image is stunning, one that most collectors are familiar with and, even though this is technically not Mantle's rookie card, it is treated as such. The card is also one of the major keys to the incredibly popular 1952 Topps set which is, arguably, the most popular set in the hobby. When you look at this card and read the name "Mickey Mantle," it's almost like he was destined to become a superstar. After slugging .530 in 1952, Mickey was well on his way. This card is of the utmost importance.

## Difficulty:

The interesting aspect of this card is, for years, people have been claiming that the 1951 Bowman Mantle was a much tougher card to locate in high-grade due to the two "finds" of 1952 Topps cards several years ago. So far, this has not been proven. The 1951 Bowman Mantle is tougher to locate in general but, as far as high-grade copies are concerned, the two issues are fairly comparable with the 1951 Bowman card only having a slight edge at this point.

The 1952 Topps Mantle, in addition to being part of the tough high-number series, is susceptible to centering problems, border toning, and variations in print quality with diamond cuts being extremely common (diamond cuts are found where the image and the border/frame seem to be misaligned, causing a tilt or angled appearance).

They may be few and far between but some examples can have amazing visual appeal. The beautiful blue background is often found with print defects that can hinder the eye-appeal. Mantle examples that originated from each "find" are usually identifiable because of the fresh appearance and white borders they possess. Keep in mind that there are actually two different versions of this card (it was a double print). Even though there is no difference in value, the line surrounding the Yankee logo box is completely blackened in on one version and only partially on the other. This is a deceptively tough card in high-grade.

## 1952 TOPPS MICKEY MANTLE

## Comments:

This card speaks for itself. The demand for this 1952 Topps Mantle should always be strong because of what the card represents. This is one of those cards that should be looked at in an entirely different light. Like the T206 Honus Wagner or 1933 Goudey Babe Ruth #53, this card is immediately recognizable and represents the classic feel of early cardboard art. On pure importance and popularity, this card would rank very high on the list. With the strength of the high-grade sportscard market, this card actually seems a bit underrated in comparison to other significant cards.

## 1952 Topps #312 Jackie Robinson

### Importance:

This is the first Topps card to feature legendary American icon Jackie Robinson. The reason I said American icon instead of sports or baseball icon is because Robinson is much, much more than a mere athlete. Few baseball players have made an impact like Jackie did. The card features Jackie's wonderful smile against a bold red background. None of us will ever know the pain Robinson had to endure but, at the same time, none of us will forget his sacrifice either. He could hit for power and average, had great speed and was a fine defensive second baseman.

In 1952, Robinson would hit .308 with 104 runs scored and a league-high .440 OBP. In his career, after nearly 5,000 at bats, he only struck out 291 times. Amazing! This card captures Jackie's great smile and it must have been hard to smile after all the torment Robinson had to endure. The red background provides a perfect backdrop to the fiery competitor, few played the game with such passion but, then again, Jackie was on a mission and had a lot to prove. This card, with the set popularity and the fact it was Jackie's first Topps card, is certainly one of his best.

### Difficulty:

As a member of the tough high-number series, this Robinson card is tougher to locate than other keys in the set like the Mays. Hey, I heard that there was a "find" or two of these cards several years ago so they must be easy to find in high-grade, right? Wrong. While these cards were the subject of two "finds" years ago, most of the cards in each "find" were off-center with many of them severely off-center. These cards are not easy at all. Centering and tilts, as indicated by the "find," are probably the most common problems.

After that, the borders seem to really range in appearance. Look for Robinson examples that have bright, white borders along with deep, red color in the background. The examples from each "find" usually exhibit these two important qualities. Finally, beware of paper wrinkles on the reverse. They are not quite creases (they don't go through the cardboard) but they will downgrade a card significantly and they are hard to see with the naked eye.

**1952 TOPPS JACKIE ROBINSON**

## Comments:

As baseball fans, we were deprived of seeing Robinson for an entire career in MLB. Who knows what kind of numbers Jackie would have amassed if he played 2,000 or more games? In his brief time, he won the Rookie of the Year and MVP Awards but forget about his pure numbers and awards for a moment. It was Jackie's impact that he will be remembered for. This wonderful portrait of this American icon should remain in very high demand for years to come as future generations learn about Jackie's sacrifice.

## 1952 Topps #314 Roy Campanella

### Importance:

This is the first Topps issue to feature legendary backstop Roy Campanella. Like Jackie Robinson, Roy Campanella was deprived of a full major league career but racism wasn't the only obstacle stopping the strong catcher. Injuries, on a few different occasions, shortened his career. A horrific car accident would end it. After the accident, almost 100,000 fans came out to honor Campy during an exhibition game in the spring of 1959. Forget about the numbers, that showing of support should tell you a lot about the man.

In 1952, Campanella would bang out 22 homers and drive in 97 runs but, one year later, Campy would have the best season of his career. He was awarded the NL MVP (one of three in his career) after hitting .312 with 41 homers, 142 RBI's (a league-high), and slugging .611. It would be his finest season and, arguably, one of the finest by any catcher in baseball history. There's no question, if Campanella could have played at least 4-5 more years, some of his numbers would be virtually untouchable for a catcher. Regardless, he was named to the Hall of Fame in 1969.

### Difficulty:

While these cards were the subject of a "find" or two years ago, most of the cards in each "find" were off-center with many of them severely off-center. These cards are not easy at all. Centering and tilts, as indicated by each "find," are probably the most common problems.

After that, the borders seem to really range in appearance. Look for Campanella examples that have bright, white borders along with a bright, yellow background (also susceptible to print defects). The examples from each "find" usually exhibit both features and the yellow color can be truly stunning. Finally, beware of paper wrinkles on the reverse. They are not quite creases (they don't go through the cardboard) but they will downgrade a card significantly and they are hard to see with the naked eye.

Photo Courtesy of the Don Louchios Collection

**1952 TOPPS ROY CAMPANELLA**

## Comments:

As baseball fans, we can argue all day long about who would be considered the top handful of outfielders or pitchers of all-time but, when it comes to great catchers, there are only a few and each one is immediately recognizable. You have Johnny Bench, Yogi Berra and Roy Campanella at the top and not necessarily in that order. Carlton Fisk and Thurman Munson were good and Mickey Cochrane was a star but only a few are considered the very best (we'll have to wait for Ivan Rodriguez and Mike Piazza before we can fairly judge them). Campanella is unquestionably one of them. The greatness of the set along with the fact he played for the Brooklyn Dodgers just adds to this card's appeal.

## 1952 Topps #407 Eddie Mathews

### Importance:
This is the last card in the incredibly popular 1952 Topps set and it features the only rookie card of 500 home run club member Eddie Mathews. Due to the amount of 1952 Topps set collectors and the focus on the 500 Home Run Club, this card is special. The fact that it is a condition rarity, as the last card in the set, makes it extra special. By the way, it doesn't hurt that Bowman didn't include Mathews as part of their set that same year. Mathews was a part of the most prolific home run duo ever. No, it wasn't Babe Ruth and Lou Gehrig; it was Hank Aaron and Eddie Mathews.

In 1952, the slugger's debut season, he jacked 25 home runs but his encore was even better. With only one year under his belt, Mathews pounded 47 homers, hit .302 and drove in 135 runs. This was, most likely, his finest season at the plate. A fiery competitor, Mathews went on to crush 512 homers and was often overshadowed by the amazing Hank Aaron but he still ranks as one of the greatest sluggers of all-time. Mathews was elected to the Hall of Fame in 1978.

### Difficulty:
This is another key card that resides in the tough high-number series and that is just the beginning of this card's difficulty. Rubber bands just loved Eddie in 1952. As the last card in the set, this card was often the one that received the brunt of the damage. Most importantly, centering is nearly impossible on this Mathews because of the location of the card on the bottom corner of the sheet. When was the last time you saw one that was nicely centered? It's probably been awhile.

Photo Courtesy of National Baseball Hall of Fame Library, Cooperstoown, NY

This card would rank high on the list of pure difficulty; you very rarely see this card centered and sharp.

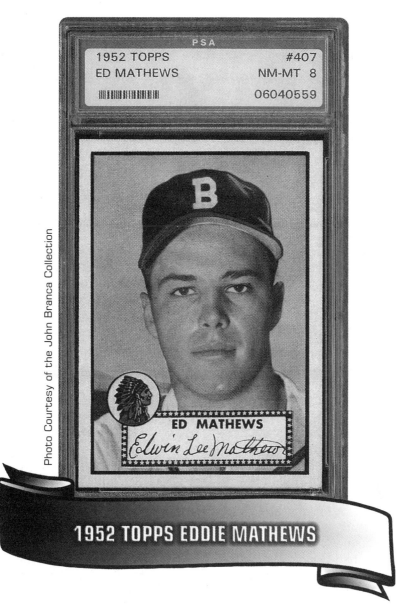

Photo Courtesy of the John Branca Collection

PSA

1952 TOPPS #407
ED MATHEWS NM-MT 8
06040559

ED MATHEWS

1952 TOPPS EDDIE MATHEWS

## Comments:

Eddie Mathews was not as popular as some of his contemporaries like Mickey Mantle or Willie Mays but his accomplishments speak for themselves. He was a great slugger and a very intense player; the kind of player any baseball fan would appreciate. Mathews will also forever be tied to his teammate Hank Aaron as one half of the most prolific slugging duo ever. In addition to the Pafko and a few other obscure rarities, this Mathews is one of the toughest keys in the set. The fact that this card is a necessity for set builders means the demand for this card should continue to be exceptionally strong.

## 1953 Bowman #33 Pee Wee Reese

### Importance:

This is one of the most classic images ever to grace a sportscard. If you had to rank the all-time list purely on the popularity of the image itself, this card would rank near the top. Reese is pictured, apparently, leaping gracefully over an incoming runner, desperately trying the break-up the double play.

Years ago, this card was often referred to as a reverse negative because the runner actually appears to going from third to second with a headfirst dive. The famous shot was taken during spring training and, if you take a close look, no other players or spectators can be seen in the background. During actual games, Reese would often "turn two" with Jackie Robinson at his side, giving Pee Wee the perfect "feed." This is the most attractive card in the set and one of the most attractive cards ever produced, a true sportscard classic.

### Difficulty:

The 1953 Bowmans, especially this Reese card, are often found off-center side to side or top to bottom. Usually, the color is fairly consistent but focus might be an issue on these cards and, if they are out of focus, the card can really lack eye-appeal. The design of the card really makes you focus on the quality of the photo because the photo takes up practically the entire face. Make sure it's nice.

Borders can sometimes be a problem in one of two ways. The borders, like most Bowmans, are commonly found with toning but it looks even worse on these Bowmans because they are so much larger than previous Bowman issues. The edges are often found with rough edges. Now, rough edges are not necessarily a bad thing. That's the way they were made but, if the rough-cut makes its way into a corner, it can really impede on the beauty of the card. These cards are not terribly difficult but tough nonetheless.

## 1953 BOWMAN PEE WEE REESE

## Comments:

This is just one of those cards that is immediately recognizable, just like the name Pee Wee. This card ranks right up there with other all-time classics, not quite on the level of the 1952 Topps Mickey Mantle or the T206 Honus Wagner, but a true classic from an image standpoint. Cards like this one always seem to perform well over time because it serves as a symbol of card collecting in general. While his 1941 Play Ball is more scarce, Reese is a very important figure in baseball history and this card is his most popular card overall. Some cards almost define themselves, this is one of those cards.

## 1953 Bowman #153 Whitey Ford

### Importance:

This is one of the key high-number stars in the set and one of Whitey's most sought after cards. In 1953, Whitey Ford emerged as a top lefty. He compiled an 18-6 record with an ERA of exactly 3.00. With the highest winning percentage in baseball history, Ford was the ultimate definition of a winner. He didn't fire 100mph fastballs or throw mesmerizing knucklers; Ford was just a true pitcher. He changed speeds, hit spots and made the hitters hit his pitch. These are skills no longer appreciated but sorely lacking in today's game. Here's a card that is tough, visually appealing  and it captures Ford at the beginning of his stardom.

### Difficulty:

This card is part of the tough high-number series that includes a few other stars on this list. While the high-numbers are considerably scarcer than the regular cards, they are also susceptible to the same condition dilemmas. The 1953 Bowmans are often found off-center side to side or top to bottom. Usually, the color is fairly consistent but focus might be an issue on these cards and, if they are out of focus, the card can look really lack eye-appeal. The design of the card really makes you focus on the quality of the photo because the photo takes up practically the entire face.  With such a close-up view of Ford's face, beware of ugly, black print defects on the surface.

The borders can sometimes be a problem in one of two ways. The borders, like most Bowmans, are commonly found with toning but it looks even worse on these Bowmans because they are so much larger than previous Bowman issues. The edges are often found with rough edges. Now, rough edges are not necessarily a bad thing. That's the way they were made but, if the rough-cut makes its way into a corner, it can really reduce the eye-appeal.

Photo Courtesy of the John Branca Collection

PSA
1953 BOWMAN COLOR #153
WHITEY FORD
NM-MT 8
08009029

1953 BOWMAN WHITEY FORD

## Comments:

Whitey Ford, like other key figures that played during his era, is easily recognized simply by his first name. Duke, Mickey, Jackie, Willie, and Yogi are a few others. We all know what their last names are but each guy is so popular that it doesn't even need to be spoken in order to identify the legend behind the name. The bottom line is that a pitcher's job is to win, period. Ford did that at a higher rate, at this point, than anyone else in baseball history. Cy Young had more total wins and Nolan Ryan had better stuff but Ford's .690 winning percentage remains untouched. This card is a necessity for any 1953 Bowman set collector and this is one of his earliest cards.

# 1953 Topps #1 Jackie Robinson

## Importance:

This is the first card in the 1953 Topps set and it features Hall of Fame legend Jackie Robinson. We have talked about the other significant #1 cards on this list such as the 1934 Goudey Jimmie Foxx, the 1940 Play Ball Joe DiMaggio and the 1951 Bowman Whitey Ford to name a few, but don't forget about this card.

The 1953 Topps set has tremendous eye-appeal and ranks very high on the list of set popularity. This card, along with cards of Willie Mays and Mickey Mantle, is a key to the set. In 1953, Robinson would hit .329 with 95 RBI's and 109 runs scored, a typical productive Robinson-like year. He was elected to the Hall of Fame in 1962. This card is important on a few different levels.

## Difficulty:

As the first card in the set, this card is a condition rarity. The fact that this card is in the 1953 Topps set makes it even more difficult. As noted many times before, the first cards in sets were often subjected to abuse stemming from general overhandling and rubber band damage. For this card, that is just the beginning.

The black bottom border is the biggest obstacle. As you might imagine, the border is very susceptible to chipping and the slightest touch is easily detected. In addition, the 1953 Topps cards have trouble with centering and paper wrinkles on the reverse. Paper wrinkles are not exactly creases (creases go through the cardboard itself), but they do lower a grade of a card significantly and are hard to see at times. This card is very tough for these reasons.

Some 1953 Topps Robinson cards were discovered as part of "finds" so eye-popping examples can be found if you are patient.

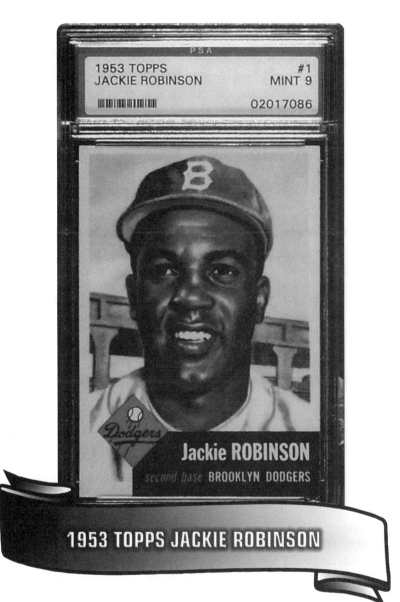

## 1953 TOPPS JACKIE ROBINSON

**Comments:**

For some reason, in comparison to other #1 cards, this card seems overlooked and underrated. It simply doesn't get the attention that the #1 Pafkos, DiMaggios or Williams cards get from collectors but I think, in the long run, that might change. Jackie Robinson is one of those players who finds himself in that upper-tier of popularity. When it comes to superstars of the 1950's, Robinson is right there with Mickey Mantle, Willie Mays and Ted Williams but he stands for something so much bigger than the game of baseball. The 1953 Topps set is extremely popular and, coupled with Robinson's significance, the demand is strong and collectors will always seek out this card.

# 1953 Topps #82 Mickey Mantle

## Importance:

This is a classic and one of Mantle's most popular cards. Topps, only one year after the production of their terrific 1952 set, came back with another gem. The 1953 Topps Mantle card does not have quite the reputation of the 1952 Topps example but this card is special. The image of Mantle is, once again, stunning as the artwork was masterfully done. The image is also powerful, much like Mantle's swing that produced several legendary drives like the 565-foot blast that struck the façade at the top of Yankee Stadium.

In 1953, Mantle was just a few years away from becoming a baseball superstar. Mantle had yet to hit 30 homers or drive in 100 runs but, eventually, he would reach those numbers routinely. In 1953, Mantle would finish with a .295 average, 21 homers, 92 RBI's and 105 runs scored. Every Mantle card is extremely popular but this one ranks very high on the list, it's a classic image of a classic Yankee.

## Difficulty:

The colored bottom border makes this one very prone to chipping but that is not the only dilemma this card faces. Centering is another major issue, as it is with most 1953 Topps cards. It's harder to judge the centering on this card, due to the design, so be careful. Also, the card has tremendous variations in eye-appeal. You can place two examples side by side and they look like entirely different cards due to color and printing variations.

Due to a "find" several years ago, though not quite as large as the 1952 Topps "find," you can find very attractive examples with booming eye-appeal. There weren't many Mantle cards in that "find" but they can be found in high-grade. Finally, Mantle's image is so large on the face of the card that print defects have little room to hide.

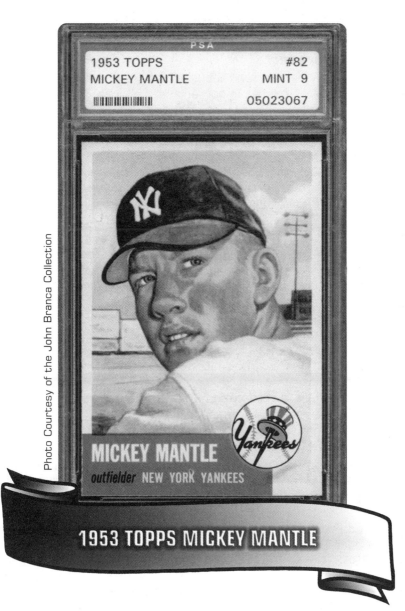

Photo Courtesy of the John Branca Collection

PSA
1953 TOPPS                    #82
MICKEY MANTLE        MINT  9
                              05023067

MICKEY MANTLE
*outfielder* NEW YORK YANKEES

**1953 TOPPS MICKEY MANTLE**

## Comments:

As a Topps issue, this card seems to be far more popular than Mantle's 1953 Bowman example and, in many cases, it commands more than double the Bowman price. That is part of the reason why I left the 1953 Bowman Mantle off the list. At the time, Topps was king and everyone knew it. The Topps Mantle is very visually appealing; part of a very popular set and is one of "The Mick's" best overall cards. The card is very striking, much like Mantle's first Topps card, you can almost sense something special. There is a large drop-off in price from the 1952 Topps Mantle to this example so collectors may want to take notice.

# 1953 Topps #244 Willie Mays

## Importance:

This is Willie's second Topps offering and, with the exception of his rookie, his most important card overall. This Mays card not only receives more attention than the 1952 Topps example but, on pure popularity, it might rank higher than even his 1951 Bowman rookie card. This card is also important because Bowman did not produce a card of Willie in 1953, making this Topps example the only mainstream issue for Mays collectors.

Granted, Mays did not play at all in 1953 because he was busy serving our country in the military. This was routine as many stars joined the service during different points in their career like Ted Williams and Yogi Berra. It's hard to believe but true. On top of all of the great qualities is the fact that this card has tremendous visual appeal and, over the years, it has become a classic image.

Mays is considered by many baseball experts to be the only true 5-tool player of his generation and perhaps in baseball history. One who can excel at hitting for average and power, running, fielding and throwing. Bonds does not have Willie's arm, Clemente did not have his power and Mantle did not have his speed (though injuries were mostly responsible for that).

## Difficulty:

According to many hobby dealers, unlike the Mantle example, this Mays card was not found at all in the famous "find" of 1953 Topps cards. In addition, this card has a solid black border at the bottom that is even more susceptible to chipping than the red border found on the Mantle or Paige cards. The slightest touch will be noticeable anywhere on the black edge. The typical 1953 Topps centering problems also contribute as a condition obstacle. This card has long been referred to as one of Willie's toughest cards and you will get no argument from me.

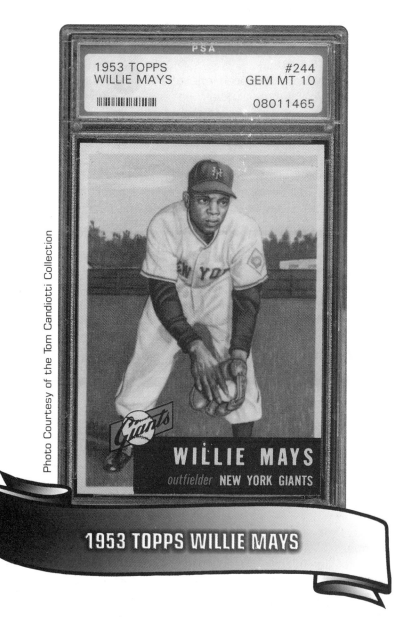

1953 TOPPS WILLIE MAYS

## Comments:

This card has a lot going for it. Willie Mays, despite his career numbers and legend, is still underrated at this point. In fact, this 1953 Topps card was actually fairly "soft" for a few years but it has started to gain more respect recently and the demand has increased accordingly over time. For all his batting prowess, Mays won 12 Gold Glove Awards in a row from 1957-1968 and stole 338 bases during his illustrious career. As one of a few major keys to the popular 1953 Topps set, this card should enjoy increased popularity in the future.

## 1954 Bowman #66 Ted Williams

### Importance:

This card is considered one of the most significant post-war rarities in the hobby. Every baseball card featuring Ted Williams is popular but this one is one of his best. The 1954 Bowman Williams card was pulled from production early due to a contract dispute so only a limited amount of these cards made it out of the Bowman factory. At the time, Topps had exclusive rights to the "Splendid Splinter." Who knew that, years later, Bowman's mistake would result in one of the great post-war sportscards? Jim Piersall eventually replaced Williams in the set as #66.

In 1954, with only 117 games under his belt, Williams hit .345 with 29 homers, 136 walks, a .516 OBP and he slugged .635. This was one of his least productive seasons overall! Ted Williams was an American hero, not just a baseball hero, as he lost nearly five years to military duty. This card is a classic and of the utmost importance.

### Difficulty:

This card, due to the contract dispute, is more scarce than other cards in the set but this card also has its problems with condition obstacles. Centering is probably the biggest problem for this card. This card is commonly found with poor centering in all directions. In addition, this card suffers from lack of eye-appeal most of the time. Just ask any advanced dealer or collector and they will tell you that it is hard to find this card with a striking look. The card is rarely found with bold color or thick gloss, so keep that in mind.

Reverse staining is also very common on all early Bowman issues. Whether it be from wax or gum, this can downgrade a card significantly based on the severity. Finally, print defects are often found in the background on the face of the card. If they gets too close to Ted's face, it may be an eyesore. Keep in mind that no Williams examples were found in the unopened pack "find" of 1954 Bowmans years ago.

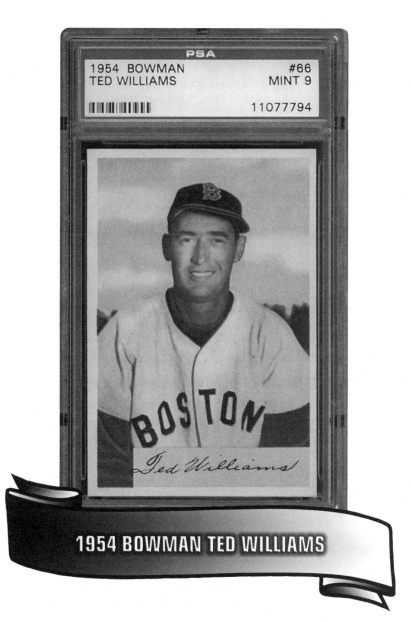

## Comments:

Even though it may not be as difficult to find as once thought, this card is still tough and it features Ted Williams. Whether the scarcity factor on this card is justified or not, the perception is that it is a major post-war rarity. The card features a classic image and, while it's not considered a necessary part of the set due to its rarity, the card is clearly the most valuable and sought after 1954 Bowman card out there. As one of the symbols of card collecting, this Williams issue should continue to enjoy great demand.

# 1954 Dan Dee Mickey Mantle

## Importance:

This is one of Mickey Mantle's toughest and most attractive cards ever produced. I know this card is not a mainstream issue like Bowman or Topps but it doesn't matter. This card is extremely desirable. First of all, Mantle was not included in the 1954 Topps set. Second, even though Mantle has a tough 1954 Bowman card, the Dan Dee is even tougher and nicer looking as well. Mantle's famous smile is plastered across the face of this beautiful regional issue. I would be smiling too if I was the starting center fielder for the New York Yankees.

In 1954, Mantle would hit .300 with 27 homers, 102 RBI's and scored a league-high 129 runs. It was the first of many big seasons to come from "The Mick." Along with the Wilson Franks Ted Williams, this is one of the most important regional cards in hobby history.

## Difficulty:

These cards were inserted into potato chip bags. What else do I need to say? The cards are commonly found with staining as a result of the potato chip oils. The staining can be a major eyesore, especially considering that the borders were white all the way around the card. In addition, centering is a major problem. I have seen very few Mantle examples that were centered, most are found with 60/40 centering or worse.

Finally, the cutting process was very crude. In fact, many of these Dan Dees are found with perforations along the edges. Sometimes, the perforations are very noticeable and actually detract from the eye-appeal of the card and, other times, you don't even notice them. Don't be afraid of them just make sure that the edges are not so jagged that you find them distracting. This card would rank very high on the pure difficulty list.

PSA

1954 DAN-DEE POTATO CHIPS
MICKEY MANTLE      MINT 9

01631115

**Mickey Mantle**

DAN-DEE

## 1954 DAN DEE MICKEY MANTLE

## Comments:

There are only a few of regional cards that made this list because very few regional cards have crossover appeal. This is certainly one of them and its popularity is without question. With no Topps issue from 1954, this card fills the void for most Mantle collectors. The 1954 Bowman Mantle is no slouch but this Dan Dee card has extreme difficulty and eye-appeal going for it. As collectors become more advanced and the focus continues to move towards rarity, this card will enjoy continued demand.

## 1954 Topps Ted Williams (#'s 1 and 250)

### Importance:

The first and last cards in the very popular 1954 Topps set and each one features "The Splendid Splinter." Both of these cards are very popular and for good reason. It was the first time that Ted Williams was featured in a Topps set and it was the only time that a vintage baseball issue let one player "bookend" the set.

The 1954 Topps set is filled with stars (with the exception of Mantle and Musial) and great rookie cards like those of Hank Aaron, Ernie Banks and Al Kaline. The cards are extremely visually appealing, especially the #250 Williams, which is the more popular of the two cards. Both cards are very desirable for a multitude of reasons.

### Difficulty:

It must have been an honor to "bookend" the set but it creates nightmares for high-grade card collectors today. As you might imagine, rubber bands found home with these two cards often. The #250 card was long believed to be the tougher of the two but the latest population numbers suggest otherwise. Both cards are very prone to poor centering and, with that undefined top border, make sure you are careful. Look for strong color, especially on the #250 example, because it makes a huge difference when it comes to eye-appeal.

Also, look for chipping on the reverse. The dark green border is almost always found with some degree of chipping so just make sure it is not too severe. This is so common that the existence of such chipping usually won't prevent a card from reaching NM-MT status but, if it is severe, it could detract from the eye-appeal. In addition, print defects are very common and, with #250, the yellow background is too light to help conceal any of them. These are both very tough 1950's cards.

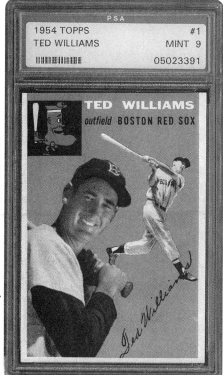

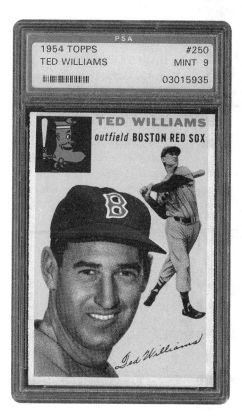

## 1954 TOPPS TED WILLIAMS

## Comments:

Demand will, most likely, never be a problem with these two cards. Ted Williams is an upper-tier Hall of Famer and the 1954 set is one of the most desirable and colorful sets from the 1950's. Add to that the fact that these cards are both tough, key cards and you have the makings of a winner. Collectors can't go wrong with either one but the #250 card is the more attractive of the two while the #1 card seems to be slightly tougher. It remains to be seen how both cards will compare over time but, then again, you can't go wrong with any card of "Teddy Ballgame."

# 1954 Topps #94 Ernie Banks

## Importance:

This is the only recognized rookie card of 500 Home Run Club member Ernie Banks. "Mr. Cub" remains one of the most popular figures in Chicago sports history along with the likes of Michael Jordan and, for the moment, Sammy Sosa. This card is one of the major keys to the set and is considered more difficult than the Hank Aaron rookie card.

In 1954, Banks gave the Cubbies a taste of his power with 19 homers but he more than doubled his output the very next year with 44 jacks. Banks, much like Aaron, used his lightning quick wrists to drive the ball out of Wrigley Field and he did that 512 times in a variety of ball parks. Banks also won back-to-back MVP awards in 1958-1959 and hit 40 or more homers five times en route to his Hall of Fame induction in 1977. This is a significant rookie card.

## Difficulty:

The two major obstacles on this card seem to be centering and print defects. The undefined top border gives some collectors trouble in determining centering and, more often than not, this card is off-center top to bottom. It's not easy to judge centering so look closely at his name. Don't let it get too close to the top. The white background provides a haven for visible print marks. In fact, most other key cards in the set have color in the background but not this one. Just make sure that the amount of print defects is not too severe or the eye-appeal will suffer.

The reverse is surrounded by green edges and the factory would often chip them during the cutting process. This is so common that the existence of such chipping usually won't prevent a card from reaching NM-MT status but, if it is severe, it could make these cards less desirable. This card is one of Ernie's tougher examples.

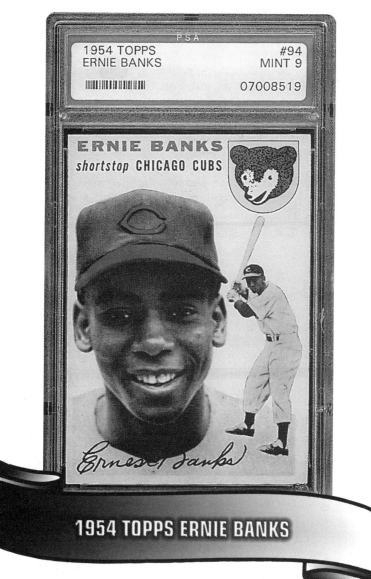

## 1954 TOPPS ERNIE BANKS

**Comments:**

The 500 Home Run Club is the most widely collected club in the hobby. Collectors and baseball fans just have an infatuation with the home run, it's something that the average person cannot do and that's what makes it special. Banks was more than just a power hitter though, he was also a great ambassador for the game because he showed unmatched enthusiasm on the field. His likable personality, much like that of Harmon Killebrew and Stan Musial, just gives people another reason to collect his cards. Banks is so young in this picture and the card itself is as recognizable as his great smile.

# 1954 Topps #128 Hank Aaron

## Importance:

This is the only recognized rookie card of baseball's all-time home run king. Hank Aaron entered the field a slender, soft-spoken man and left it as "The Hammer." Aaron didn't fit the mold of a pure power hitter and it made sense because he was much more than that. His consistency and lifetime numbers are nothing less than amazing.

In 1954, Aaron's debut season, he hit a mere 13 homers in 122 games. From that point on, he would not hit less than 20 homers in a season until 1975! His tremendous hand and wrist strength enabled Aaron to turn on inside fastballs with the incredible quickness.

With all his home runs, believe it or not, he never struck out 100 times in a season. Aaron was also a fine base stealer (240 career steals), currently ranks 3rd in career hits with 3,771, is the all-time leader in RBI's with 2,297, was a fine defensive player and he also had a career average over .300. Some numbers are recognized by themselves and Hank's 755 is one of them. Aaron entered the Hall in 1982. This card is of the utmost importance.

## Difficulty:

While this card is not the most difficult card to find in near mint condition or lower, it is virtually impossible to find in strict mint condition. This card is often found with print defects in the orange background (the orange background can sometimes be dull or faint) and, if they are severe, the stray marks can significantly hurt the eye-appeal. Centering is always an issue when it comes to the 1954 Topps cards, especially with the undefined top border. It doesn't make it easy to judge centering so look closely at his name. Don't let it get too close to the top.

The reverse is surrounded by green edges and the factory would often chip them during the cutting process. This is so common that the existence of such chipping usually won't prevent a card from reaching NM-MT status but, if it is severe, it could prevent a card from reaching higher grades. Finally, this card is one card from the set that is often found with a rough-cut. As long as the cut isn't too jagged, it shouldn't detract from the visual appeal.

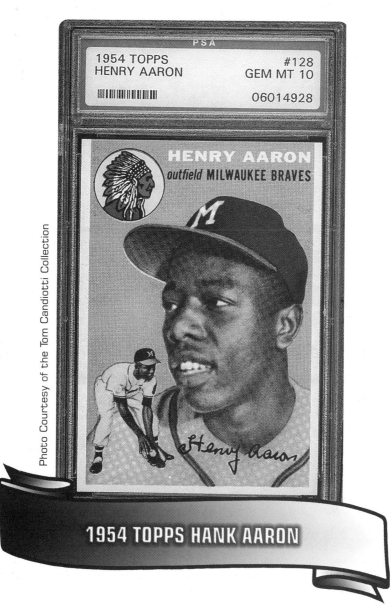

Photo Courtesy of the Tom Candiotti Collection

PSA

1954 TOPPS
HENRY AARON

#128

GEM MT 10

06014928

HENRY AARON
*outfield* MILWAUKEE BRAVES

## 1954 TOPPS HANK AARON

## Comments:

The Aaron rookie card is a classic. When you think of collecting baseball cards, this one comes to mind. Like the 1952 Topps Mickey Mantle, the Aaron rookie is a symbol of the hobby. Hank Aaron, even if his career home run record falls someday, will always be remembered as one of the best sluggers in baseball history. His name, like Babe Ruth, is synonymous with the home run. So as sluggers approach home run milestones and records, Aaron's name will remain in the limelight. Aaron never had the following of Mickey Mantle or Ted Williams, but his numbers speak for themselves.

## 1954 Topps #201 Al Kaline

### Importance:

This is the only recognized rookie card of the Detroit Tiger legend. Despite being such a well-rounded player, Kaline remains a very underrated player. He won 11 Gold Gloves, was the youngest player to ever win a batting title with a .340 average at the young age of 20, collected 3,007 hits and crushed 399 homers en route to Hall of Fame induction in 1980.

After years of mediocrity, the Tigers finally won a World Series in 1968 and Kaline chipped in with a .379 series average. Kaline, believe it or not, only hit 4 homers and drove in 43 runs in 1954 during his first full season. The very next year, Kaline would lead the league with a .340 average and 200 hits while smacking 27 homers, driving in 102 runs and scoring 121. What a turnaround! Along with the Hank Aaron and Ernie Banks rookie cards and the two Williams cards, this Kaline rookie is a key to a very popular set.

### Difficulty:

The Kaline rookie card, while not a very difficult card, it is still more difficult than some other star cards in the set including the Aaron rookie card. Like most 1954 Topps cards, this card suffers from centering, print and toning problems. The undefined top border doesn't make it easy to judge centering so look closely at his name. Don't let it get too close to the top. Make sure you look for nice cherry-red color in the background, it can really make this card jump out at you but, usually, print defects are lurking.

When it comes to print defects, keep in mind that you don't want the print marks to be located near his face or the eye-appeal can be severely reduced. Finally, the reverse is surrounded by green edges and the factory would often chip them during the cutting process. This is so common that the existence of such chipping usually won't prevent a card from reaching NM-MT status but, if it is severe, it could make the card less desirable.

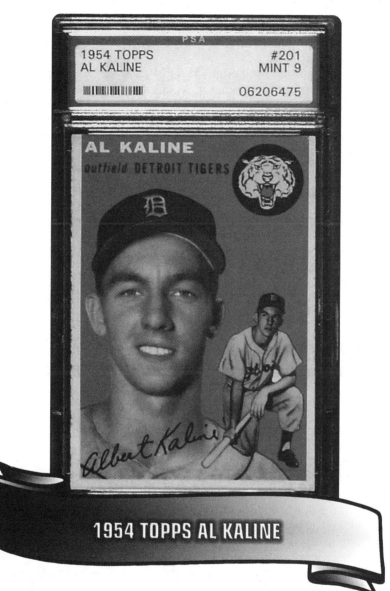

**1954 TOPPS AL KALINE**

## Comments:

Al Kaline, while not considered an upper-tier Hall of Famer, is a Detroit Tiger favorite and a 3,000 Hit Club member. Team or exclusive club association can be just as important as individual player popularity and, in Kaline's case, all three apply. Add to that the fact that this set is one of the favorites of the 1950's with the beautiful designs and great selection of star cards and you have a winner. Kaline has a reputation much like that of Harmon Killebrew and Brooks Robinson, Kaline is an extremely likable person and his career was free from any real controversy. His accomplishments speak for themselves and his only rookie card is a keeper.

## 1954 Wilson Franks Ted Williams

### Importance:

By far, this is the toughest Ted Williams card in the hobby and one of the toughest cards on the list. There were two regional baseball cards selected for this list and each of them is significant but this one is, in my opinion, the best. No offense intended to Mr. Dan Dee Mantle. This card is not only incredibly difficult but it is also an extremely attractive card. To put things in perspective, the 1954 Bowman Williams is considered a great post-war rarity but it pales in comparison to the difficulty of this one.

Most regional cards are considered very obscure and, usually, the designs themselves are equally as obscure. This card defies all the stereotypes of regional issues. It is a very attractive card and it is so difficult that it is nearly impossible to acquire in near mint or better condition. Ted Williams is not only a Hall of Famer; he is an icon of the sport.

### Difficulty:

This card is unbelievably difficult. From the almost non-existent borders placed around the edges to the fact that these cards were inserted into packages of hot dogs, this card is a major challenge. It's not only difficult to find in high-grade; it's difficult to find in any grade! Because of those pesky, narrow borders mentioned above, poor centering is the major reason that most of the existing copies suffer in the grading process. The few high-grade copies that have surfaced in the last several years have

Photo Courtesy of National Baseball Hall of Fame Library, Cooperstoown, NY

sold for tremendous sums and rightfully so. This card is tough, tough, tough!

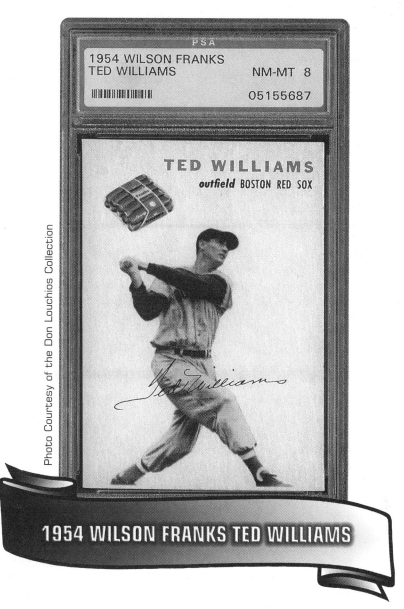

Photo Courtesy of the Don Louchios Collection

PSA

**1954 WILSON FRANKS TED WILLIAMS**

NM-MT 8

05155687

**TED WILLIAMS**

*outfield* BOSTON RED SOX

## 1954 WILSON FRANKS TED WILLIAMS

## Comments:

I am still waiting for the "Ted Williams Movie" because his life has been storybook-like. Ted's plane was hit by enemy fire and crashed during his military duty and he still came back to baseball and crushed major league pitching. Can you imagine a modern superstar fighting for our country in a war? Neither can I but this guy was a true American hero and this card is part of a legendary regional issue. You can't complete a run of Ted Williams cards without it. This is not only the key to the set but it is also considered the most significant regional card ever produced in any sport.

# 1955 Topps #123 Sandy Koufax

## Importance:

This is the only recognized rookie card of, arguably, the most dominating lefty in baseball history. This card, like the 1952 Topps Mickey Mantle or the 1954 Topps Hank Aaron, is a symbol of card collecting. The card, like most cards in the extremely popular 1955 Topps set, has a very attractive design. Koufax led the National League in ERA for five consecutive seasons and, during that run, went 111-34 and threw four no-hitters before arthritis damaged his pitching arm. During that incredible, dominating streak, Koufax was earned three Cy Youngs and one MVP Award.

After going 36-40 in his first 6 years, Koufax started to shine. In 1965, he would throw a perfect game and strikeout 382 batters (a record until Nolan Ryan broke it with 383). With a World Series ERA under 1.00, Koufax proved he was a clutch performer.

He was forced to retire at only 30 years of age. Due to his early retirement, Koufax became the youngest man to be elected to the Hall of Fame in 1972. Who knows what Koufax could have done if his arm would have held up, regardless, he is a legend.

## Difficulty:

While this card is not overly difficult, there are a few obstacles to look for. The yellow background is a haven for print defects so beware. With 1955 Topps cards, centering is also an issue and this Koufax is rarely found with 50/50 centering. With the yellow background, the centering can be deceiving in the upper portion of the card so make sure the white area of the border is balanced. Finally, the reverse on these cards is sometimes seen with major toning. The reverse doesn't have to be sparkling white but make sure the back isn't too "dirty" looking or some collectors will see it as a detractor.

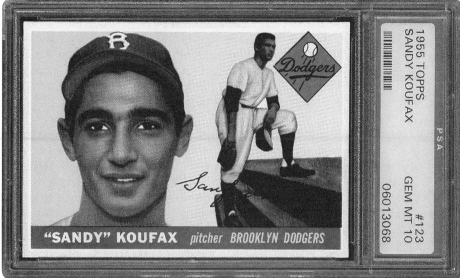

1955 TOPPS
SANDY KOUFAX

PSA

#123

GEM MT 10

06013068

"SANDY" KOUFAX  pitcher BROOKLYN DODGERS

## 1955 TOPPS SANDY KOUFAX

## Comments:

As it was mentioned above, this card is not overly difficult, but it doesn't have to be because it's a classic card in a great set. The set is filled with stars and key rookie cards like the Roberto Clemente and Harmon Killebrew examples. The colors are outstanding and the image of Koufax is one that is ingrained in the advanced collector's mind. In the overall scheme of things, Koufax is perhaps a bit overrated as a player due to his short tenure on the mound but, more importantly, Koufax had such great talent that he captivated the baseball world.

# 1955 Topps #124 Harmon Killebrew

## Importance:

This is the only recognized rookie card of super slugger Harmon Killebrew. This guy could absolutely mash! Killebrew, when it came to brute power, was right there with Mickey Mantle throughout his career and he is still the all-time leader for American League right handed batters with 573 titanic clouts. Even though his debut came in 1954, Killebrew did not play a full season until 1959 and boy did he take advantage of the opportunity. He led the league with 42 homers!

Overall, he crushed 40 or more homers in 8 different seasons and led the league in homers 6 times en route to Hall of Fame induction in 1984. Killebrew earned the AL MVP in 1969 by hitting 49 homers and driving in 140 runs. This card is one of the most attractive rookie cards of the 1950's and it fits nicely in a set that includes the ever-popular Sandy Koufax and Roberto Clemente rookies.

## Difficulty:

This card, like the 1955 Topps Koufax, is not very tough to find in high-grade. While this card is not overly difficult, there are a few obstacles to look for. The yellow background is a haven for print defects so beware. With 1955 Topps cards, centering is also an issue. With the yellow background, the centering can be deceiving in the upper portion of the card so make sure the white area of the border is balanced. Finally, the reverse on these cards is sometimes seen with major toning. The reverse doesn't have to be sparkling white but make sure the back isn't too "dirty" looking as some collectors see this as a detractor.

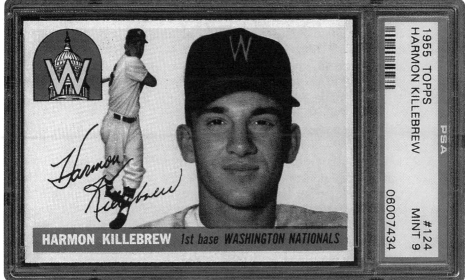

## Comments:

This card is not the toughest one on the list but Killebrew's significance and popularity as a player overrides this card's lack of scarcity. If you ask anyone who has had the pleasure of meeting Harmon Killebrew, they will tell you that this man is one of the nicest men they have ever met. Notice that I did not say that he is one of the nicest baseball players, but one of the nicest men. His likable personality has gone a long way in this hobby and fans enjoy that in a day of $100 million contracts and egos galore. The bottom line is that this card is part of a beautiful set and the guy crushed. Case closed.

## 1955 Topps #164 Roberto Clemente

### Importance:

This is the only recognized rookie card of baseball icon Roberto Clemente. At the time, Clemente was yet to emerge as a major star for the Pittsburgh Pirates but his talents would be show-cased soon. Despite having inferior numbers when compared to the likes of Willie Mays and Hank Aaron, Clemente's name is always raised when discussing the best players of the 1950's and 1960's. His fiery approach on the field and his kind ways off the field made him a fan favorite.

Clemente could do it all. He could field, throw, hit, hit with power and run. The only thing that overshadowed his ability on the field was his giving personality off the field. Clemente was unfortu-nately killed during one of his charitable missions when the plane, carrying supplies to the earthquake victims, crashed before ar-rival. He finished his career with exactly 3,000 hits and was inducted into the Hall of Fame in 1973 but, more importantly, he was beloved by millions of fans. This card, like the Koufax rookie from the same set, is a hobby classic.

### Difficulty:

This card, as opposed to the Koufax, is much tougher as part of the high-number series. Centering seems to be the biggest problem here and, with the green background, an off-center card is much more noticeable. You can find this card sharp but the card is usually 70/30 or worse. Also, look for deep colors on this one. The combination of colors on this one can be a real asset to the eye-appeal but a "washed out" appearance can be an eyesore. This is not a terribly difficult card but it is tougher than the Koufax or Killebrew rookies from the same set.

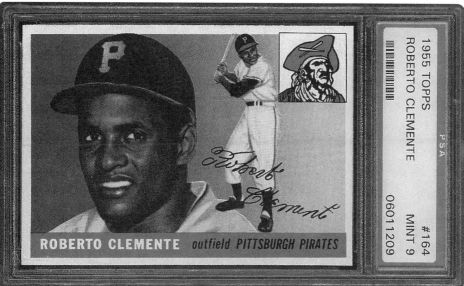

## 1955 TOPPS ROBERTO CLEMENTE

## Comments:

On pure statistics, Clemente does not match up well against the likes of Mays or Aaron but his personality takes him to a new level. He was simply a beloved player. He played with a lot of heart and showed a big heart off the field as well. Clemente cards provide a valuable lesson to collectors. Athletic accomplishment is what makes you a great player on the field but the collecting world is entirely different. The more likable the player, the more desirable are his items. There are exceptions like Ty Cobb but a personable nature, or lack of one, can dramatically change the way collectors view certain cards. This rookie card ranks high on the list of pure importance and, as one of the top keys to the 1955 Topps set, it should enjoy great demand for a long time.

## 1955 Topps #210 Duke Snider

### Importance:

This is the last card in the tremendously popular 1955 Topps set. This card rarely comes up for sale in high-grade, it's very tough. Duke Snider will always be remembered as one of the great center fielders in baseball history. Snider held his own with the likes of Willie Mays and Mickey Mantle for several years as part of the "Mickey, Willie and the Duke" legacy. All you have to say is his first name (Duke) and you immediately know who it is. With five straight 40-plus home run seasons (1953-1957), it's no wonder.

With the possible exception of Sandy Koufax or Jackie Robinson, Snider is the most recognizable Dodger in history. Snider's 407 career home runs made him the key power threat in a lineup filled with stars. In 1955, in perhaps his best season, Duke hit .309 with 42 homers, had a slugging percentage of .628, 136 RBI's and 126 runs scored (both league-highs). His likable personality just adds to his appeal and his induction into the Hall of Fame in 1980 solidified it.

### Difficulty:

This card is clearly the toughest 1955 Topps card on the list. I just never see this card, period. When you can find it, it is very tough to find centered with centering usually bordering on 65/35 or worse. The yellow background is a haven for print defects and is usually faded so beware. The yellow background can also cause the centering to be deceiving in the upper portion of the card so make sure the white area of the border is balanced.

Finally, the reverse on these cards is sometimes seen with major toning. The reverse doesn't have to be sparkling white but make sure the back isn't too "dirty" looking as some collectors see this as a problem. Very few of these cards have surfaced in high-grade over the years.

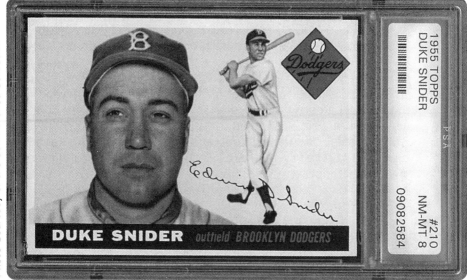

Photo Courtesy of the John Branca Collection

1955 TOPPS DUKE SNIDER

## Comments:

I can't emphasize the demand for this card enough. I pay close attention to all the major auctions and retail offerings each year and very rarely do I see this card come up for sale in high-grade. In fact, I can't remember seeing more than a couple of these surfacing in the last few years. The reason behind this is that so many collectors are assembling this set and everyone seems to need this card. The card is usually sold very quickly. Even non-set collectors can appreciate this card as the last card in the set and the fact it features Duke Snider.

# 1956 Topps #135 Mickey Mantle

## Importance:

This is one of "The Mick's" most attractive and popular cards. A smiling Mantle graces the front of the ever-popular card and you would be too if you just had a season like his. In 1956, Mantle would win the elusive Triple Crown by leading the league in batting average (.353), homers (52) and RBI's (130). Oh, by the way, he also led the league with 132 runs scored and slugging average (.705).

This card is also significant in that 1956 was the year that Mantle became a true superstar, it was also the year that unreachable expectations began to be placed on the former small town prodigy. This card captures Mantle in his prime and it is certainly the key to the 1956 Topps set which lacks significant rookie card power.

## Difficulty:

This card might be one of the easier 1950's cards on the list. Mantle is so popular that it just doesn't seem to matter how many of them are in existence. Keep in mind that there are actually two variations of this card, the white back and the grey-back Mantle. The white backs often sell for a premium due to their superior scarcity over the grey backs. The grey backs, however, are traditionally noted for having superior eye-appeal on the front. Take your pick.

The few obstacles to look for on this card are centering, print and edge problems. The centering on the 1956 Topps cards seems to range much like the 1955 Topps cards, so dead-centered cards are not easy to find. In addition, scattered print defects are often found, even in the facial area of Mick's image. The action photo in the background can help hide them so beware. Finally, I have seen some 1956 Topps cards with edges that are so rough it looks like they were cut with my dog's teeth. Stay away from overly rough-cut cards, slight rough-cuts are actually evidence of an unaltered state.

MICKEY MANTLE

*outfield* NEW YORK YANKEES

1956 TOPPS
MICKEY MANTLE
PSA
#135
MINT 9
07115145

1956 TOPPS MICKEY MANTLE

## Comments:

On strict difficulty, this is not one of the Mick's highest-ranking cards but, on pure popularity, this one is near the top. The 1956 season is seemingly when Mantle rose to another level with his brilliant Triple Crown accomplishment. When you look at this card, the image almost speaks to you. The image helps us understand what it must have been like to be Mickey Mantle during that time period. Just look at how huge that smile is. He's got to be the happiest man on earth. He played center field and hit jacks for the New York Yankees, he's "The Mick."

# 1957 Topps #1 Ted Williams

## Importance:

This is the first card in one of the most popular sets of the 1950's. This wasn't the first time Ted Williams was chosen to be the leadoff man in a Topps set and it also wasn't his last either. Williams was given the honor, by Topps, three times. This card features an older "Splendid Splinter" but the man could still crush.

After hitting 38 homers, with an OBP of .528 and slugging .731 (both league-highs), Williams somehow finished second to Mickey Mantle in the MVP voting. This was, seemingly, a theme to Ted's career. He did win two MVP's (1946 and 1949) but, according to many baseball historians, he should have been awarded a few more. His second to last Topps card is very popular and the fact that Williams hit .388, at the age of 39, and won another batting title in 1957, doesn't hurt.

## Difficulty:

By now, you all probably realize the dilemma that most number one cards pose to high-grade collectors. They were the cards that many collectors strangled with rubber bands and the cards that bore the brunt of the damage when being stored away in boxes. These number one cards were like the front line in battle.

The 1957 Topps Williams suffers from two distinct problems, lack of eye-appeal and toned borders. This card always seems to lack nice picture focus, gloss

Photo Courtesy of Troy Kinunen

and color in the photo. You will notice a big difference when you find an eye-popping example. Also, the borders are commonly found with a "dirty" appearance. White borders can do a lot for this condition sensitive card.

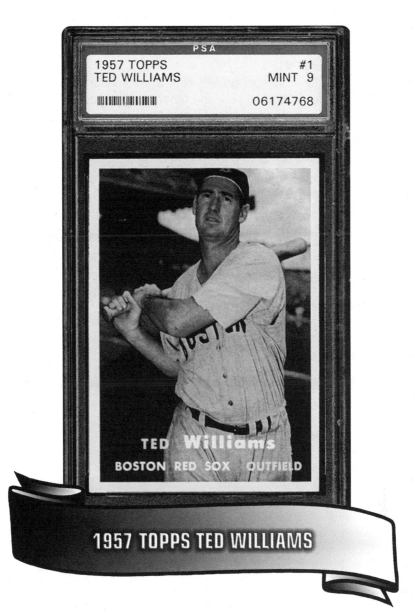

1957 TOPPS TED WILLIAMS

## Comments:

This card seems to be have been a bit overlooked in recent years. It's not as colorful and attractive as some of his other 1950's Topps examples but, as the first card in a great set, it deserves more respect. Collectors have always found the 1957 Topps set appealing due to the great photos found on the front, much like the 1953 Bowmans. As the set continues to remain popular, look for this Williams card to gain more attention. It may not be the type of number one card that captures the collector's imagination, like the 1952 Topps Pafko or 1934 Goudey Foxx, but it still shares that ever-important spot.

## 1957 Topps #35 Frank Robinson

### Importance:

This is the only recognized rookie card of one baseball's best sluggers. If I had to pick the most underrated player in baseball history, it might be Frank Robinson. He was the first player to win the MVP award in both leagues, he clubbed 586 homers, just missed 3,000 hits with 2,943, won the Triple Crown in 1966, had good speed, was a good outfielder, became the first African-American manager in major league history and was elected to the Hall of Fame in 1982.

This card is also significant in that, during his rookie campaign of 1956, Robinson jacked 38 home runs. Those 38 homers remained a rookie record for decades until a big lumberjack came along by the name of McGwire in 1987. His rookie card is one of the keys to the very popular 1957 Topps set that also features rookie cards of Brooks Robinson and Don Drysdale. Need I say more?

### Difficulty:

The 1957 Topps cards all seem to suffer from similar problems. Centering is a key with these cards, especially the Robinson rookie, as many of them are found with tilts that cause the borders to be uneven. In addition, the borders are often found toned and that can be a real eyesore. With the extremely dark background, white borders can really assist in the visual appeal department.

Print "snow" can be a "killer" to these examples. The dark background, if filled with white print specks known as "snow," becomes utterly destroyed. Last, but not least, look for solid focus and color in regards to the images. More often than not, this Robinson card is found with lackluster colors and poor registration. Many of these cards simply lack pizzazz, the image is the key.

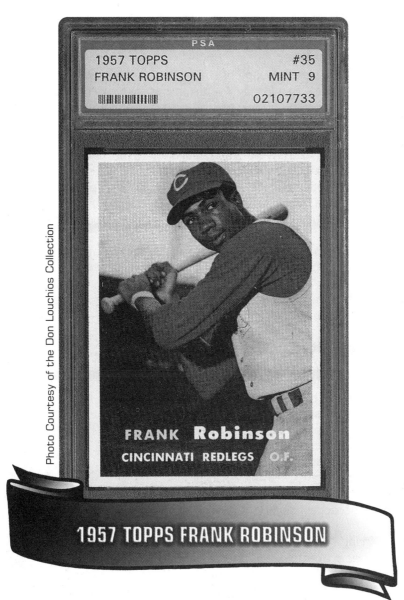

**1957 TOPPS FRANK ROBINSON**

## Comments:

Frank Robinson does not have the following that players like Willie Mays or Mickey Mantle have but, after looking at his numbers, you have to be left asking, "Why?" Robinson was a tough competitor and a fine ballplayer. In fact, he really was one of the finest of his era. While this is somewhat of a problem(the fact that he is so overlooked), it is also the beauty of his rookie card. It's extremely affordable in comparison to other comparable players of the era. Due to his great career numbers, this rookie card of Frank Robinson will enjoy great collector demand for many years as his accomplishments are put into perspective.

## 1957 Topps #302 Sandy Koufax

### Importance:

This is a classic image of the most devastating left handed pitcher of his era. This Sandy Koufax card is just one of those cards that symbolizes the hobby, an image that stands out. If you are a collector of vintage cards, you are familiar with the big smile of Sandy.

In 1957, Sandy was still learning to harness his phenomenal stuff and it wouldn't be long before he would start embarrassing hitters at the plate. In fact, during batting practice for the Los Angeles Dodgers, Koufax, well into his 50's at the time, frustrated batters so much that they ask him to stop throwing.

It's too bad that an arm injury took Koufax away from the game he loved but he was here long enough to show fans his devastating assortment of pitches. I am sure the National League hitters were happy to see him go. This is simply a legendary card of a legendary man.

### Difficulty:

The 1957 Topps cards all seem to suffer from similar problems. Centering is a key with these cards as many of them are found with tilts that cause the borders to be uneven. In addition, the borders are often found toned and that can be a real eyesore. With the extremely dark background, white borders can really assist in the visual appeal department.

Print "snow" can be a "killer" to these examples. The dark background, if filled with white print specks known as "snow," becomes utterly destroyed. Last, but not least, look for solid focus and color in regards to the images. This large photo of Koufax is usually found with slight focus problems and lackluster color. Many of these cards just lack eye-appeal in comparison to other Topps issues, the image is the key.

Image Courtesy of A.K. Miller

**Comments:**

This is just a great card in all respects. It's an early Koufax example in a great set and it's part of a tough high-number series. The "icing on the cake" is that it really is one of those card that collectors immediately recognize. Sometimes, an individual card will go as the entire set does, whether it's hot or cold. The 1957 Topps set has always been popular due to the difficulty in finding nicely centered examples and the overall star selection. Like the Williams in the same set, if this set continues to enjoy solid demand, look for increased interest in this Koufax card. Fortunately for Koufax collectors, this card stands alone regardless of the set outlook.

## 1957 Topps #328 Brooks Robinson

### Importance:

This is the only recognized rookie card of one of baseball's most popular players. Brooks Robinson is widely regarded as one of the finest fielding 3rd basemen of all-time. He was rewarded for his fielding with 16 Gold Gloves and he appeared in 15 straight All-Star games. Robinson was also a solid hitter. He would hit .317 with 28 homers and 118 RBI's in 1964, which helped earn him A.L. MVP honors. In 1957, Robinson had yet to play a full season at the big league level but the 1960's would be his decade to shine.

When Robinson was inducted into the Hall of Fame in 1983, the crowd was one of the largest ever for a player. This card, perhaps more than any other in his career, captures the man who so many fans adore. He just looks like a nice guy, don't you think? This card, much like the Koufax example, is instantly recognizable to many collectors and that's important because collectors associate this card with the hobby. It's not a major classic like a 1952 Topps Mantle or 1933 Goudey Ruth but it's still a great card.

### Difficulty:

The 1957 Topps cards all seem to suffer from similar problems. Centering is a key with these cards as many of them are found with tilts that cause the borders to be uneven. In addition, the borders are often found toned and that can be a real eyesore. With the extremely dark background, white borders can really assist in the visual appeal department.

Print "snow" can be a "killer" to these examples. The dark background, if filled with white print specks known as "snow," becomes utterly destroyed. Last, but not least, look for solid focus and color in regards to the images. This card can actually be fairly eye-appealing in comparison to the Williams and Frank Robinson in the same set due to the overall brightness of the photo.

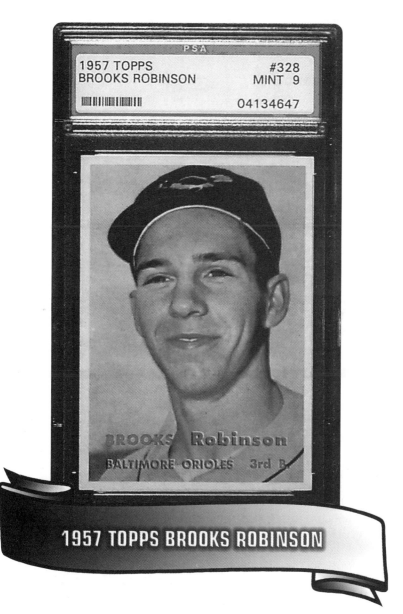

1957 TOPPS BROOKS ROBINSON

## Comments:

The "Human Vacuum" could really pick it at third base and he was a solid hitter as well but, with Robinson, his statistics are secondary. He is admired, much like Killebrew, as much for his contributions to the game as he is for his personable nature off the field. He just makes you want to own one of his cards, he's that nice. The image on this card says it all. As a player, fans can still see Brooks range wide to his right and fire across his body, robbing hitter after hitter of base hits. Imagine Ozzie Smith at third base but add some real pop to his bat, that's Brooks Robinson.

# 1957 Topps #407 Yankee Power Hitters (Berra and Mantle)

## Importance:

This is a great card that features the two key components to the New York Yankees offensive attack in the 1950's and 1960's. The stage was set in New York and these two guys really took advantage of it. Between the two of them, these guys could fill a room with just their World Series rings alone and, with 6 MVP's between them (three each), the room might overflow. They were opposites in many ways yet similar when it came to playing the game. One was the poster boy for all of baseball while the other one remained lovable but odd to say the least.

This card represents Yankee domination, the confidence of a true dynasty and it symbolized the beginning of multi-player star cards for Topps. With those classic Yankee pinstripes almost covering the entire face of the card, the image remains an all-time classic. This is, quite possibly, the most popular multi-player card in the hobby.

## Difficulty:

The 1957 Topps cards all seem to suffer from similar problems. Centering is a key with these cards as many of them are found with tilts that cause the borders to be uneven. In addition, the borders are often found toned and that can be a real eyesore. With the extremely dark background, white borders can really assist in the visual appeal department.

Print "snow" can be a "killer" to these examples and this is often found on this Yankee Power Hitters card. The dark background, if filled with white print specks known as "snow," will cause a loss of eye-appeal. Last, but not least, look for solid focus and color in regards to the images. Many of these cards just lack pizzazz, the image is the key. If you can find this example where the image is crisp and bright, you've got a great card. This card does reside in the high-number series but that series is actually not quite as difficult as the 265-352 series. In any event, this is a tough card to find with strong eye-appeal.

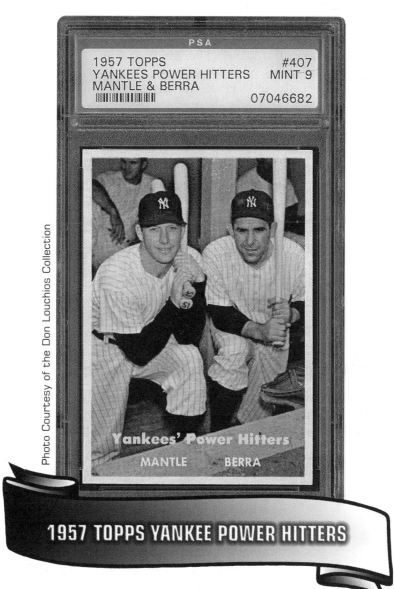

# 1957 TOPPS YANKEE POWER HITTERS

## Comments:

Collectors just love this card. Here's the recipe. Take one Mantle and one Berra, mix them together in one of the hobby's favorite sets and you have a winner. This card features 2/3 of the legendary Yankee trio. If only Whitey Ford was standing in the background, it would be complete. I chose this card over the 1962 Topps Manager's Dream card (Mantle/Mays – another great card) because of the significance as the first superstar combo card created by Topps and the fact that it resides in a better overall set. Combo cards have really been surging in demand over the last few years because collectors started to realize that they could get multiple players for the price of one or, in many cases, less. What a great card.

## 1958 Topps #1 Ted Williams

### Importance:

This is Ted's last Topps regular issue card and it's the first card in the set. Topps, once again, devoted the number one slot to the great Ted Williams. It was the last time he would appear in a Topps set and, even though there are two other Williams cards in the set, this is the most significant. Williams, at 40, won the batting title again with a .328 average in 1958.

Incredibly, despite winning the batting title, the average was about 20 points below his career mark. Still, Williams ended his stay with Topps with a bang and he always had a way to end things with a dramatic twist. How about the time he ended the 1941 All-Star Game with a home run or when he blasted a pitch over the right field wall in Fenway during his final career at bat, he always had that flair for the dramatic. Pitchers were not too fond of him and this 1958 Topps card features the scowl that Williams gave to many of his victims. He was elected to the Hall of Fame in 1966.

### Difficulty:

By now, you all probably realize the dilemma that most number one cards pose to high-grade collectors. They were the cards that many collectors strangled with rubber bands and the cards that bore the brunt of the damage when being stored away in boxes. These number one cards were like the front line in battle. There are a few other key condition problems to look for. The yellow background on this card can create an illusion of nice centering. Look closely and keep this in mind before purchasing.

The yellow background is also, as mentioned with other issues, a haven for print defects because there is no where for them to hide. Finally, the 1958 Topps cards were printed so inconsistently that the range of picture, color and cut quality is all over the place. This was not one of the company's better years when it came to quality control.

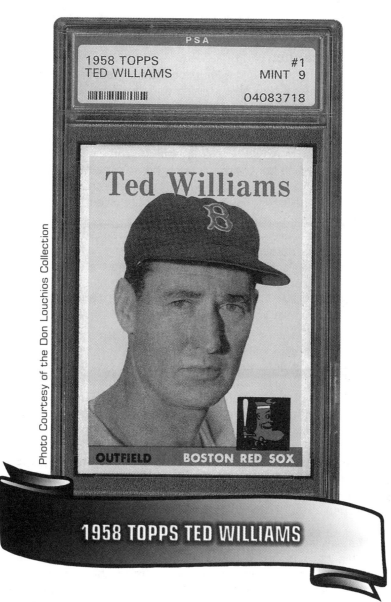

Ted Williams

OUTFIELD     BOSTON RED SOX

1958 TOPPS TED WILLIAMS

## Comments:

If you want difficulty and importance, you found the right card. Williams almost looks sad in this picture, it was his last appearance on a Topps card. This card, unlike the 1957 Topps example, can exhibit great color and is slightly tougher as well. This set, once considered "soft" in the market, has really begun to reestablish itself as a hobby favorite in recent times. This is one of those sets that will benefit from collector education. The more they learn about the set, the more the set will look attractive as an option. It has been said that Williams wanted to be remembered as the greatest hitter who ever lived, you will get no argument from me.

# 1958 Topps #418 World Series Batting Foes

## Importance:

This is the only card ever produced to feature baseball's Home Run King and New York's pride and joy. This card carries a lot of power. Between Mickey Mantle and Hank Aaron, 1291 homers were blasted making these two sluggers responsible for a lot of souvenirs. If Mickey Mantle had not suffered so many injuries, that number would be much higher. The two sluggers were really a study in contrast. One hit home runs because of his brute strength and raw power while the other methodically piled up the long balls with quickness and consistency.

This card takes on extra importance because, in 1957, both men were named MVP but it was Aaron who would walk away with a World Championship as a member of the Braves. This card has remained extremely popular over the years for its beauty and difficulty. This card is one of only a handful of multi-player cards to make the list.

## Difficulty:

This card is notorious for being hard to find in high-grade. First of all, you have to contend with very inconsistent centering. Very few examples are found dead-centered and, due to the design, a slight shift one way or the other makes the centering actually appear much worse than it is. Second, you have to contend with print spots that haunt the image. I am not sure if I have ever seen an example devoid of print spots. Usually, you see the image plagued with print "snow" or light specks across the dark background. As long as they are not too severe, the card's eye-appeal should not suffer dramatically.

Finally, because of the poor paper used to make these cards, this card is often found with soft corners. Razor sharp examples sell for a significant premium as this card is rarely found nice. Also, look for bold yellow and blue colors, it can make a big difference in the quality of the image.

PSA
1958 TOPPS                    #418
SERIES BATTING FOES    MINT 9
MANTLE & AARON
08162030

WORLD SERIES BATTING FOES
MICKEY MANTLE • HANK AARON

## 1958 TOPPS WORLD SERIES BATTING FOES

## Comments:

While not quite as popular as the 1957 Topps Power Hitters card, this card is tougher overall. This set is filled with other interesting multi-player cards like that of Ted Williams and Ted Kluszewski but none of them have the raw power that this one holds. In addition, the 1958 Topps set has enjoyed increased demand in recent years, so this card will naturally receive more attention as an important key. This card, admittedly, was a borderline choice and I am sure some collectors are wondering why it made this exclusive list. The card just has a very strong, almost "cult-like" following. This is simply a collector favorite of two vintage mashers.

## 1959 Fleer #68 Ted Signs for 1959

### Importance:

This is the toughest card in a set entirely devoted to Ted Williams. It was Fleer's first offering and they chose one man to represent their entire launch. If you ask me, they chose wisely. Fleer was able to sign Ted Williams to an exclusive deal and, for the duration of Ted's career, Topps would never produce another card featuring the "Splendid Splinter." This set has always been very popular with collectors due to its storytelling ability and affordability.

This is, by far, the most valuable card in the set as it was pulled from production early with only a limited amount escaping into the market. In 1959, Williams was only one year away from retirement and, after the 1960 season (a season in which Ted hit 29 homers in a mere 310 at bats), he called it quits. The image is a familiar one and, while the card may not be as difficult as once thought, it still remains a classic.

### Difficulty:

This card is not one of the tougher cards to find in high-grade on this list but the key here is that you have to find it first. This card was pulled from production early and does not exist in the same quantities as the rest of the cards in the set do. According to most experts, Bucky Harris, the other man pictured on card #68, was under contract with Topps at the time. Before you could say, "Legal Action," the card was removed from production. While some examples did escape the factory, the number was limited.

Two major condition problems seem to affect this card, centering and corner blunting. You can find clean examples of this card but rarely do you find this card with perfect centering (it's usually 60/40 or worse). In addition, these cards will usually be found with blunt corners because of the way the cards were cut and packaged. They are not round, they just lack the pointed quality of a truly sharp corner. Difficulty, in terms of condition, is not the strong suit of this card but it's not easy find.

Jan. 23, 1959 — Ted Signs For 1959

1959 FLEER TED SIGNS FOR 1959

## Comments:

This card, like a few others on the list, is one of those classic images that remains familiar to many collectors. Always considered a post-war rarity, this card has had its share of attention but, lately, the attention has waned. We now know that this card, while not easy to find by any means, is not as difficult as once thought. It may not be as scarce as rumor had it but the significance of the card has remained as the key card in a set devoted to the "Splendid Splinter." Sometimes, perception is greater than reality.

## 1959 Topps #514 Bob Gibson

### Importance:

This is the only recognized rookie card of one of baseball's best, but nastiest, right-handed power pitchers. The last thing a hitter would want to do is to disrespect Mr. Gibson. If a hitter decided to make such a foolish choice, the next pitch would be a 95mph fastball coming straight for his "nugget." Bob Gibson was one of the most respected pitchers in his era and his devastating slider made hitting a nightmare for right-handed batters. He would win 20 or more games 7 times in his career (twice winning 19) with two Cy Youngs and one MVP Award to his credit.

In 1968, Gibson may have turned in the greatest single season performance in pitching history. He won the Cy Young and MVP awards with a 22-9 record, 13 shutouts and an amazing 1.12 ERA! That's an ERA that may never be matched and Gibson certainly is one of a kind. The pitchers mound was lowered after his great season, due in large part to Gibson's performance. He was elected to the Hall of Fame in 1981.

### Difficulty:

The Gibson rookie is usually found with a few different condition problems. The first problem is centering. Like all 1959 Topps cards, due to the design and inconsistent cuts, the Gibson is usually off-center. With the exception of the 1959 Topps cards that have yellow backgrounds, the contrast between the white borders and colorful backgrounds leaves no room for error. Poor centering is easily noticed. The second problem is the existence of print marks. Again, this is common to most 1959 Topps cards, but the light pink background of the Gibson card makes this problem even worse. Any dark spots are clearly visible thereby reducing the eye-appeal.

Finally, the coloring of the background and whiteness of the borders seem to be all over the place. Some 1959 Topps cards are found with toned borders and bland color while other are found with bright white borders and bold color. Be patient and look for the card with outstanding colors and you will be rewarded.

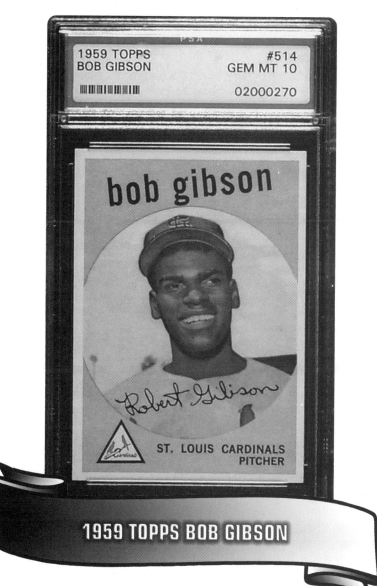

| | |
|---|---|
| 1959 TOPPS<br>BOB GIBSON | #514<br>GEM MT 10 |
| | 02000270 |

bob gibson

Robert Gibson

ST. LOUIS CARDINALS
PITCHER

**1959 TOPPS BOB GIBSON**

## Comments:

Gibson was as tough as they come and, although he wasn't necessarily considered the most likable guy in the league, his pitching dominance is legendary. In a day of super sluggers and run scoring jubilees across the country, Gibson takes us back to a time when runs were scarce and the game was played a little differently. He's the guy you would want on the hill in the big game and this is the most important trait of the fierce pitcher. It is also important to note that Gibson cards, in general, have been experienced heightened demand in recent years so it seems as if collectors are finally taken notice of his track record. Keep in mind that this card is indeed the key rookie card in the set. Don't be fooled by the smile, this guy means business.

# 1960 Topps #148 Carl Yastrzemski

## Importance:

This is the only recognized rookie card of the legendary Boston left fielder. "Yaz" had one of the most difficult jobs in baseball history in the early 1960's. He would have to replace the best hitter in baseball history, Ted Williams. While no one could ever replace Williams, Yastrzemski came about as close as anyone could hope. The powerful slugger finished his career with 3,419 hits, 452 homers and 1,844 RBI's. In fact, he was the first American League player in history to reach 400 homers and 3,000 hits.

Along the way, Yaz would win a few batting titles and, more importantly, is still the last man to win the Triple Crown Award. In 1967, his .326 average, 44 homers and 121 RBI's gave him that honor as well as the A.L. MVP Award. Also a great outfielder, Yaz would lead the league in assists six times, an astonishing defensive accomplishment. He was elected to the Hall of Fame in 1989.

## Difficulty:

The 1960 Topps Yastrzemski rookie card is tough for a number of reasons. While you can find this card very sharp on occasion due to a "find" of cello packs years ago, the centering and print problems overwhelm the card. Often times, you will find the Yaz rookie with black print defects (also known as "peppering") in the orange-colored background. These print spots can really damage the eye-appeal of the card. In addition, the centering is virtually all over the place.

One thing to keep in mind is that this issue was produced with rough edges some of the time. Cards pulled from the cello "find" were sometimes seen with severe rough-cuts. While rough-cuts do not technically downgrade a card, make sure it is not so severe that it reduces the visual appeal of what is really a beautiful card.

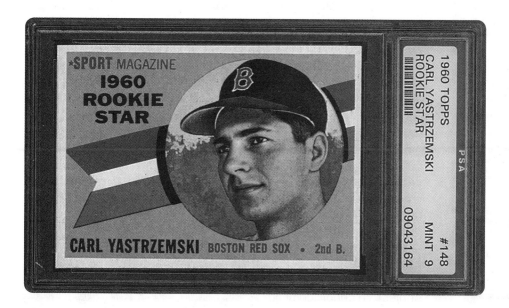

## Comments:

Carl Yastrzemski was never considered a legend during his playing days. He was often overshadowed by the likes of Aaron and Mays and the ghost of Ted Williams was always lurking near the Green Monster. Despite all the pressure, Yaz compiled an outstanding career and truthfully, when you look at his numbers, he seems a bit underrated in the sportscard market. Yastrzemski's numbers should keep his name in the minds of collectors for generations and being a part of Red Sox lore should enhance his place in history much like team association has helped others on the list. A World Championship is the only thing that eluded Yaz during his great career. Red Sox fans are still waiting.

## 1962 Topps #1 Roger Maris

### Importance:

This is the first card in the 1962 Topps set and, perhaps, the most desirable card of Roger Maris. Many people will say that, if you were going to choose the best card of Maris, it would have to be his rookie card. I disagree.

First of all, Maris is basically known for his miracle 1961 season when he broke Babe Ruth's single season record for home runs with 61 jacks and this is the card that commemorates that season. Second, this card features Maris on the Yankees while his rookie card features him on the Cleveland Indians. Third, this card is the first card in the set and a condition rarity. His rookie card is tough to find in high-grade but so is this one. Finally, the image on this card is great and it is one of the most attractive cards in the entire set. His chase for immortality was legendary and this card captures that magical season.

### Difficulty:

All 1962 Topps cards are subject to condition problems but this card is even tougher. The brown borders that frame the card are very susceptible to chipping and, when chipping is present, it can be a real problem. The damage to the eye-appeal can be a major detractor if the chipping is significant. Centering is another major obstacle. Several of

Photo Courtesy of National Baseball Hall of Fame Library, Cooperstoown, NY

the star cards in the set are prone to poor centering and this one is no exception. Be careful because centering can be deceptive due to the design of the card.

The next obstacle would be black print marks that are commonly found on this issue. If the print defects affect the facial area of Maris, they will downgrade the card significantly. Finally, the fact that this card is the first card in the set means that the card was often subject to overhandling and, in some cases, rubber band strangulation. This is one of the toughest Maris cards in the hobby and it rarely comes up for sale in high-grade.

PSA

| 1962 TOPPS | #1 |
| ROGER MARIS | MINT 9 |
| | 09019744 |

## 1962 TOPPS ROGER MARIS

## Comments:

The outlook for Maris is an interesting topic. I used to think that his popularity might fade because, truthfully, his numbers are no where near Hall of Fame consideration and one or two seasons don't make a player. While he will never make it to the Hall as an individual, it's like he's there anyway. He will always be associated with the first memorable home run chase and forever linked to Mickey Mantle. The fact that he was a Yankee, a team with such a rich history, just adds to the demand for his cards. He was even the focal point of a wonderful baseball movie entitled *61* that chronicled the pressure Maris endured. Maris will never fade, his legend just burns too bright.

## 1963 Topps #537 Pete Rose

### Importance:

This is the only recognized rookie card of baseball's all-time Hit King. All right, so Pete Rose is not in the Hall of Fame because of some gambling that took place. Collectors don't seem to care. Like Shoeless Joe Jackson a few eras back, Rose is treated like he is a part of the Hall because his accomplishments on the field put him in a league by himself. Rose was never the most talented man to take the field but his heart and determination helped him reach the unthinkable hit total of 4,256. Rose would reach 200 hits 10 times in his career and reach a .300 batting average 14 times.

After being named Rookie of the Year in 1963, Rose would also be named to 17 All-Star teams and MVP (1973) along the way. This card features three other players on the front, none of major note, but the card is classic. From his daring head-first slides to his nickname of "Charlie Hustle," Rose was the ideal baseball idol for the average fan.

### Difficulty:

Just think for a moment. When was the last time you saw a true mint copy of this great rookie card? It's probably been awhile. The blue colored border, located at the top of the card, is very easily chipped. In fact, this card might be more susceptible to chipping than the 1962 Topps cards are.

The light-colored background is a haven for print marks and the fact that there are four different images on the front leaves little room to hide these potential defects. The mixture of various colors just increases the chance of print spots. Because of the undefined border at the top, take a close look at the centering. An example may be off-center and you might not even realize it, pay close attention to the size of the white border at the base. This is a tough card of the all-time career hit leader.

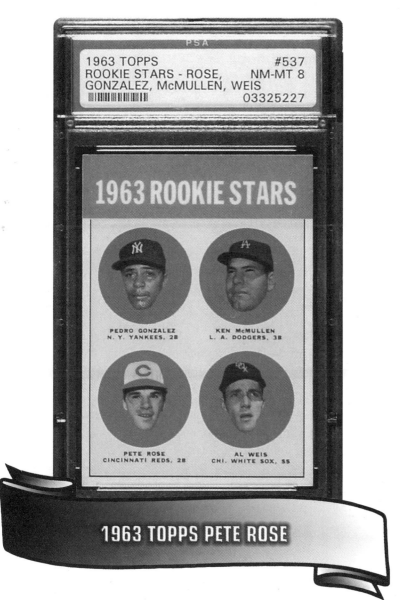

1963 ROOKIE STARS

PEDRO GONZALEZ
N. Y. YANKEES, 2B

KEN McMULLEN
L. A. DODGERS, 3B

PETE ROSE
CINCINNATI REDS, 2B

AL WEIS
CHI. WHITE SOX, SS

**1963 TOPPS PETE ROSE**

## Comments:

Forget about the Hall of Fame, Rose is treated like he's in there anyway. As the all-time hit leader, it's no wonder. Rose was the hero for the average fan. He wasn't overly big or incredibly fast. No "rocket" arm and no dynamic fielding here, just a guy who went all out to win. His appeal is constantly increasing. Even his haircut represents the working class. It's going to take a lot of determination and longevity to approach his hit record. With today's salaries, who's going to stick around long enough and take the physical pounding in order to do it? This card is tough, colorful and a key for most collectors.

# 1965 Topps #477 Steve Carlton

## Importance:

This is a key rookie card of one of baseball's best all-time hurlers. Carlton is recognized as, perhaps, the best left-handed pitcher in baseball history. Some critics may argue that Sandy Koufax deserves that distinction or that Warren Spahn is worthy of consideration but neither pitcher combined the strengths that Carlton possessed. Carlton showed dominance and longevity. He finished with 329 victories, 4,136 strikeouts and a 3.22 ERA after pitching over 5,000 innings.

"Lefty" also had six seasons with 20 or more wins, including a 27-10 season for the last place Philadelphia Phillies in 1972 (he remains the only pitcher in history to win the Cy Young for a last place team). Carlton was rewarded for his mound mastery with four total Cy Young Awards over the course of his career and an election to the Hall of Fame in 1994.

## Difficulty:

While this rookie card might not be the most difficult on the list, this Carlton example does have a few condition obstacles of note. First, beware of reverse chipping along the edges. The dark (blue/green) reverse is very susceptible to wear. In addition, centering is always an issue when discussing vintage specimens and this issue has very narrow borders making room for error very slim. Finally, the print quality is very inconsistent. Not only are print defects a possibility but overall color and registration seem to be a problem. Some Carlton rookies have very nice eye-appeal while others look very bland. This card is not overly difficult, but deceptive.

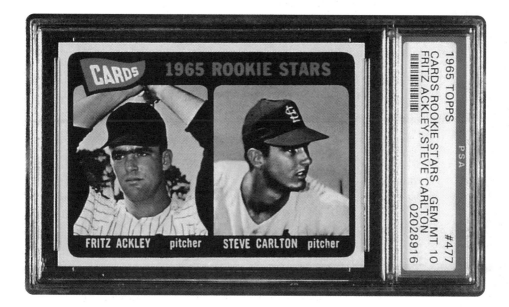

1965 TOPPS STEVE CARLTON

## Comments:

Steve Carlton was just one of those guys who really never embraced the media so the perception of Carlton is often skewed. The fact of the matter is, as time goes on, no one will remember Carlton's ability or inability to handle the press. All collectors will care about are his numbers and those numbers are awfully strong. When people talk about assembling an all-time pitching staff, his name always comes up as the man who possessed that wicked slider. This classic card should remain a part of most collector wantlists.

## 1967 Topps #569 Rod Carew

### Importance:

This is the only recognized rookie card of one of the best hitters of his generation. Rod Carew was not a physical powerhouse but his bat control was certainly lethal as his .328 career batting average would indicate. Those who saw him play will never forget Carew's unique hitting style as little leaguers emulated his stance across the country. Crouched over at the plate, Carew would appear extremely relaxed as he waved his bat slightly as the pitch was delivered. Carew's lighting quick hands took over from there as he could slap the ball in any direction at any time.

A tremendous bunter and blessed with terrific speed, Carew used many tools in order to compile 3,053 total hits. Carew won 7 batting titles in all and, after batting .388 in 1977, was honored with the A.L. MVP Award. He was elected to the Hall of Fame in 1991. This card is one of two key rookie cards, along with the Seaver rookie, in the 1967 Topps set.

### Difficulty:

The Carew rookie card is part of a set not known for substantial difficulty. The 1967 Topps issue does not have the colored borders of the 1962 or 1963 set and it is not rare by 1960's standards but there are a few condition obstacles to look for. You can find this card sharp, much like the Yastrzemski rookie, but centering is a problem due to very narrow borders on this Topps issue.

In addition, 1967 Topps cards, in general, have been known to exhibit black print defects along the white borders and in the backgrounds. Finally, and for good measure, the Carew rookie seems to come up for sale less often than the Seaver perhaps due to Seaver's popularity. This is not a very tough card by vintage standards but it does have some condition obstacles to overcome.

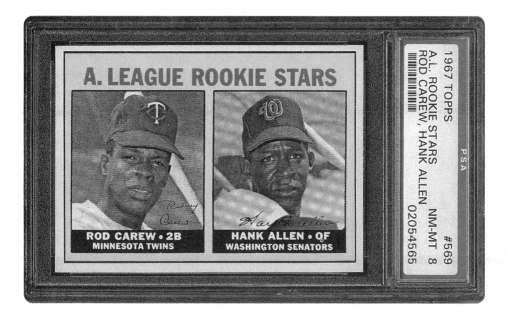

## Comments:

As a 3,000 Hit Club member, Carew will always be at the top of many wantlists. He did not possess the incredible power of Mantle or Williams, but this second/first baseman reached an exclusive club that eluded both legends. Carew also proved that he brought more to the game than just batting average, he could also run. Carew was so fast that he stole home 7 times in 1969. Now that's exciting. One thing is for certain, Carew brought a style to the game that will not soon be forgotten and his rookie card, while not that difficult overall, is one of the biggest keys to one of the more attractive sets of the decade.

## 1967 Topps #581 Tom Seaver

### Importance:

This is the only recognized rookie card of "Tom Terrific." This 3-time Cy Young Award winner won 311 games in his career, had a 2.86 ERA and a .603 winning percentage. He also struck out 3,640 batters including 10 seasons of 200 or more and a single game-high of 19.

In 1967, Seaver would finish with 16 victories in just his first big league season. When it came time for Hall of Fame voting, Seaver was named on a record 98.8% of the ballots in 1992. His ability to use his legs during his windup enabled Seaver to generate tremendous velocity from the mound. His fastball was one of the best in the league. Seaver's rookie card is a key to the attractive 1967 Topps set along with the Mickey Mantle, Brooks Robinson and Rod Carew (rookie) cards.

### Difficulty:

Despite being a part of the high-number series, this Seaver rookie is not the hardest card to find in nice shape. That being said, two problems exist that are worth noting. The problems are centering and print defects. The card has somewhat narrow borders, which means a slight shift in any direction will be immediately noticeable.

The other problem, print defects, are usually black and are frequently found sprayed across the image or on the white border. When print defects appear on the borders, collectors take notice and often hesitate about purchasing the card. If the print defects are minimal, the eye-appeal should not be damaged too badly.

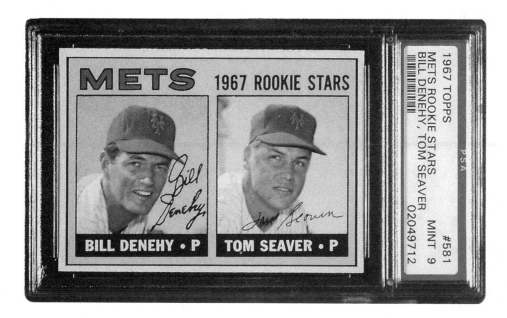

1967 TOPPS TOM SEAVER

## Comments:

When this card is found with a bright, crisp look, it's great to look at. The card is not overly tough but the accomplishments of Seaver override the lack of difficulty. The card is also helped by the fact that he played in New York as part of the "Amazing Mets" in 1969 (going 25-7) and he was very likable as well. Fans that watched him pitch can still remember that high leg kick from the mound which was only to be followed by an overpowering fastball. This is a key rookie card for any collection of high-profile Hall of Famers, especially pitchers.

## 1968 Topps #177 Nolan Ryan

### Importance:

This is the only recognized rookie card of baseball's all-time strikeout king. What can you say about the importance of Nolan Ryan and this card? The guy defied all natural law. He still threw in the mid-90's when he retired in his mid-40's! If Ryan had not suffered a career-ending elbow tear in 1993, he might still be pitching today. All right, maybe not, but you get my point. He was actually a better pitcher at age 40 than he was at 25 because he was able to gain control of his blistering heater. He finished with 324 wins, a 3.19 ERA, 5,714 strikeouts and 7 no-hitters.

The 5,714 number is the one that defies logic. If you struck out 250 batters per year for 20 years, that gets you to 5,000. Then you need to sprinkle in another 714 k's! He was elected to the Hall of Fame in 1999. This humble cowboy from Texas holds more records than you can imagine and this card is the key to the 1968 Topps set.

### Difficulty:

Like the Seaver rookie, this card is not very tough overall. On the other hand, this card is not easy to locate in strict mint condition. You can find this rookie card without much effort but not with all the attributes of a mint card. If it's sharp, it's usually off-center and, if it's centered, it's usually soft along the edges. In addition, the reverse is colored, a yellow-orange shade. This reverse is susceptible to chipping so make sure you look at the back edges. Many collectors ignore the reverse but you shouldn't, especially with this one.

Finally, this card is found with a very wide range of eye-appeal and beware of print defects in the background of the two photos (Ryan and Koosman). Some of these Ryan rookies have a very light colored background (in the patterned area) and some have a rich, dark color. This can make a big difference.

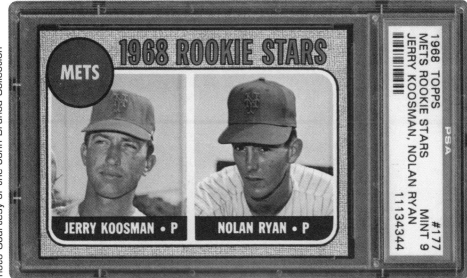

1968 TOPPS NOLAN RYAN

## Comments:

There are legends of the game and then there are legends of the game. Nolan Ryan was one of the most entertaining pitchers ever to pitch. He threw harder in the 9th inning than he did in the first and, once he got his curveball over, forget it. He would make great hitters look like little leaguers at the plate. The numbers go on and on for Ryan making this card especially important. By the way, another fine pitcher by the name of Jerry Koosman is coupled with Ryan on the card. It was one of the only times that two star players were placed on the same vintage rookie card. This card may not be overly difficult but it's deceptively tough in strict mint condition. This card is just a must for most collectors.

# 1968 Topps #247 Johnny Bench

## Importance:

This is the only recognized rookie card of one of baseball's best catchers. If you ask most baseball experts, they consider Johnny Bench the best all-around catcher in baseball history. From his rocket arm to his lethal bat, Bench offered a rare combination of stellar offense and defense from the backstop position. In fact, he was so dominant behind the plate that the Gold Glove Award went to Bench each and every year from 1968-1977.

At the plate, he led the league in homers twice and RBI's three times, a rarity for a catcher. Bench was awarded the MVP in 1970 (the youngest ever at the age of 22) and 1972. He was also named to the All-Star Team 14 times en route to Hall of Fame induction in 1989. The card itself is one of two key rookies, along with the Ryan rookie, in the very popular 1968 Topps set.

## Difficulty:

Like the Ryan rookie card, this Bench example is not terribly difficult by vintage standards but there are a few condition obstacles to look for. First, the patterned background can mask corner and edge wear on the card. Take a close look at those corners or you will be sorry. In addition, the reverse is a yellow-orange color and it is also very susceptible to chipping or wear. Do not ignore the reverse on this card.

Finally, the eye-appeal on these 1968 Topps cards in general really varies. Make sure, if you are seeking a high-end copy, to look for deeper colors because dull copies are seen quite often and beware of print defects in the background of the two photos of Bench and Tompkins. Not a tough card but you shouldn't underestimate it either.

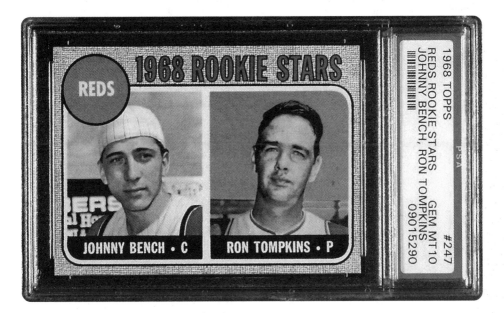

## Comment:

Considering Bench's importance as a player, his popularity and his status as a catcher, inclusion of his rookie card in this book is mandatory. Anytime the media, players or fans assemble an all-time list team, Johnny Bench is the name they pick as the starter behind the plate. In the future, that may change with superstar players like Mike Piazza and Ivan Rodriguez becoming possible candidates but, as it stands, Bench is the man. This card may not rank high in pure difficulty but the importance of Bench was just overwhelming. The "quarterback" of the *Big Red Machine* has earned his spot.

# 1968 Topps 3-D Roberto Clemente

## Importance:

This is, perhaps, the toughest Clemente card in the hobby and the key to an extremely tough set. Some collectors label this card as "mainstream" because it was made by Topps. Beyond that, this card is anything but mainstream. This was actually a test issue produced by Topps that never made it to the market. A few examples escaped from the factory and a legendary set was born. Clemente was, by far, the biggest star to be included in the set. There was no Mantle, Aaron or Mays, just a sincere looking Roberto.

When this card was produced, Clemente was just coming off one of his best years. In 1967, he hit .357 with 209 hits (both league-highs), 110 RBI's and 103 runs scored. The year before that, he won the MVP. Two World Championships, four N.L. batting titles and 12 straight Gold Glove Awards later, Clemente became legend. The image is classic, but one not seen too often.

## Difficulty:

Once you find this card, you may notice some distinct flaws that are unique to the issue. The trouble is that you rarely can find it! This was a test issue and very few cards were released from the factory. There are no exact numbers as to how many exist, but all experts agree that the number is small. The top layer of the card was coated in plastic to give the card a 3-D effect. That plastic coating can be susceptible to cracking, so some examples that appear NM-MT at first glance can actually conceal a major defect. The defect usually results in a downgrade of the card, usually to EX-MT status depending on the severity of the crack.

Another thing that you should be aware of is the printing on the reverse. I have seen a few examples where the printing is out of focus and the back appears tilted. This doesn't seem to bother most collectors and it usually will not result in a major downgrade. The card is so tough to find that most people focus on the front. A small "find" in the late-1990's is responsible for most of the high-grade examples that exist today.

PSA

1968 TOPPS 3-D
BOB CLEMENTE

GEM MT10

04216415

## 1968 TOPPS 3-D ROBERTO CLEMENTE

## Comments:

With Clemente, like a few other noted players on this list, you almost have to forget about the numbers and focus on his impact. With Clemente, his numbers were more than adequate as he ripped exactly 3,000 hits to go along with occasional power, great speed and a rifle for an arm but the statistics do not do him any justice. You just need to ask those who saw him play if he was one of the best. The answer is always, yes. Keep in mind that he was still going strong (.312 average) in 1972 before he perished in a plane crash bound for Nicaragua. This card will be a tremendous challenge for many collectors because of the extreme rarity but it is certainly worth the chase.

# 1969 Topps #260 Reggie Jackson

## Importance:

This is the key rookie card of one of baseball's all-time great performers. Let's face it, baseball is a form of entertainment. When you buy a seat at the ballpark, you want to be entertained. No one, during his era, was a better entertainer than Reggie Jackson. Everyone knew when Reggie was coming to the plate. He received booming cheers when he homered and thunderous boos when he struck out (and vice versa depending on what ballpark you were at), you either loved him or hated him.

Who can forget the three consecutive homers he hit against the Dodgers during the 1977 World Series? With 563 homers, over 1,700 RBI's, five World Series titles and a MVP in 1973, Reggie had plenty of accomplishments to warrant his admission to the Hall in 1993. Even though Reggie does have a 1969 Topps Supers card, this regular Topps card is his most important rookie.

## Difficulty:

The 1969 Topps cards are very deceptive in terms of difficulty. The centering is truly horrendous for the issue, many Jackson rookies are found with 70/30 centering or worse. In addition, look out for a variety of print defects on the front. Due to the light-colored background and white borders, black print spots can disturb the eye-appeal. This card is also known for lacking great eye-appeal to begin with so the additional problems simply add a layer to the condition sensitivity.

Photo Courtesy of National Baseball Hall of Fame Library, Cooperstoown, NY

Also, beware of wear, chipping or fading along the pink-colored reverse. This can possibly prevent an otherwise mint copy from reaching top grading levels. You can find Reggie sharp but not always on the mark. This is a very deceptively tough card.

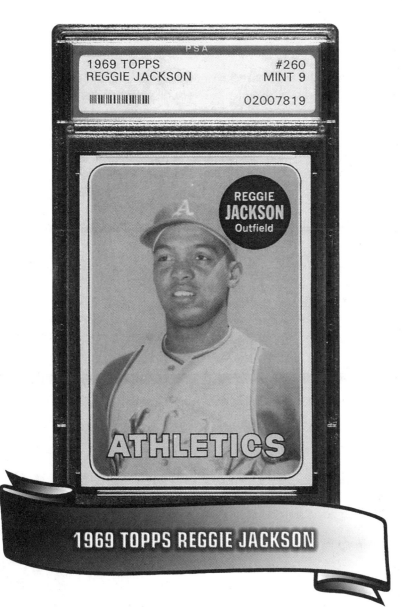

1969 TOPPS REGGIE JACKSON

## Comments:

Reggie Jackson is one of those players whose name evokes emotion from collectors and fans. For better or for worse, Reggie was always in the headlines and knew how to grab the spotlight. For that reason, in addition to his inclusion into the elite 500 Home Run Club, this Reggie rookie should be a fixture on many wantlists. It also doesn't hurt that Reggie was a member of the New York Yankees during some great years. The 1969 Topps set is also very popular in its own right and, with Reggie as one of the keys driving the demand along with Mantle, it should remain a very popular set.

## 1969 Topps #500 Mickey Mantle White Letter

### Importance:

This is the last card and one of the most difficult cards of hobby legend Mickey Mantle. The white letter variation is just plain tough. No one seems to know for sure why these cards were produced this way. Was it a mistake? Was it intentional in order to generate more interest in packs? It's a mystery but there's no mystery when it comes to how important this card is. It's the card that has all of Mickey's statistics, from start to finish.

This card, in any grade, seems to be in high demand and what a way for New York's most beloved son to leave the collecting world. He left us with a mysterious rarity on almost everyone's wantlist. It is Mantle's rarest regular issue card.

### Difficulty:

The 1969 Topps cards are all very tough to find centered. It seems like no one cared about the cutting process that year. Most examples, of any player, are found with tilts and this can, in some cases, severely affect centering. Also, because of the white borders and light background, black print marks are very commonly seen. The print marks that reside inside a border can be a real distraction.

Photo Courtesy of National Baseball Hall of Fame Library, Cooperstoown, NY

Add to that the fact that these white letter variations are significantly scarcer than the yellow letter or regular issued cards. No one seems to know why the white letters were made but the rarity created a stir. They only appear from card #400-511 but Mickey Mantle's last card happened to appear in that run. Coincidence?

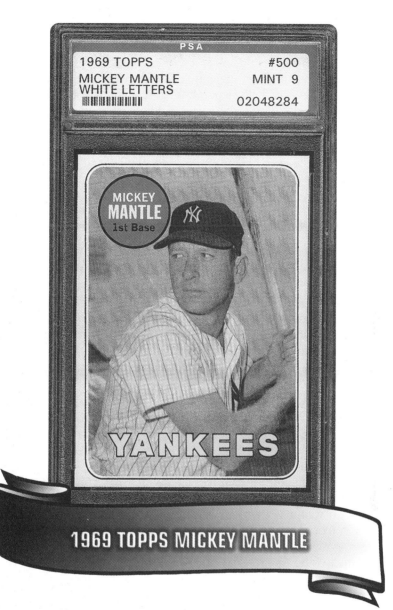

**1969 TOPPS MICKEY MANTLE**

## Comments:

The last card, for any player, always seems to be collectible but this one is special for a couple of reasons. First, it features superstar Mickey Mantle who has been the symbol of Topps and collecting in general for two decades. Second, it is a very rare variation of a card that is already extremely popular without the variation. Because of the inherent problems with all 1969 Topps cards, this variation is rarely found in strict mint condition or centered. You can never go wrong with Mantle and this one is a key for, not just Mantle collectors, but also those who are interested in pure rarity.

## 1973 Topps #615 Mike Schmidt

### Importance:

This is the only recognized rookie card of the best 3rd baseman of all-time. It's an argument that many fans have. Who's the best 3rd baseman in history? Eddie Mathews had a lot of "pop" in his bat and was one heck of a competitor. Brooks Robinson was a good hitter with an unrivaled glove at the "hot corner." George Brett combined the skills of both men to some degree with his outstanding bat control.

All of those men were great ballplayers but no one could match Schmidt all the way around. He could match and beat Mathews at the power game, Schmidt had 8 home run crowns and 548 total homers under his belt at retirement. He could also match Robinson with his glove as Schmidt won 10 Gold Gloves, breaking numerous fielding records along the way. Brett, while a legend himself, could only surpass Schmidt in batting average but not in power or defense. Schmidt could also run as he stole 174 bases, won 6 division titles as a member of the Philadelphia Phillies, three MVP's and he was elected to the All-Star squad 12 times. He was elected to the Hall of Fame in 1995.

### Difficulty:

Much like the Seaver rookie card, this card is short printed but it is not one of the more difficult cards on the list. On the other hand, there are a few notable condition obstacles to look for. The centering can not only be poor but also deceptive due to the 3-player design on the front. In addition, the most problematic obstacle may be the print quality. These Schmidt rookies are often found with a variety of print defects that scatter about the front, especially along the white borders.

Finally, the reverse is surrounded by black-colored borders so chipping and general edge wear may be an issue, especially if you are trying to obtain a super high-end copy. Again, it's not extremely tough but this card has a lot of other things going for it.

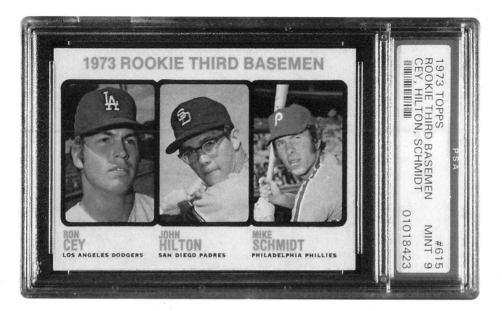

## 1973 TOPPS MIKE SCHMIDT

## Comments:

Schmidt has set the standard for all 3<sup>rd</sup> basemen to shoot for. Power, speed and great fielding, Schmidt could do it all. His rookie card entered the collecting world in a set that will never win the award for most attractive issue but his accomplishments override the lackluster design. If you collect 500 home run hitters, you need this card. If you collect Gold Glove winners, you need this card. If you collect MVP's, you need this card. If you collect all-time or all-Century teams, you need this card. With so many things going for this card, you simply can't avoid it.

# 1975 Topps #228 George Brett

## Importance:

This is the key rookie card in a star-filled 1970's set. George Brett was considered a solid ballplayer for years but, when he made a run at the elusive .400 batting average in 1980, he became a star. He would finally finish that year at .390, a level that no player has reached since in a full season.

Brett won the MVP that year for his outstanding performance and became known for his clutch hitting during regular and postseason play. Brett also became the first player in history to win batting crowns in three different decades (1976, 1980 and 1990). Despite being known for the famous "Pine Tar Incident," Brett's two greatest accomplishments might be his 3,154 hits and his induction to the Hall of Fame in 1999.

The famous incident, which took place at Yankee Stadium in 1983, was the result of a disputed rule by Yankee manager Billy Martin. After Brett homered off Rich Gossage in the 9th inning to give the Kansas City Royals a one-run lead, Martin emerged from the dugout. He pointed to Brett's bat and told the umpire that the pine tar exceeded the 17-inch limit allowed in the rulebook. Brett was ruled out after the umpire measured the coating of tar and Brett stormed out of the dugout in protest. The Yankees won the game 4-3 only to have the ruling changed by A.L. President Lee MacPhail. MacPhail, after stating that the rule should be clarified in the books, ordered that the home run should stand and the game be resumed from that point on.

## Difficulty:

The 1975 Topps cards are very tough in comparison to other issues of the decade. The multicolored borders are not only easily chipped but the variety of colors opens the door for print defects to wreck the image. In addition, the centering was very poor and many cards are often found with "tilts" creating a slew of off-center examples. There was a limited, mini version produced that very same year. The cards are identical in appearance with the exception of the noticeable size difference. Again, the card may be found sharp, as it is not very old in comparison to other issues on the list but, for a 1970's production, it is fairly challenging with the mini having the edge.

1975 TOPPS MINI     #228
GEORGE BRETT     MINT 9
08003437

ROYALS

3rd Base

GEORGE BRETT

## 1975 TOPPS GEORGE BRETT

## Comments:

This card is one of the few classics from the 1970's. Let's face it, the decade of the 70's wasn't exactly the most memorable 10-year span for sportscards. The designs were poor and the manufacturing process was even worse but a few keys are left embedded in the collecting mind and this is one of them. George Brett, as a member of the 3,000 Hit Club, is automatically included on many wantlists but his memorable performances as a clutch hitter make him a standout to most baseball fans. This card, one of two major keys in the 1975 Topps set (the Yount rookie being the other), is one of the decade's few bright spots.

## 1980 Topps #482 Rickey Henderson

### Importance:

This is the only official rookie card of the best leadoff man in baseball history. Rickey Henderson may not be the fan favorite that Derek Jeter is today but I couldn't leave this man off the top 200 considering the impact he made on the game. The fact that he is the all-time stolen base leader with almost 1,400 bags and counting is just one part of his impressive baseball legacy.

At the time of publication, Henderson surpassed 3,000 hits, is the all-time leader in walks (surpassing Babe Ruth) and runs scored (surpassing Ty Cobb) and was named the AL's Most Valuable Player in 1990 as the spark plug for the Oakland A's. By the way, he could also hit for power. Henderson is the all-time leader in leadoff home runs and has nearly 300 career homers to boot. He also made fans realize that OBP (.402 at the end of 2001) was more important than raw batting average (about .280). Forget about his "I'm the Greatest" speech, his numbers speak volumes.

By the way, who is going to break his stolen base mark? With nearly 1400 at the time of this writing, you would need to steal about 93 bases for 15 years in a row. The league leaders today usually don't come close to 93 stolen bases in their best years!

### Difficulty:

This card is one of those cards that is somewhat deceptive. While no modern card is tough in comparison to vintage cardboard, this Henderson rookie is not easy to find in strict mint condition. Poor centering leads the way as the biggest condition obstacle. In addition, the edges and corners on this issue are often found with a blunt appearance causing the card to be downgraded.

Last but not least, you will occasionally run across examples that exhibit print defects in the background. Luckily, the image of Rickey is taken from a distance so it may not be as much of an eyesore as might be expected on portrait-style cards. This is not a very tough card in NM-MT but it provides a solid challenge in mint condition. This card has been counterfeited, so beware!

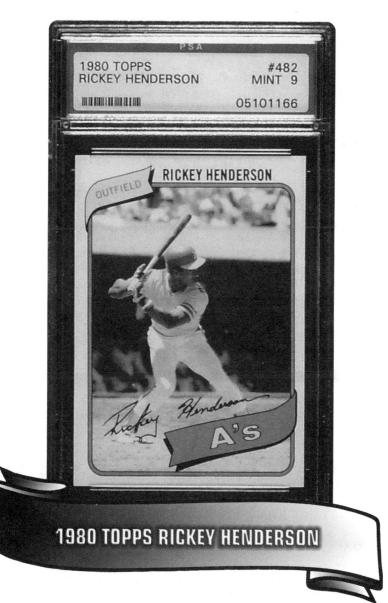

PSA

1980 TOPPS #482
RICKEY HENDERSON MINT 9
05101166

OUTFIELD RICKEY HENDERSON

A'S

## 1980 TOPPS RICKEY HENDERSON

**Comments:**

Like with many other great athletes who were not fan favorites of their day, Rickey's accomplishments will become increasingly important as time goes on. Keep in mind that even Reggie Jackson was booed incessantly during his prime but, as time went on, people began to appreciate Reggie for what he was, an entertainer. That's exactly what Rickey brought to the game and, with the way the game has changed with power being the focus, don't look for anyone to approach his stolen base mark for a long, long time. Looking ahead, collectors will come to appreciate the impact he had on the game, like him or not.

## 1982 Topps Traded #98 Cal Ripken Jr.

### Importance:

This is the most desirable rookie card of the modern day "Iron Man." Cal Ripken Jr. was a player that took fans back to another time. He played hard at all times, you never hear a bad word about him and he signs autographs for hours on end until every last youngster gets his wish. Needless to say, there is simply no one like Mr. Ripken.

Breaking Lou Gehrig's consecutive games played streak is just a part of what Ripken has accomplished even though that is what he will always be remembered for. He hit for power with 431 homers, is a member of the 3,000 Hit Club (3,184), drove in runs (1,695), fielded his position with the best (Gold Glove winner) and he was a great team leader. His two American League MVP's (1983 and 1991) are proof that he was among the best. While Ripken does have other popular rookie cards like the Donruss, Fleer and regular Topps versions, this card, in the semi-limited Topps Traded series, is his toughest and most important best rookie card.

### Difficulty:

The paper stock on this issue, by modern card standards, was not of the highest quality. Taking that into consideration, the red reverse can reveal wear with minimal touching. Print marks are fairly common along the white edges but centering does not appear to be of major concern. Finally, these cards were somewhat limited in comparison to the regular issue Topps cards from the same year as part of the separate boxed set. This is a semi-tough card by modern standards.

1982 TOPPS TRADED CAL RIPKEN

## Comments:

Ripken is an amazing athlete and man but there is one thing more amazing than his accomplishments, his appeal. I really have seen nothing like it in the hobby. Usually, no matter how great a player is, when they go into a slump, their collectibles take a turn for the worse. With Ripken, I have noticed that his collectibles would remain in demand over the years even when he would struggle at the plate, it was amazing. I guess when you have accomplished so much in the game and you are so well-liked, the demand naturally follows. His plaque has already been made in Cooperstown, this guy is a classic.

## 1983 Topps #482 Tony Gwynn

### Importance:

This is the key rookie card of one of baseball's most consistent hitters and personable players. Tony Gwynn is often referred to as the best pure hitter of the last two decades and his numbers can certainly support that argument. With a career batting average of .338 and 8 batting titles to his credit (only Ty Cobb had more), Gwynn has been a symbol of consistency in the National League. He is also one of the few players to start and finish his career with the same team (San Diego Padres), another fact that endears him to fans everywhere.

Gwynn made a run at .400 with a .394 average in August of 1994 but a strike-shortened season halted the chase. Don't forget that Gwynn was an excellent base stealer (over 300 career steals with a high of 56 in 1987) and outfielder (several Gold Gloves) as well. While Gwynn has Fleer and Donruss rookie cards, the Topps rookie is the most desirable.

### Difficulty:

The 1983 Topps Gwynn rookie card is actually fairly tough to locate in top grades due to extremely inconsistent centering. Whether it's top to bottom or left to right, these Gwynn rookies are found with very poor centering. Print spots are considered a lesser issue and you can find these cards with very sharp corners because of all the vending and unopened packs in circulation. This is not a very tough card in NM-MT condition but it is somewhat of a chore to find centered, truly mint examples.

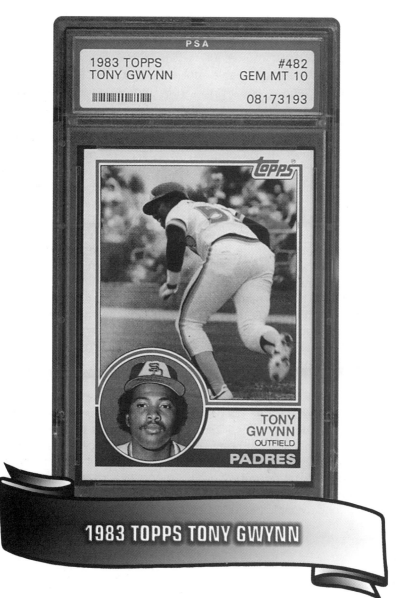

## 1983 TOPPS TONY GWYNN

## Comments:

Tony Gwynn had the personality and work ethic that made him one of the most likable baseball stars in a generation of multimillion dollar baseball celebrities. Gwynn was a real throwback in more ways than one. He wasn't flashy, he stayed with one team his whole career, he was the first guy at the ballpark every day, his ego didn't override his ability and he remained a genuinely nice guy through all the success. You want to root for a guy like Gwynn and it is sad that baseball lost two of its throwbacks to retirement, along with Ripken, in 2001. Gwynn will be missed by many, but his rookie card will remain a modern hobby staple.

## 1984 Fleer Update #27 Roger Clemens

### Importance:

This is the most valuable rookie card of one of modern baseball's most dominant pitchers. "The Rocket" has been striking out batters and racking up wins for nearly 20 years now and he shows little sign of slowing. After six Cy Young Awards, the most ever by a pitcher from any generation, Clemens has paved a road straight to Cooperstown.

What makes his mound domination all the more impressive is the fact that we are playing in an era of offense. Almost every player in the lineup can hit today as the size and strength of hitters are significantly improved from yesteryear. Clemens has been able to stand out in a time when the once tiny shortstops have evolved into 6'3, 200-pound power monsters and that says a lot. The mark of 300 wins in certainly within his grasp and Clemens has already moved into the top 5 on the strikeout list with 3,717 and counting. Who can forget his two, that's two, 20-strikeout performances in a single game?

### Difficulty:

By modern card standards, this card is actually fairly difficult. The set was subject to a very limited print run by modern card standards. There was a buzz about this set before the cards reached hobby stores and collectors gobbled the set up once it hit the market. In addition to the limited print run, the cards, for whatever reason, were packed in such a way that some of them are found with tearing along the reverse. You see this more often near the corners than anywhere else on the reverse. By modern standards, once again, a reasonably tough card.

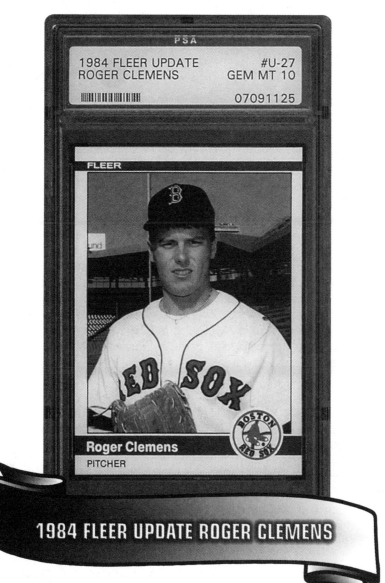

**1984 FLEER UPDATE ROGER CLEMENS**

## Comments:

Roger Clemens has already ensured admission to the Hall, but his numbers are still climbing and his final legacy is not yet set in stone. What Clemens represents is far more intriguing than his actual career pitching numbers. While Hall of Fame pitchers like Don Sutton, Jim Palmer and Fergie Jenkins were left off the list, Clemens has that something extra that makes him a marquee draw. Clemens was the premier power pitcher of the modern era and the successor to Nolan Ryan, the greatest power pitcher in baseball history. There's something about the power pitcher, much like the power hitter, than appeals to us. Maybe we will never fire a fastball at 98mph but we can own "The Rocket's" rookie card.

## 1985 Topps #401 Mark McGwire

### Importance:

This is the only true rookie card of baseball's modern home run hero. Mark McGwire had a roller coaster of a career but, now that it's over, he will be remembered as perhaps the greatest pure home run hitter this game has ever seen. From his record-breaking rookie season of 49 homers, to being overshadowed by Jose Canseco and Rickey Henderson in the late 1980's and early 1990's and almost quitting after batting .201 in 1991, McGwire went through it all. His home run frequency is astonishing. If it were not for injury, McGwire might have reached 800-1,000 homers.

In 2001, he showed no signs of slowing either but injuries finally forced Big Mac into sudden, unexpected retirement but he did finish with 583 career homers. In fact, he was a much better hitter late in his career than he was as a part of the "Bash Brothers" in Oakland. Even though Bonds has eclipsed Big Mac's single season mark, McGwire is still considered the best overall home run hitter in the game's history, not to mention a solid defensive player. I don't think we can appreciate what he has accomplished in his career until he is long gone.

### Difficulty:

This card is actually a fairly tough modern issue for several reasons. First, this card is found off-center the majority of the time. Second, the 1985 Topps cards exhibit very inconsistent print quality. This card has a very wide range of appearances. The colored frame can range from pink to orange to red and the picture of McGwire has registration issues to be aware of. Third, these cards did have some trouble with wax and gum staining, seemingly more so than other Topps issues of the era.

Finally, beware of a wide variety of counterfeits. When McGwire reached 70 in 1998, a few variations came out of the wood-work. The most common counterfeit has a perfectly sharp name box at the bottom. Remember that the box, on authentic examples, was never made perfectly square. The box should have some slight rounding at the corners. A Tiffany or Glossy version was produced the same year and limited to 5,000 and this example sells for a premium.

1985 TOPPS MARK MCGWIRE

## Comments:

Was Mark McGwire the modern-day equivalent of Babe Ruth? Not really, but his legacy remains. McGwire simply looks like the ultimate home run hitter. When he stood at the plate, he looked like a giant among boys. The images from the 1998 season will be remembered for a long time. Despite falling to Bonds in 2001, Mac's moment was much more memorable. When you look at his photo on the 1985 Topps rookie card, he doesn't look like the man we witnessed destroying fastballs into the outer limits of stadiums in the late 1990's, but that is part of the card's charm. It reminds me a lot of the 1954 Topps Ernie Banks rookie card in that we see the transformation of a baby-faced kid into a super slugger. McGwire was the prototype of power.

## 1987 Donruss #36 Greg Maddux

### Importance:

This is the most popular rookie card of the man who best exemplifies pitching in the modern era. Greg Maddux is a true artist on the mound. Maddux doesn't possess a 95mph fastball or a devastating breaking ball, he wins with precision and grit. With five Cy Young Awards to his credit, including four in a row (1992-95), Maddux has proved to the baseball world that drive is more important than talent.

It's amazing to think that, in his first full season, Maddux was 6-14 with a 5.61 ERA. His mound dominance has helped lead the Atlanta Braves to postseason play year in and year out. A lock for the Hall of Fame and an almost certain lock for 300 wins, Maddux has been one of the few consistent mound aces during an era dominated by power hitters. His 2.84 career ERA provides the best proof.

It is hard to compare players from different eras but, when you consider the offensive firepower that Maddux has to face today in comparison to the lineups faced by pitchers of the past, it just makes his accomplishments all the more impressive. While Maddux does have Fleer Update and Donruss Rookies examples, this is his most popular card.

### Difficulty:

Overall, this is one of the easier cards on the list but there are a few notes to pass along. First of all, the black borders that frame the youthful image of Maddux are susceptible to chipping as most colored borders are. In addition, keep in mind that there are two different versions of the 1987 Donruss rookie card. There's a wax pack version and a factory set version. The factory set version is slightly smaller than the wax pack version and the corners are usually blunted due to the cellophane wrap that housed the "card bricks" (small groupings of cards that are sealed together) in the boxes. This card is not very tough but gem mint examples are not easy to find by any means.

PSA

1987 DONRUSS      #36
GREG MADDUX    GEM MT10

04054811

GREG MADDUX P

**1987 DONRUSS GREG MADDUX**

## Comments:

I have to admit, I do not get all that excited to go to the ballpark and watch Greg Maddux spot his changeup, but his lack of flash simply allows his cards to remain more affordable. Nolan Ryan and Sandy Koufax had the kind of fastball that could leave a crowd in awe but, if there were one pitcher in baseball history that I would recommend emulating as a young-ster, it would be Greg Maddux. Maddux has made pitching a craft more than any other in the modern era. If you want a representative collection of all-time great pitchers, you have to own this card.

## 1987 Fleer #604 Barry Bonds

### Importance:

Barry Bonds, despite what some people feel about him on a personal level, is quite simply one of the best players in the history of the game and this is his most popular rookie card. Not just a Hall of Famer, Bonds is one of the very, very best the game has ever seen. He can hit, hit with power, run and field. The only thing lacking from Barry's game is a powerful throwing arm but, when you can excel is so many other areas, no one seems to notice your shortcomings.

Bonds has been an MVP four times (a record), he will certainly make a run at 600 homers or more, he was the first National League player to accomplish the 40/40 (40 homers/40 steals), he will most likely exceed 500 stolen bases, he has won numerous Gold Glove Awards and he has a solid career batting average near .300. By the way, he just happened to hit 73 homers in a season while breaking Babe Ruth's single season walks and slugging mark. Need I say more? Bonds does have other popular early cards like his 1986 Donruss Rookies, Topps Traded and Fleer Update cards but this is his most desirable.

### Difficulty:

By modern card standards, this rookie card is fairly tough to find in true mint or gem mint condition due to the inconsistent centering and chipping along the solid blue border, the border that surrounds the youthful image of Bonds. This card, while not as scarce as the Glossy Fleer version, is actually tougher to find in top shape. The gloss actually helped preserve the cards, especially the borders, while the regular Bonds rookie was manufactured with inferior paper stock. You will also occasionally find white print spots on the front as well. This is not a very tough card but there are some obstacles to consider.

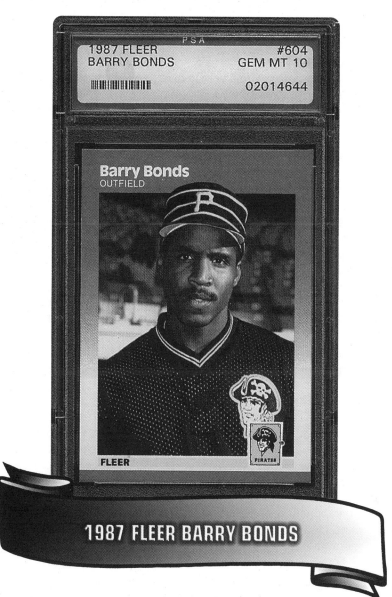

1987 FLEER BARRY BONDS

## Comments:

Again, forget about what you hear about the man, Bonds has accomplished so much that you can't deny his importance in baseball history. Whether he is simply misunderstood or arrogant, the numbers are astonishing. If Bonds was embraced by the media and the fans in the same way that they embrace Sammy Sosa or Mark McGwire, his rookie card would sell for multiple times the current market value. What does this mean for collectors? Well, it could mean that his rookie should enjoy solid long-term demand because, as time goes on, collectors tend to forget the bad things and focus on pure numbers.

## 1989 Upper Deck #1 Ken Griffey Jr.

### Importance:

This is the most desirable rookie card of modern baseball's best all-around player. Now, you might get a great argument from Barry Bonds supporters but, while they both have similar skills, Griffey possesses something that Bonds doesn't. Griffey has mass-appeal. You can just tell by watching Griffey that he loves to play. It's a big part of his charm.

Griffey's mannerisms are like that of a youngster playing ball with his friends, he just makes everything look so easy and fun. His stroke is smooth and he runs down deep drives with such ease and grace, it's incredible to see. He gives modern fans a chance to imagine what watching Willie Mays was like. His pile of Gold Gloves (10 consecutive) and home runs (460 and counting), at this point anyway, will lead the 1997 A.L. MVP straight to the Hall one day. Griffey does have an assortment of other rookie cards, including Bowman, Donruss and Fleer, but this is his most popular card. This premier set, from Upper Deck, challenged the other card manufacturers to upgrade the quality of their offerings.

### Difficulty:

This card is not very tough, even by modern standards but there is one hidden, factory defect to be wary of. There is a common wrinkle found on the reverse of the card that most collectors don't take notice of until it's too late. This was caused by the factory and most of the wrinkled Griffey's originated from factory sealed sets. Beyond that, and maybe slight centering variations that will prevent examples from reaching the exclusive gem mint club, this card can be acquired in high-grade without too much difficulty and is not on the list as a condition rarity.

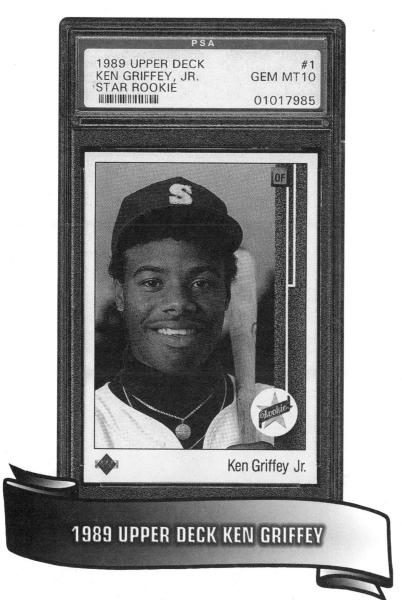

**1989 UPPER DECK KEN GRIFFEY**

## Comments:

This card serves as a reminder of the enthusiasm Griffey brings to the game. His smile is so big on the front of this Upper Deck rookie card, it almost looks like he just can't stop laughing. Maybe he is laughing at the pitchers who keep trying to get him out? Probably not, but when he gets hot at the plate, he might as well be laughing. Most baseball experts think it is Griffey, now that McGwire is gone, who might have the best chance of breaking Hank Aaron's all-time home run mark because of Griffey's young age. We can only wait and see if the record falls someday but, in the meantime, we can pick up a great modern rookie card of one of baseball's best all-around players.

## 1990 Leaf #220 Sammy Sosa

### Importance:

This is the most popular rookie card of the Chicago Cub's greatest power hitter. When Sammy Sosa entered the Major Leagues, scouts thought he would evolve into a solid player but no one, including myself, ever thought Sosa would become the power hitter we see today. As a member of the Texas Rangers and Chicago White Sox, Sosa would not make much of an impact. Once traded to the Cubs, Sosa would begin a steady climb to stardom.

Even before his magical 1998 MVP season, a season in which he batted .308 with 66 home runs and 158 RBI's, Sosa would become a 30-30 man (30 homers and 30 stolen bases) twice. Many thought that 1998 may have been a fluke for Sosa but they couldn't have been more wrong.

Sosa has put together a string of home run seasons that can match or beat anyone in baseball history. The year 2001 marked the 4th consecutive year that Sosa would crush 50 or more homers and the 3rd time overall that he would hit 60 or more. With over 450 homers and 231 steals, Sosa is one of the better all-around players in the game. He is simply unreal. Sosa does have other rookie cards produced by companies like Bowman, Donruss, Fleer, Score, Topps and Upper Deck but this is his most popular.

### Difficulty:

This is truly one of the easier cards on the list but one condition obstacle may be a bit deceiving. Keep an eye on the reverse. The grey-colored backs are often chipped and reveal wear at the tips of the corners. In addition, due to the grey color, any surface defect (such as any type of impression left by a fingernail, etc.) is immediately noticeable unlike the white backs that are found on many modern cards.

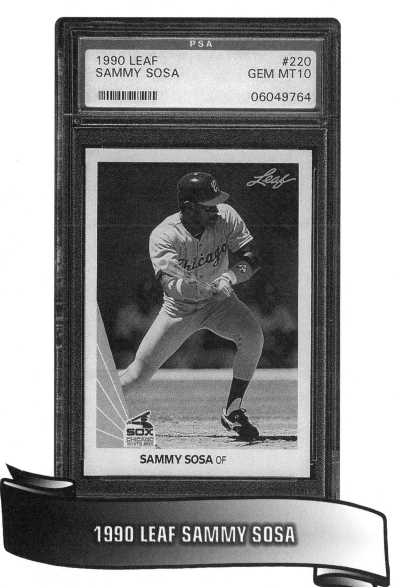

**SAMMY SOSA** OF

**1990 LEAF SAMMY SOSA**

## Comments:

I have to admit that I was one of those people who felt Sosa was not the real thing back in 1998. Boy was I wrong! I do not think we can appreciate Sosa's accomplishments enough right now because of the influx of great home run specialists, but what he has done is nothing short of amazing. Yes, he hits in Wrigley Field (a hitter-friendly ballpark). Yes, he didn't do much his first few seasons in the majors, but Sosa has proved, without question, that he is indeed the real thing. More importantly, he's a true fan favorite because of his endearing personality. For that reason alone, he will remain a popular player for future generations. By the way, is Sammy bunting in the photo? That will never happen again.

## 1992 Fleer Update #92 Mike Piazza

### Importance:

This is the most popular rookie card of baseball history's most prolific offensive catcher. Love him or hate him, Mike Piazza is quite simply the greatest hitter to ever play backstop. To think he wasn't drafted until the 62nd round? It's amazing. With an uncanny ability to drive the ball with authority to the opposite field, Piazza's swing is left with few holes, if any.

For a man of his strength, Piazza's bat control is incredible. At the time of publication, Piazza had a career batting average over .320, a slugging average of nearly .580, over 300 home runs, nearly 1,000 RBI's and numerous All-Star Game selections in his brief 10-year career. With more productive seasons ahead, Piazza is sure to rewrite the record books at his position, a position that traditionally produces little offensive support.

Each year the rumors spread about Piazza moving to another position on the field. With such incredible potential at the plate, many baseball experts feel that Piazza will succumb to the wear and tear that catchers are subject to and cut his career short. Piazza has refused a position change and, while some feel he is an average defender at best, you cannot deny his determination and heart. Piazza does have a popular Bowman rookie card as well but this is his most desirable.

### Difficulty:

This card, it terms of difficulty, would not rank very high on this list but there are two keys to keep in mind. First, and perhaps most importantly, this issue was subject to limited production by modern card standards much like the 1984 Fleer Update set 10 years earlier. The relative scarcity is probably the most difficult aspect to this card. The other aspect, while not nearly as important, is the existence of moderate centering problems. This Piazza rookie card has the type of centering problems that may not prevent the card from reaching mint levels but the gem mint grade may still remain a challenge.

1992 FLEER UPDATE MIKE PIAZZA

## Comments:

Piazza is a workhorse who plays with pain and provides a fearless wall against incoming baserunners. Piazza also has something extra going for him, marquee value. Much like Derek Jeter, Piazza is now one of New York's own, which never hurts card values. He's not just a great player, he's also a marketable personality. The amazing aspect of Piazza's legacy is that he could never play another game and still be considered the best offensive catcher in history. So few catchers have been able to provide clout at the plate, with Yogi Berra, Roy Campanella, Johnny Bench, Carlton Fisk, Gary Carter, Mickey Cochrane and Ivan Rodriguez being the most notable names. In the end, Piazza's final numbers should dwarf the rest.

## 1993 SP #279 Derek Jeter

### Importance:

This is one of the toughest modern rookie cards to find in strict mint condition and it features New York sensation Derek Jeter. This guy has yet to reach the halfway point of his career yet he already has more World Series rings than most grizzled veterans combined. While this man is an incredible athlete, it's not the only reason why Jeter has such a loyal following.

Jeter, much like Cal Ripken, is a humble guy that gives his all every time he steps on the field. He's just one of those guys that you just can't help rooting for. It doesn't hurt that he plays in New York, is a great shortstop, has a great bat (a .320 career average), occasional power and the ladies seem to like him too. He should be a shoe-in for 3,000 hits barring injury. What else do you want? Jeter does have other rookie card produced by companies like Pinnacle, Score and Topps but this one is his most desirable.

### Difficulty:

This card is not tough in NM-MT condition but finding it in gem mint shape is another story. The dark edges, in combination with the foil coating, are easily chipped, scratched and will reveal wear with ease. The packaging process was the problem. These SP's can be removed straight from the pack with corner touches or edge chipping. Both inherent defects will prevent a card from reaching the mint level. Some gem mint examples have brought incredible prices on the market, you would think it was a card from the 1960's.

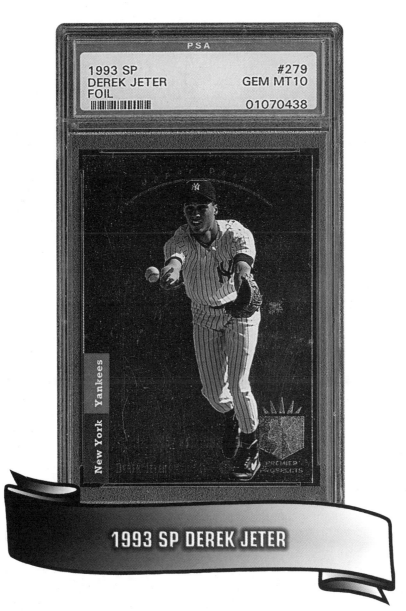

PSA

1993 SP #279
DEREK JETER GEM MT 10
FOIL
01070438

New York Yankees

## 1993 SP DEREK JETER

**Comments:**

Very few players come around with the overall appeal that Derek Jeter has. It's true that playing in New York, especially for the Yankees, has a lot to do with it but the way he has handled the pressure of playing there just adds to his appeal. The fact that he is so young makes the future of this card even more promising. Will he have the desire to play for another 10 years? Does it matter to Jeter if he reaches certain individual milestones? Nobody knows for sure, but I would bet that Jeter will be around for a long time, he has the desire to do great things in this game. Isn't it obvious?

## 1994 SP #15 Alex Rodriguez

### Importance:
This is one of the toughest modern-day rookie cards to find in mint condition and it features slugging shortstop Alex Rodriguez. This guy is a perfect example of the new athlete seen in baseball today. Shortstops used to be little guys who were fine fielders but had very little hitting ability at the plate. Not anymore.

At 6'4, 215 pounds, Rodriguez has redefined the position along with fellow shortstops Cal Ripken and Derek Jeter but no one has had the effect of "A-Rod." This guy ranks right up there with the best defensive shortstops in the game but where he stands out is with a bat in his hands. He can do it all at the plate and on the bases.

In 2001, A-Rod broke the single season record for home runs by a shortstop (previously held by Ernie Banks) with 52 dingers. Rodriguez has been a 40-40 man (40 homers/40 steals) and only 2 other men have ever done it (Canseco and Bonds). Both of those guys were outfielders, this guy's a shortstop! His potential seems limitless. A-Rod does have other popular rookie cards produced by companies like Leaf and Score but this is the most desirable.

### Difficulty:
This card, like the 1993 SP Derek Jeter rookie, is not tough in NM-MT condition but finding it in gem mint shape is another story. The dark edges, in combination with the foil coating, are easily chipped, scratched and will reveal wear with ease. The packaging process was the problem, these SP's can be removed straight from the pack with corner touches or edge chipping. Both inherent defects will prevent a card from reaching the mint level. Some gem mint examples have brought incredible prices on the market, you would think it was a card from the vintage era. Keep in mind that there is also a Die-Cut version of this card that was produced in more limited numbers.

PSA

1994 SP
ALEX RODRIGUEZ
FOIL

#15

MINT 9

08015183

## 1994 SP ALEX RODRIGUEZ

## Comments:

The 1950's was the decade of the center fielder but this is the era of the shortstop. Jeter might be more popular and Omar Vizquel might be better defensively but, if you ask most baseball experts who the best overall short-stop in the game is, their answer always seems to be Alex Rodriguez. Much like Jeter, it will be interesting to see how many years Rodriguez will stick around. The one encouraging aspect to Rodriguez is that he really appreciates and enjoys the game, so longevity shouldn't be a concern bar-ring injury. It's scary how good this guy is and his rookie card owners should benefit.

# 1948 Bowman #69 George Mikan

## Importance:

This is a classic rookie card of basketball's first marquee player. George Mikan is more responsible than any other player of his generation for making basketball a nationally recognized sport. On the face of this ever-popular card, Mikan is pictured storming towards the basket with relentless fury. At 6-10, 245 pounds, Mikan was the game's first dominant center. He led his team, the Minneapolis Lakers, to five NBA Championships in six years. It was the first time the word "Dynasty" was used to describe a professional basketball team.

Mikan averaged 22.6 points per game during his career, leading the NBA on four separate occasions and he retired as the all-time scoring leader. Mikan also led the NBA in rebounding twice. After his retirement, Mikan came back to the game as the ABA's first commissioner. This card is quite simply the most desirable basketball card in the hobby.

## Difficulty:

Like the Goudeys, the Bowmans are often found with toning around the edges and on the reverse. That is not the biggest problem though. Centering is a true nightmare on this card. Many Mikan rookies are found with tilts causing the card to qualify as off-center. With the great contrast between the borders and the dark-blue background, poor centering is very noticeable and affects the eye-appeal. Remember that these cards are also often found with rough-cuts. The existence of a rough-cut is not necessarily a problem, just make sure the cut doesn't affect the corners or distract from what otherwise is a beautiful card.

Photo Courtesy of the Tom Candiotti Collection

PSA

| 1948 BOWMAN | #69 |
| GEORGE MIKAN | GEM MT10 |
| | 02075060 |

**1948 BOWMAN GEORGE MIKAN**

## Comments:

George Mikan is very important to basketball history because he paved the way for future centers like Wilt Chamberlain and Bill Russell. Mikan was the first dominating center the game ever saw and it is fitting that his rookie card is the most desirable basketball card in the hobby. The image is such a classic that it becomes permanently ingrained in your mind. This card has so many things going for it that it's scary. The card resides in a tough set, features a true superstar, has great visual appeal and is widely recognized as the "crown jewel" of basketball cards. Outstanding future demand should accompany this card.

## 1957 Topps #17 Bob Cousy

### Importance:

This is the only recognized rookie card of basketball's "Houdini of the Hardwood." Until Cousy's arrival, basketball had been a methodical game with pre-planned plays and little innovation. Cousy, on the other hand, was unpredictable and his new style of play got fans excited about the game. He seemed to have the ability to do virtually anything with the basketball.

As the point guard for the Boston Celtics, Cousy led his team to six NBA Championships. He was also named the NBA's Most Valuable Player in 1957 before retiring in 1963. Cousy entered the game with little promise but left with a permanent mark on the game showing a flair never seen before.

### Difficulty:

This story will sum up the level of difficulty for sure. A well-known dealer discovered a small find of these cards, all in un-opened vending boxes, with well over 1,000 total cards in all. It became known as the "Tyler Texas Find." Out of the huge hoard of 1957 Topps cards, only 50 were believed to be suitable for high-grade collections. In other words, only 50 were expected to grade at NM-MT or better.

These were preserved in untouched form for decades and they still had major condition problems. The centering and print quality for this issue is totally inconsistent. Usually cut off-center and covered in print defects, this issue ranks near the top of the basketball list when it comes to pure difficulty. Finding a Cousy rookie card without "snow" in the background, centered and in focus is a real challenge.

**1957 TOPPS BOB COUSY**

## Comments:

The 1957 Topps issue is one of the most difficult vintage basketball issues in the hobby and this set has a major following. The set features several major rookie cards and this Cousy rookie, along with the Bill Russell example, is one of two major keys to the entire set. During an era when basketball was methodical and lackluster, Cousy brought about a radical style that helped to increase fan interest in the sport. As the second most valuable card in the set, this tough rookie is a card that should enjoy solid future demand.

# 1957 Topps #77 Bill Russell

## Importance:

This is the only recognized rookie card of the NBA's biggest winner. This card is the key to the 1957 Topps basketball set, considered one of the toughest basketball issues ever produced. In 13 seasons with the Boston Celtics, Bill Russell won 11 championships. Need I say more? Russell's focus on tenacious defensive changed the way fans perceived star players. Russell made defense an art, even his shot-blocking ability was legendary and he led the league in rebounds four times but his legacy cannot be measured by statistics.

Known as an extremely physical player, Russell's reputation alone would cause opposing players to alter their shots. During his career, Russell made 12 All-Star teams and won an amazing five Most Valuable Player Awards. As an amateur, Russell won two NCAA titles and he even won a Gold Medal during the 1956 Olympics. Russell is one of the true legends.

## Difficulty:

This story will sum the level of difficulty up for sure. A well known dealer discovered a small find of these cards, all in unopened vending boxes, with well over 1,000 total cards in all. It became known as the "Tyler Texas Find." Out of the huge hoard of 1957 Topps cards, only 50 were believed to be suitable for high-grade collections. In other words, only 50 were expected to grade at NM-MT or better.

These were preserved in untouched form for decades and they still had major condition problems. The centering and print quality for this issue is totally inconsistent. Usually cut off-center and covered in print defects (mainly print "snow" in the dark background), this issue ranks near the top of the basketball list when it comes to pure difficulty. Locating a Russell rookie card that is free of the above-mentioned defects is a real chore, even for the most advanced collector.

**1957 TOPPS BILL RUSSELL**

## Comments:

There are stars and there are superstars. Bill Russell was a superstar. I can't think of any other player who dominated the game, from the defensive end of the court, the way Russell did. The fact that Russell is constantly linked to fellow legend Wilt Chamberlain just adds to Russell's mystique. Like Magic and Bird or Mantle and Mays, most legendary players have a comparable foe. Russell's rookie card still, to this day, seems underrated when you consider the difficulty and desirability of the set overall. There's just not much else to say about this card, it is as solid as can be.

## 1961 Fleer #3 Elgin Baylor

### Importance:

This is the only recognized rookie card of the one of basketball's most exciting players of the 1960's. Elgin Baylor was fast, powerful and inventive. In today's game, powerful dunks and acrobatic shots fill the highlight reels but Baylor was the first player to do it routinely. During his 14 seasons as a part of the Los Angeles Lakers, Baylor averaged 27.4 points and 13.5 rebounds per game.

Baylor was also a very well-rounded player. At the end of the 1962-63 NBA season, Baylor ranked in the top five in four major categories. The categories were scoring, rebounding, assists and free throw percentage. It was first time in history that a player reached such lofty heights. His rookie card is one of four major keys to the 1961-62 Fleer set and his unreal performances make Baylor a collector favorite.

### Difficulty:

There was a find of these Fleer cards years ago so sharp examples do exist but that doesn't solve all the condition obstacles. These cards have very inconsistent centering, creating major demand for nicely centered copies. Also, keep an eye out for stray print in the bright-colored background. Dark print marks are very apparent on these cards and can detract from the eye-appeal in a major way. Keep in mind that all Baylor 1961-62 Fleer cards exhibit a print defect on the right side of his face. Like the early Bowman issues, rough-cuts are fairly common so make sure the cut doesn't severely affect the corners. Again, you can find them sharp but overall they are still tough.

PSA

1961 FLEER                    #3
ELGIN BAYLOR

NM-MT 8

08135720

LOS ANGELES
LAKERS

FORWARD
**ELGIN BAYLOR**

**1961 FLEER ELGIN BAYLOR**

## Comments:

The 1961-62 Fleer basketball set is not nearly as difficult as the 1957 Topps issue but, when it comes to demand, it stands alone. The combination of colors and key rookies make this set the most desirable vintage set in the basketball card hobby. As a player, Elgin Baylor is clearly underrated. When you consider his numbers coupled with his early impact on the game, his card should enjoy even more demand than it currently does. That's great news for collectors as Baylor's rookie card has remained affordable in comparison to other stars of the game. It might not be the most difficult card on the list, but it is certainly one that should appeal to many collectors.

## 1961 Fleer #8 Wilt Chamberlain

### Importance:

This is the only recognized rookie card of the most dominant player to ever play the game. Who is the best player in basketball history? Some might say Michael Jordan or Magic Johnson but statistics don't lie. If you want pure dominance, dominance of "Ruthian" proportions, your choice has to be Wilt Chamberlain. At 7'1, 275 pounds of pure muscle, he was just so much bigger and stronger than everyone else was. He looked like a man playing amongst boys on the court. No one could stop him.

Take a look at these numbers; he was the only player to score 4,000 points in a season and averaged 50.4 points during the 1961-62 season, he holds the record for points in a game with 100, the record for rebounds with 55, he led the league in scoring for 7 straight seasons, in rebounding 11 of his 14 seasons, and holds numerous other offensive records. By the way, Chamberlain won two championships as well. This card is just a classic. The confident stare of "The Stilt" graces the front of one of the hobby's most recognizable cards.

### Difficulty:

This card is seen more frequently in high-grade than the other 1961 Fleer cards on the list and this is possibly due to the fact that Wilt is so popular, bringing more rookies into the hobby limelight in comparison to the other rookies in the set. There was a find of these Fleer cards years ago so sharp examples do exist but that doesn't solve all the condition obstacles. These cards have very inconsistent centering, creating major demand for nicely centered copies.

Also, keep an eye out for stray print in the bright-colored background. Dark print marks are very apparent on these cards and can detract from the eye-appeal in a major way. Like the early Bowman issues, rough-cuts are fairly common so make sure the cut doesn't severely affect the corners. Again, you can find them sharp but overall they are still tough.

**1961 FLEER WILT CHAMBERLIN**

PSA
1961 FLEER #8
WILT CHAMBERLAIN NM-MT 8
01428058

PHILADELPHIA WARRIORS
CENTER
WILT CHAMBERLAIN

## Comments:

Wilt Chamberlain's dominance is hard to imagine. Even though many of us have seen Michael Jordan play, Wilt was more dominant for sure. While he was an incredibly dominant player, he was also very hard to figure out as a person. Wilt was not really disliked but he was often misunderstood. Regardless, his card is a classic in the basketball card hobby. Along with the Mikan and Jordan rookie cards, this one is a must for the serious collector. It's not as tough as the Russell rookie but, as an offensive force, Wilt receives more demand because collectors are often drawn to offensive stars. Wilt was a true giant of the hardwood.

## 1961 Fleer #36 Oscar Robertson

### Importance:

This is the only recognized rookie card of basketball's most well-rounded legend. Oscar Robertson could beat his opponents in many ways whether it was on the offensive or defensive end. He could do it all. Perhaps his most defining moment came at the end of the 1961-62 season, only his second year in the NBA. Robertson averaged 30.8 points, 12.5 rebounds and 11.4 assists per game for the entire year. That's a triple-double for the whole year! In fact, he came within a whisper of doing it again on four separate occasions. Wow!

At 6'5, 220 pounds, Robertson was a powerful guard and he helped revolutionize the position. He was selected to the All-Star team in 12 of his 14 seasons in the NBA and was named MVP for his outstanding performance during the 1963-64 season. This card joins three other major keys on this all-time list, all of them part of the most popular basketball card set ever produced.

### Difficulty:

There was a find of these Fleer cards years ago so sharp examples do exist but that doesn't solve all the condition obstacles. These cards have very inconsistent centering, creating major demand for nicely centered copies. Also, keep an eye out for stray print in the bright-colored background. Dark print marks are very apparent on these cards and can detract from the eye-appeal in a major way. Like the early Bowman issues, rough-cuts are fairly common so make sure the cut doesn't severely affect the corners. Again, you can find them sharp but overall they are still tough.

1961 FLEER OSCAR ROBERTSON

## Comments:

Here's another great rookie card from the 1961 Fleer set and, much like Elgin Baylor, Oscar Robertson is seemingly underrated. Add to that the fact that this set is in such high-demand and you have a winner. Like the Baylor rookie, this card offers an affordable alternative to other great players of the era. A Bill Russell rookie card, while it is more difficult, will cost you multiple times the price of Oscar's rookie and they are both Hall of Fame legends. Again, this card is not the most difficult on the list but it certainly has a lot going for it. Keep an eye on it.

## 1961 Fleer #43 Jerry West

### Importance:

This is the only recognized rookie card of one of basketball's all-time great shooters. During West's career as a member of the Los Angeles Lakers, the team reached the NBA finals 9 times in 14 years. Known as "Mr. Clutch" for his ability to come through with the big shot, West finished his career with a 27-point scoring average and a selection to the All-Star team in each of his 14 seasons. When he retired, West held the highest playoff scoring average in history at 29.1 points per game.

During the 1971-72 season, West averaged 25.8 points and led the league in assists at 9.7 per game en route to the NBA title. Their record of 69-13 was the best ever until the Chicago Bulls went 72-10, coming two decades later. When his career came to a close, West was one of only three players to reach the 25,000-point mark. His rookie card is one of four major keys in the set and ranks second in popularity only to the rookie card of Wilt Chamberlain.

### Difficulty:

There was a find of these Fleer cards years ago so sharp examples do exist but that doesn't solve all the condition obstacles. These cards have very inconsistent centering, creating major demand for nicely centered copies. Also, keep an eye out for stray print in the bright-colored background. Dark print marks are very apparent on these cards and can detract from the eye-appeal in a major way. Like the early Bowman issues, rough-cuts are fairly common so make sure the cut doesn't severely affect the corners. Again, you can find them sharp but overall they are still tough.

**1961 FLEER JERRY WEST**

## Comments:

Offense is what excites fans and collectors. Jerry West was the ultimate offensive player. While Wilt Chamberlain simply overpowered his opponents, West had to launch long bombs from all points on the court. The pure shooter is sorely lacking in the current game and West offers a glimpse of what used to be. If you were a youngster growing up in Southern California during West's era, there's a pretty good chance that you emulated him at some point or another. His rookie card, along with the other three major keys on the list, makes up a fearsome foursome. This great rookie card, due to the desirability of the set, is a key that should enjoy solid long-term demand.

# 1969 Topps #25 Lew Alcindor
# (Kareem Abdul-Jabbar)

## Importance:

This is the only recognized rookie card of the most prolific offensive player in NBA history. Close your eyes and, for those of us who were lucky enough to have seen him play, imagine that famous sky hook. It was his trademark weapon and no one has been able to perfect it since. At 7'2, Lew Alcindor, later known as Kareem Abdul-Jabbar, would take his outstretched arm and gracefully toss the ball into the basket, no one could stop it. During his time at UCLA and under the direction of legendary coach John Wooden, he led the Bruins to an unreal 88-2 record and 3 NCAA championships.

Now, let's look at some other notable accomplishments. He won six NBA championships as a member of the Milwaukee Bucks and Los Angeles Lakers, he was named Rookie of the Year in 1970, he won six NBA Most Valuable Player Awards (a record), two NBA Finals MVP's and he was a 19-time All-Star. His rookie card is a classic. Topps decided to produce larger cards by the late 1960's and this card, literally, towers above the rest just like Kareem did over his opponents for two decades.

## Difficulty:

This is one of the toughest cards on the basketball list. The oversized design prevented collectors from preserving these vintage gems. The corners and edges took a lot of abuse over the years. To complicate matters, these cards were designed very poorly. In fact, even if you were able to acquire unopened packs of this issue, most of the cards are severely off-center. The absence of defined borders make for additional problem, the slightest move to any one edge causes the image to appear even more off-center than it actually is. Like the Namath rookie card on the football list, this card is subject to print defects, so beware.

PSA
1969 TOPPS          #25
LEW ALCINDOR       NM-MT 8
                   01847992

LEW ALCINDOR
*center*

MILWAUKEE

## 1969 TOPPS LEW ALCINDOR

## Comments:

Kareem is one of the most recognizable figures in sports history. From those unmistakable goggles to that graceful sky hook, he was just one of those athletes that comes along once in a lifetime. The numbers are there for Kareem but, when it comes to collector popularity, people seem to either love him or hate him. When it comes to his rookie card, the demand is solid due to his place in NBA history. The unique, large design is fitting for one of the game's most feared big men and unique players. From a pure aesthetic standpoint, this card is really appealing, especially in top grades. With the focus on condition and rarity in today's market, this card offers wonderful future potential for demand.

## 1970 Topps #123 Pete Maravich

### Importance:

This is the only recognized rookie card featuring one of basketball's greatest entertainers. "Pistol Pete" was a crowd favorite. He mesmerized defenders with his incredibly quick hands and had the ability to fool just about anyone who stepped on the court. As a collegiate player, Maravich averaged 44.2 points per game! That number was achieved without the benefit of the three-pointer. He also set records for total season and career points, field goals and attempts.

After a brilliant college career, Maravich went on to play 10 years in the NBA. He was named to the All-Star team for five of those seasons and led the league with 31.1 PPG in 1977. For his career, he averaged 24.2 PPG and, more importantly, changed the game with his creative play. His rookie card remains a collector favorite and, on pure popularity, this card would rank near the very top of the basketball list.

### Difficulty:

This is one of the tougher cards on the basketball list. The oversized design, like the Jabbar rookie, prevented collectors from preserving these vintage gems. The corners and edges took a lot of abuse over the years. To complicate matters, these cards were designed very poorly. In fact, even if you were able to acquire unopened packs of this issue, most of the cards are severely off-center. The narrow white borders make for additional problem, the slightest move to any one edge causes the image to appear even more off-center than it actually is. Like the Namath rookie card on the football list, this card is subject to print defects so beware. This is a very desirable card in top grades.

## Comments:

The bottom line is that Pete Maravich has a cult-like following. In reality, Maravich was not as good as most other players on this list but his exciting brand of play put people in the seats. Technically, there were better all-around players but few players of his era generated the excitement that "Pistol Pete" could. As sports fans, there are certain athletes that we identify with and others that we don't. For whatever reason, Maravich appealed to a lot of fans. His rookie card, with the large style format and legitimate difficulty, should remain in high demand for years to come. The overall set is lacking in rookie power but that makes this card even more of a standout. Very few of these cards ever surface in high-grade, it's at the top of many wantlists.

# 1972 Topps #195 Julius Erving

## Importance:

This is the only recognized rookie card of one of basketball's most exciting players. "Dr. J" was able to leap to unreachable heights and dunk with power and grace long before players like Dominique Wilkins and Michael Jordan came along. After a short time in the ABA, Dr. J was lured away to the big show. When you watch any NBA highlight reel, "Dr. J" is sure to make a few appearances, whether he is defying gravity above the rim or launching a shot from the far reaches of the court.

For several years, "Dr. J" *was* basketball, no player was more iemulated by kids until Jordan came along. In 16 total seasons (NBA and ABA combined), Erving scored 30,026 points, which was 3rd on the all-time list at the time of his retirement and was named to the NBA All-Star team every year. With Philadelphia, he averaged 22 points per game during his perennial All-Star career. In 1996, Erving was named as one of the 50 best players in NBA history. Erving's rookie card is, by far, the key to the 1972 Topps set and is perhaps the most desirable card from the 1970's.

## Difficulty:

While 1970's sportscards issues lack the pure age of pre-1970's material, the manufacturing process can make them just as tough and sometimes tougher. For whatever reason, most 1970's Topps issues were produced with an assortment of problems.

This particular card, while not one of the toughest 1970's issues, does have its problems. Poor centering and print defects seem to be the biggest offenders. The bright yellow background and white borders provide the perfect backdrop for nasty print sports, there's nowhere to hide. Keep in mind that there is an infamous print dot next to Dr. J's left elbow on almost every example, which should not downgrade the card because of its commonality. This is not a very tough card overall, in comparison to some other vintage issues, but a few condition obstacles remain in the way.

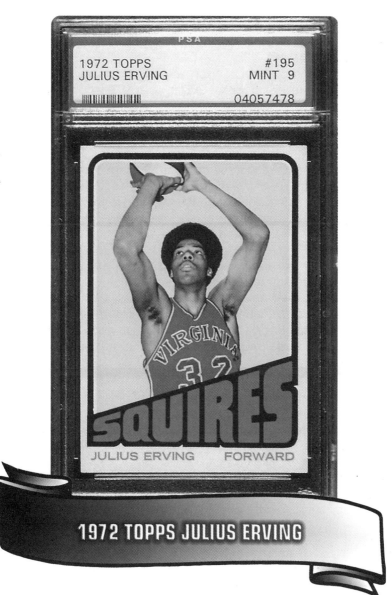

## 1972 TOPPS JULIUS ERVING

## Comments:

Many young people today can relate to the unreal leaping ability of Michael Jordan but, for those who grew up in the 1970's and early 1980's, "Dr. J" was the biggest draw. Much like Mr. Jordan, Erving was a gentleman and an outstanding athlete all wrapped up into one package. The image of "Dr. J" soaring through the air with his trademark hair and unmatched grace is ingrained into the minds of those who saw him play. He made it look so easy. His rookie card is, without question, the most significant card in the entire set by a large margin. As one of the most exciting players to ever step on the court, this "Dr. J" rookie card should always remain in high demand.

## 1980 Topps Larry Bird/Magic Johnson

### Importance:

This is the only recognized rookie card featuring the two most popular players of the 1980's. Larry Bird and Magic Johnson, two of the greatest competitors the NBA has ever seen, share a rookie card. It started at the college level. After Bird led his team, Indiana State, to the NCAA finals during the 1978-79 season, Johnson and Michigan State destroyed Bird's otherwise perfect season by defeating Indiana in the final game. The rivalry was on and, for the next decade, these two would raise the NBA to new heights with their drive to win. Bird would lead the Boston Celtics to three titles while Magic would lead the Los Angeles Lakers to five.

Forget about the numbers, All-Star appearances and MVP's for a moment, the effect these two had on the game was immeasurable. Their ability to excel in virtually every facet of the game was only overshadowed by their desire to win. This multi-player rookie card is one of a kind in the basketball section and it will remain a classic, two legends for the price of one.

### Difficulty:

This card, like most modern issues, is not difficult by vintage card standards but there are a few key condition obstacles to be wary of. First, this card is often found with poor centering, making it very difficult for many modern collectors to find that gem mint specimen. In addition, this card is often found with black print defects scattered across the face of the three-player card. Again, this card did not make the list based on pure difficulty but it is nearly impossible to find virtually perfect examples.

## Comments:

This card has as much star power as virtually any card on the list. The card features three superstars (including Dr. J), not just generic Hall of Famers, real superstars of the game. The two key figures, Magic and Bird, were able to raise basketball to a new level. When they entered the league, basketball was struggling. When they retired, it was the most popular sport in the country. The only problem with this card is that it is not the most visually appealing card in the hobby (maybe that was a slight under-statement) but you can't ignore the star power. No two opposing players, in any sport, have ever been linked so closely. This card has been surprisingly overlooked.

## 1986 Fleer #57 Michael Jordan

### Importance:

This is the most recognizable basketball card and the most important modern sportscard in the entire hobby. Michael Jordan is, quite simply, the most recognizable face on the planet. As a basketball player, he is a phenom but, as a figure in our country's history, he means even more. Believe it or not, this guy was cut by his high school coach as a sophomore! Boy, does that guy feel stupid. A couple of years later, Jordan would make the game-winning basket in the NCAA finals for North Carolina. The legend was just beginning.

The accomplishments are endless. Jordan has won six NBA titles, eight scoring titles, four MVP's, four NBA Finals MVP's, two All-Star Game MVP's, one Defensive Player of the Year award and the list goes on and on. His ability to come through in the clutch and dazzle fans with moves that defied natural laws makes Jordan a legend in his own time. Recently, Jordan came back to the NBA with the Washington Wizards. After taking some time off, Jordan looked to add to his legacy. This card defines modern basketball card collecting; it's the most popular basketball card on the list.

### Difficulty:

As far as modern cards go, this one is fairly tough. The colored borders surround the entire card, making chipping a major issue to contend with. The slightest chip will be very apparent to the collector because the edges are bright red, leaving a white spot on the card. Perfectly centered copies are also in high-demand as well as copies void of print marks or "snow" in the dark background. Finally, this card might be the most heavily counterfeited card in the hobby.

**1986 FLEER MICHAEL JORDAN**

## Comments:

Some people will say it's Ruth or Woods and others will say it's Ali but Michael Jordan is the most recognizable sports figure on the face of the planet. In a day when the media watches a celebrity's every move, Jordan took center stage. Unlike some other basketball stars from the past, Jordan has major crossover appeal. In other words, he is not just a basketball player to the average citizen. Sports fan or not, he is a major American icon. Not too many modern cards are worthy of a spot on the list but this one is not only worthy, it's one of the most popular cards overall in the top 200.

# 1992 Upper Deck #1 Shaquille O'Neal

## Importance:

This is the most popular rookie card of the most dominating center of the modern era. Before he laced up his gigantic shoes and stepped into the NBA, everyone knew Shaq was going to be something special. With nearly a decade under his belt, Shaq has been just that. At 7-1, 300 plus pounds, Shaq moves up and down the court like a small guard at times, bringing a level of athleticism never seen before for a man of his size. After a few seasons as the star of the often overlooked Orlando Magic, Shaq packed his bags for Hollywood. Could there have been a more perfect match?

Always an offensive force, Shaq has averaged just under 28 points per game in his career to go along with nearly 12.5 rebounds per game but his career is far from over. After winning three consecutive NBA Championships in LA, including three consecutive Finals MVP Awards (Michael Jordan is the only other player in history to accomplish this feat), Shaq is certain to add some more jewelry to his huge hands before his career is over.

Wilt may have been more dominant when you look at his numbers but Wilt did not have to match up against many other big men who challenged him on a physical level. It is hard to compare players from different eras but Shaq's performance needs to be appreciated in context and, when you do that, he becomes even more impressive.

## Difficulty:

The high gloss surface on this card is very, very sensitive. This allows very minor surface wear to be readily apparent to the collector. In addition, chipping along the black edges and wear at the tips of the corners are also easily detected. Many of these O'Neal rookie cards are found with a natural rough-cut, which can enhance the chances of chipping in this area. This card offers a true challenge in gem mint condition.

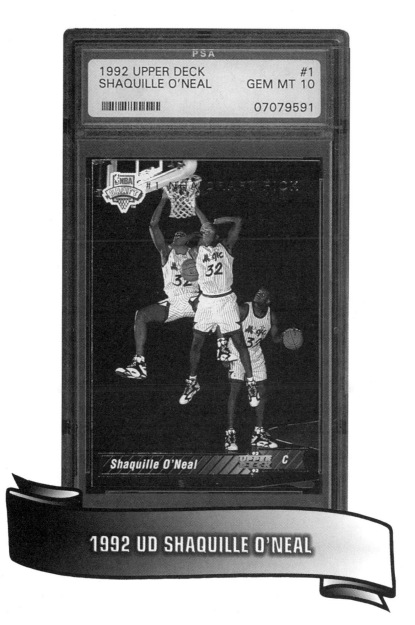

**1992 UD SHAQUILLE O'NEAL**

## Comments:

Forget about the pure numbers, Shaquille O'Neal represents so much more than that. From his monster jams to his music jams, Shaq has a magnetic personality. His love for life, great sense of humor and unique style only enhance the incredible ability Shaq has on the basketball court. Shaq just appears to be a big kid who is having the time of his life and fans are drawn to him because of it. One thing to consider about his NBA performance is that he is playing in an era that features much bigger players and a more athletic style of play. This fact should confirm his place as an NBA legend.

# 1996 Topps Chrome #138 Kobe Bryant

## Importance:

This is the most popular rookie card of the heir apparent to Michael Jordan. Kobe Bryant, much like Shaquille O'Neal, was seemingly destined for greatness. Entering the NBA straight out of high school, for one, was amazing in itself. Furthermore, his ability to mature so quickly has been, perhaps, his most impressive showing yet. Bryant did not have the luxury of refining his skills in college, he was thrown right in with the best in the world while still in his teens. It is truly a remarkable story with more chapters to be written.

After six seasons on the court, Bryant has not only proved that he belongs, but he has rapidly become the biggest draw in the game. From his high-flying dunks and natural flair to his ability to score from virtually anywhere on the court, Bryant is now the main attraction. Teaming up with Shaq, Bryant already has three NBA Championships under his belt with more certainly within sight. There are a number of other Bryant rookie card produced by other companies but this is his most desirable.

## Difficulty:

The Bryant rookie card suffers from two major condition obstacles, poor centering and surface scratches. The technology on modern cards, in comparison to vintage issues, is superior in many ways but the high gloss, chrome finish is very prone to scratching and wear. The presence of these defects will prevent the card from reaching gem mint status, but centering might be a bigger issue for those who seek top of the line specimens.

**1996 TOPPS CHROME KOBE BRYANT**

## Comments:

Kobe Bryant has always been subject to pressure due to unreachable expectations. Yet, through it all, he has shown maturity and progression as a player each year in the league. The scary thing is that Bryant should only improve as he is still very young and has many years ahead of him. While Bryant doesn't have quite the charisma that Shaq has, he does have a style all his own and it is very comparable to that of Michael Jordan, quiet and classy. He is one of those athletes that is recognizable by the mere mention of his first name. The future looks bright, we should all just sit back and enjoy the ride.

# 1933 Goudey Sport Kings #4 Red Grange

## Importance:

This legendary football star has one of the more visually appealing cards in this classic set. If you ask any 1933 Goudey Sport Kings set collector, they will probably tell you that this is one of their favorite cards. As another tough card in high-grade, the price for quality examples seems to be moving fast like Grange through a defensive line. Grange was able to help bring football, as a sport, to a new level after a spectacular career at the University of Illinois as a 3-time All-American.

Known as the "Galloping Ghost," Grange would use his tremendous speed and deceptive moves to make him the biggest football draw of the 1920's. As a junior, Grange ran for four touchdowns in the first 12 minutes against Michigan, totaling over 250 yards. As a college senior, he graced the cover of *Time* in 1925, a year in which Grange had his best overall performance (gaining 363 yards on 36 carries in one game). Throughout his career, Grange piled up the endorsements much like Tiger Woods and Michael Jordan today. As the card featuring the man who truly put pro football on the map, this issue is of the utmost importance.

## Difficulty:

As beautiful as the Goudeys are, they pose a real challenge when it comes to condition. All of the Goudey Sport Kings are susceptible to toning along the edges and reverse and centering problems. The toning issue is a significant one because most Goudeys are found with some degree of toning. The key is to avoid those examples that exhibit extreme toning. When you can find an example that has nice clean borders and at least a semi-white reverse, the cards becomes much more attractive.

The reverse may also be hindered by "bleeding". When the sheets of cards were laid on top of each other, the moist ink would sometimes stick to the reverse of the cards above. If the bleeding is not severe, then it should not detract from the appearance in a substantial way. As you might notice, the borders are extremely narrow on these cards and, due to the colors chosen on most of the cards, poor centering is an obvious flaw when present. Overall, this is one of the tougher football issues on the list.

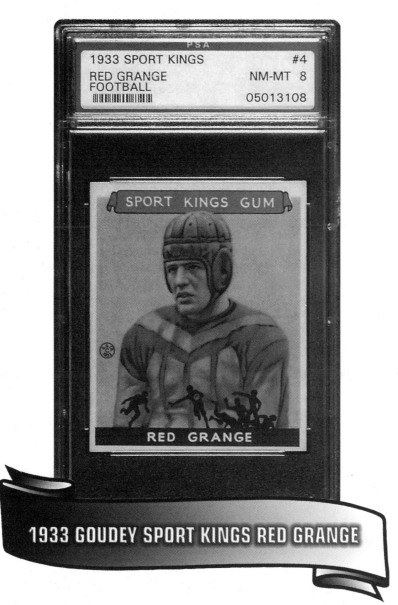

1933 GOUDEY SPORT KINGS RED GRANGE

## Comments:

This iconic figure is part of, perhaps, the most interesting sportscard set in the hobby. With such a vast array of sports stars from so many different competitive fields, this set provides a rare combination. The great colors featured, not only on this card, but in the overall set make it one of the best looking issues in sportscard history. Some younger collectors might not recognize the "Galloping Ghost" but, due to the set's popularity, this key football figure automatically gains major attention. As one of the cards that exhibits immense eye-appeal, this card should always enjoy solid demand.

# 1935 National Chicle #9 Knute Rockne

## Importance:

One of the keys to the first widely distributed football set and Rockne's most valuable card overall. Knute Rockne is simply the most popular coach in football history. Even though he was a very discipline-oriented coach and known for practicing plays until they could be perfectly executed, his was more well-known for his ability to motivate players with simple words. Rockne's speeches were his trademark. One of the more notable speeches came when, after trailing at the half, Rockne stormed into the locker room where his Notre Dame players awaited a major lashing. Instead, Rockne simply said, in a calm voice, "Let's go, girls." The Irish went on to victory.

His famous "Win one for the Gipper" speech is considered one of his most memorable orations as Notre Dame went on to upset Army. Rockne's coaching strategy was also legendary. He was known for his "brains over brawn" mentality, speed and deception over size. He went on to finish his 13-year coaching career with an amazing 105-12-5 record including three National Championships and five undefeated teams. In the prime of his coaching career, he perished in a plane crash in 1931.

## Difficulty:

The National Chicle issue is one of the toughest on the list, not just the football list, but the entire sportscard list. I liken this issue, in many ways, to the early Goudeys and Leaf issues. All are undersized and very, very tough. The key condition obstacle for this issue is the poor centering. These cards are almost always found off-center. As you might expect, as with the early Goudey and Leaf cards, toning and general wear are also a problem.

Don't expect to find these cards with bright, white borders. If you do, the card has, most likely, been bleached. As long as the borders are not extremely dark, the eye-appeal shouldn't be affected too badly. All in all, this issue is a true challenge in Near Mint condition or better.

1935 NATIONAL CHICLE KNUTE ROCKNE

## Comments:

The 1935 National Chicle set is widely regarded as the most difficult football issue in the hobby. With Rockne's card being one of the major keys to the set and his most valuable card overall, the potential for future demand is terrific for this example. Not too many coaches are as recognizable as the athletes themselves but Rockne was, and still is, the exception. As college football seems to gain in popularity each and every year, Rockne's legacy should be placed in the limelight more and more often. His collegiate record (a lifetime .881 winning percentage) is almost unthinkable and, in today's game, probably unattainable. Rockne is, and forever will be, the standard for all football coaches.

# 1935 National Chicle #34 Bronko Nagurski

## Importance:

This is the pinnacle of the football card sector, football's equivalent to the T206 Honus Wagner. If Red Grange was the "Galloping Ghost" then this guy was a tank. One of the charter members of the NFL Hall of Fame (1963), Bronko did not bother to use deception or trickery in order to avoid defenders, he simply ran over them. Steve Owen, of the New York Giants, once said of Bronko, "The only way to stop Nagurski is to shoot him before he leaves the dressing room." Ernie Nevers, a Hall of Famer himself, added, "Tackling Bronko is like tackling a freight train going downhill."

He was also an outstanding athlete and one of the most versatile players in NFL history. Many experts believe that he could have been inducted into the Hall of Fame as a linebacker, without ever carrying the ball. This guy even passed for a few touchdowns, including the game-winner in the NFL's first official championship game.

## Difficulty:

The National Chicle issue is one of the toughest on the list, not just the football list, but the entire sportscard list. This card happens to reside in the virtually impossible high-number series, making it hard to find in any grade. I liken this issue, in many ways, to the early Goudeys and Leaf issues. All are undersized and very, very tough. The key condition obstacle for this issue is the poor centering. These cards are almost always found off-center. As you might expect, as with the early Goudey and Leaf cards, toning and general wear are also a problem.

Don't expect to find these cards with bright, white borders. If you do, the card has, most likely, been bleached. As long as the borders are not extremely dark, the eye-appeal shouldn't be affected too badly. All in all, this issue is a true challenge in any condition.

## Comments:

This is, without question, the "crown jewel" of all football card collecting. Even the guy's name is a classic, "Bronko Nagurski." Just his name alone scares me. Much like Dick Butkus or Mike Ditka, he just sounds like a football player. In terms of value, this card has no rival in the football card world. There are players who are certainly more popular like Joe Montana or Jim Brown but this Nagurski card has extreme rarity and set importance going for it. The image of Nagurski, charging like a bull, is so memorable that it almost brings the viewer back to a time when players wore little equipment and end zone dances weren't tolerated. This card symbolizes football card collecting.

## 1948 Leaf #1 Sid Luckman

### Importance:

A key rookie card and the first card in a difficult set. Sid Luckman, with a powerful arm and mind, led the Chicago Bears to four NFL titles and five division championships during the 1940's.     It wasn't just the number of titles that was so impressive, it was the pure dominance.  The Bears, behind Luckman's vast array of offensive plays, simply destroyed teams.  They mauled the Washington Redskins 73-0 in the 1940 championship game.  Luckman would also throw 7 touchdown passes against the New York Giants during his 1943 MVP campaign.  He was the ultimate field general.

### Difficulty:

All of the early football issues on this list have major condition obstacles and this one is no exception.  The Leaf cards, whether we are talking about football or baseball, are extremely difficult to find in high-grade.  When it comes to poor centering, the Leaf issue might be the chief offender.  The overwhelming majority of these cards were cut off the mark and exhibit image tilting.  In fact, a few years back, after opening several unopened packs of Leafs, I couldn't find one card with better than 60/40 centering with most of them much, much worse.   The bright background on these cards are very, very susceptible to print defects.  The combination and contrast of light and dark colors make it easy to detect stray spots or blotches on the front.

Finally, like the National Chicles, toning is almost assumed.  One interesting aspect of these cards is the fact that each card exhibits such a wide range of eye-appeal.  Due to the poor quality control in the manufacturing process, you will find some Leafs that are bright and bold while others have faint color and poor registration.  Keep this in mind as you search for a quality specimen, there's a wide range in the eye-appeal department.  With Leafs, if you are patient, eye-popping examples can be found but they are few and far between.

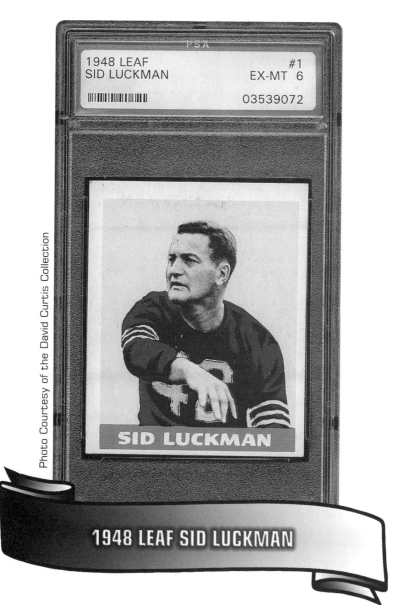

1948 LEAF
SID LUCKMAN

PSA

#1

EX-MT 6

03539072

SID LUCKMAN

**1948 LEAF SID LUCKMAN**

## Comments:

Quarterbacks have always been at the top of most football wantlists, this card is no exception. In fact, the difficulty of the set and the #1 slot position, make this card extremely desirable. The Bobby Layne rookie card might be more popular but this card has rarity on its side. As the game changes and new quarterbacks come into the league, they are always compared to the legends of the past. The constant comparisons allow for players like Luckman to share the spotlight decades after they are gone. While it's true that Luckman is not as popular as other quarterback legends, this card has other significantly positive attributes for vintage football collectors.

## 1948 Leaf #6 Bobby Layne

### Importance:

The only recognized rookie card of the "Blonde Bomber." Bobby Layne has always been a collector favorite and his rookie card is featured in one of the most difficult and desirable football sets in the hobby. As a leader, Layne was second to none. Layne was known for his clutch drives late in the game. In fact, Layne's last-second touchdown pass during the 1953 Title Game made the Detroit Lions champions. Layne would lead his team to four divisional titles and three NFL titles during the 1950's. In his career, Layne threw for over 26,000 yards and nearly 200 touchdowns. Did you know that this Hall of Famer also kicked field goals?

### Difficulty:

All of the early football issues on this list have major condition obstacles and this one is no exception. The Leaf cards, whether we are talking about football or baseball, are extremely difficult to find in high-grade. When it comes to poor centering, the Leaf issue might be the chief offender. The overwhelming majority of these cards were cut off the mark and exhibit image tilting. In fact, a few years back, after opening several unopened packs of Leafs, I couldn't find one card with better than 60/40 centering with most of them much, much worse. The bright background on these cards are very, very susceptible to print defects. The combination and contrast of light and dark colors make it easy to detect stray spots or blotches on the front.

Finally, like the National Chicles, toning is almost assumed. One interesting aspect of these cards is the fact that each card exhibits such a wide range of eye-appeal. Due to the poor quality control in the manufacturing process, you will find some Leafs that are bright and bold while others have faint color and poor registration. Keep this in mind as you search for a quality specimen, there's a wide range in the eye-appeal department. With Leafs, if you are patient, eye-popping examples can be found but they are few and far between.

## Comments:

Bobby Layne, like a few other athletes on this list, has a "cult-like" following. When you envision what a prototypical quarterback should be and look like, Layne's image appears. The 1948 Leaf football set, much like the 1948 Leaf baseball set, is very tough and desirable. As the set goes, so do the cards within and, when you consider the importance of Layne's rookie card, the demand for the set just adds to the appeal of this key. Even though this card is not in the scarce high-number series, it is still a real challenge. The fact that it is not in that high-number series, just makes this card more affordable to collectors.

## 1948 Leaf #34 Sammy Baugh

### Importance:

This is the key to the 1948 Leaf set and an important rookie card of a quarterback legend. Accuracy, accuracy, accuracy, that is what "Slingin Sammy" Baugh was all about. Not until his arrival, did the NFL witness such great "touch" from the quarterback position. He would lead the NFL in passing six times with a combination of short passes and long bombs. He helped lead the Washington Redskins to five championship games and was one of the charter members of the NFL Hall of Fame. Like Nagurski, Baugh was extremely versatile. Believe this or not, he led the NFL in passing, punting and interceptions in 1943. Are you kidding me? As a punter, he is still regarded as one of the best ever, maybe the best. Baugh does have a Bowman rookie card but this is his most desirable.

### Difficulty:

All of the early football issues on this list have major condition obstacles and this one is no exception. The Leaf cards, whether we are talking about football or baseball, are extremely difficult to find in high-grade. When it comes to poor centering, the Leaf issue might be the chief offender. The overwhelming majority of these cards were cut off the mark and exhibit image tilting. In fact, a few years back, after opening several unopened packs of Leafs, I couldn't find one card with better than 60/40 centering with most of them much, much worse. The bright background on these cards are very, very susceptible to print defects. The combination and contrast of light and dark colors make it easy to detect stray spots or blotches on the front.

Finally, like the National Chicles, toning is almost assumed. One interesting aspect of these cards is the fact that each card exhibits such a wide range of eye-appeal. Due to the poor quality control in the manufacturing process, you will find some Leafs that are bright and bold while others have faint color and poor registration. Keep this in mind as you search for a quality specimen, there's a wide range in the eye-appeal department. With Leafs, if you are patient, eye-popping examples can be found but they are few and far between.

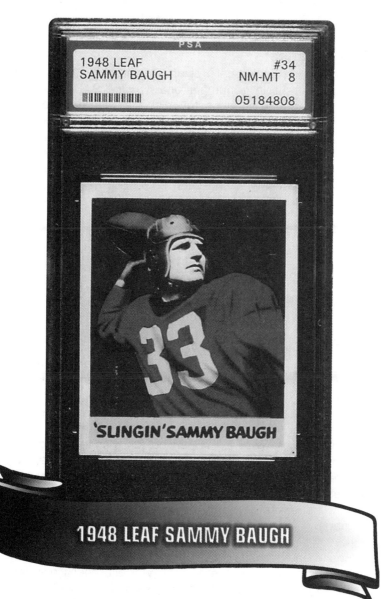

'SLINGIN' SAMMY BAUGH

**1948 LEAF SAMMY BAUGH**

## Comments:

Baugh is simply another example of the versatility required of players from a time long past. In Baugh's case, he was not only versatile, he excelled at it. As a charter member of the NFL Hall of Fame, Baugh's rookie card becomes extremely important. In the baseball sector of the hobby, you always hear people talking about forming collections around the original inductees to the Hall of Fame. It is a very popular collecting theme. In football, this theme is not nearly as popular but that might be a blessing for collectors. A comparable rookie card in the baseball issue would probably cost you a lot more. Regardless, this Baugh rookie is one of the most significant cards on the football list.

## 1950 Bowman #5 Y.A. Tittle

### Importance:

This is a key rookie card of one of the NFL's best all-time quarterbacks. Tittle, a number one pick in 1948, never won a NFL title but his individual performance led him down a path for Hall of Fame inclusion. As a quarterback for the Baltimore Colts, San Francisco 49ers and New York Giants, Tittle would pass for 33,070 yards and 242 touchdowns. He would twice be named the NFL's Player of the Year. The first time, in 1962, he passed for 33 touchdowns and then, in 1963, he would earn another award by throwing 36.

After he was traded to New York, Tittle led the Giants to three consecutive title games despite being labeled "over the hill." After being named to 6 Pro Bowl squads, Tittle was eventually inducted into the Pro Football Hall of Fame in 1971. Tittle was one of the game's first big passers and this card is his only recognized rookie.

### Difficulty:

The vintage Bowman issues have three major problems that prevent most examples from reaching the upper echelon of the grading ranks. Those three obstacles are staining on the reverse, print defects and poor centering. The grey-colored backs, just like the early Bowman baseball issues, are often found with dark staining from wax. Wax can be fairly easily removed from the surface on the front of most cards but the reverse is an entirely different story. The wax penetrates the cardboard, causing a deeper stain. Print defects are nothing new to the vintage Bowman issues as a variety of spots, usually black, can spray the image.

Finally, and perhaps most importantly, centering is tough due to the very narrow borders. The white borders are very narrow and contrast greatly with the framed image. This causes the slightest centering problem to appear worse than it actually is. There's no place for the centering shift to blend in. It can blend in on some issues like the 1955 Topps baseball cards that have yellow backgrounds (the frame appears less defined there).

1950 BOWMAN Y.A. TITTLE

## Comments:

It seems like many of these football legends have such great names and Y.A. Tittle is no exception. As you may have noticed, this list is mainly comprised of quarterbacks. The key with this card is that Tittle was one of the first big passers and that is what fans and collectors are drawn to. It is similar to the appeal of the home run hitter who not only hits them frequently, but hits them further than anyone else. Tittle's numbers, for the era, made him a standout, especially those career passing yards. This Bowman issue is a real favorite, not only for its selection of stars, but also for the artwork. The artwork on 1950's football cards, especially Bowmans, make them very appealing. There is certainly no lack of appeal when it comes to Tittle's rookie card.

## 1950 Bowman #45 Otto Graham

### Importance:

This is a significant rookie card and one of the keys to the 1950 Bowman set. Otto Graham was the starting quarterback for the Cleveland Browns between 1946-1955. Even though his passing numbers are extremely impressive, it was Otto's ability to win that made him a legend. In a brief 10-year career, he led the Browns to four conference, six division and three NFL Championship crowns. Otto was also named All-League in 9 of his 10 seasons.

When his career came to an end, he finished with 174 passing touchdowns and 44 rushing touchdowns. This legendary quarterback was elected to the Hall of Fame in 1965 and this is one of his most valuable cards.

### Difficulty:

The vintage Bowman issues have three major problems that prevent most examples from reaching the upper echelon of the grading ranks. Those three obstacles are staining on the reverse, print defects and poor centering. The grey-colored backs, just like the early Bowman baseball issues, are often found with dark staining from wax. Wax can be fairly easily removed from the surface on the front of most cards but the reverse is an entirely different story. The wax penetrates the cardboard, causing a deeper stain. Print defects are nothing new to the vintage Bowman issues as a variety of spots, usually black, can spray the image.

Finally, and perhaps most importantly, centering is tough due to the very narrow borders. The white borders are very narrow and contrast greatly with the framed image. This causes the slightest centering problem to appear worse than it actually is. There's no place for the centering shift to blend in. It can blend in on some issues like the 1955 Topps baseball cards that have yellow backgrounds (the frame appears less defined there).

PSA

| 1950 BOWMAN | #45 |
| OTTO GRAHAM | MINT 9 |
| ‖‖‖‖‖‖‖‖‖‖ | 04005253 |

## 1950 BOWMAN OTTO GRAHAM

## Comments:

This card, along with many early Bowman keys, represents a key time in football card history. No matter what sport you collect or follow, you cannot deny the visual appeal of these vintage football gems. This Graham is a perfect example of the quality artwork produced during Bowman's reign as the football card leader. The modern card technology is, without question, far superior but you would be hard pressed to favor that technology over the vintage artwork. Graham is also a key quarterback in football history and, due to the focus on quarterbacks, this card takes on extra importance. Much like the power hitters in baseball, quarterbacks seem to generate more demand than any other position player on the field and that demand should stay strong with Mr. Graham.

## 1951 Bowman #4 Norm Van Brocklin

### Importance:

This is the only recognized rookie card of legendary quarterback Norm Van Brocklin and the key to the 1951 Bowman set. Norm wasn't the most graceful, scrambling quarterback the game has ever seen but could he ever throw. In his 12 years at quarterback, some of those years only part-time, he threw for a total of 23,611 yards and 173 touchdowns. He was also one of the league's best punters with an average well over 40 yards per kick. Norm would win NFL championships with the Los Angeles Rams and the Philadelphia Eagles in 1951 and 1960 respectively. The 1960 championship was especially pleasing for Norm as he led a perennial loser to the title after the Rams sent him packing.

### Difficulty:

The vintage Bowman issues have three major problems that prevent most examples from reaching the upper echelon of the grading ranks. Those three obstacles are staining on the reverse, print defects and poor centering. The grey-colored backs, just like the early Bowman baseball issues, are often found with dark staining from wax. Wax can be fairly easily removed from the surface on the front of most cards but the reverse is an entirely different story. The wax penetrates the cardboard, causing a deeper stain. Print defects are nothing new to the vintage Bowman issues as a variety of spots, usually black, can spray the image.

Finally, and perhaps most importantly, centering is tough due to the very narrow borders. The white borders are very narrow and contrast greatly with the framed image. This causes the slightest centering problem to appear worse than it actually is. There's no place for the centering shift to blend in. It can blend in on some issues like the 1955 Topps baseball cards that have yellow backgrounds (the frame appears less defined there).

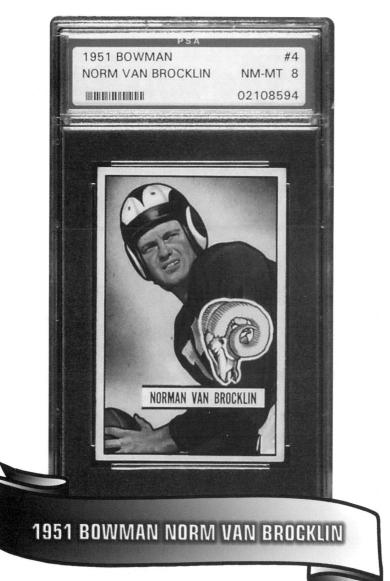

## 1951 BOWMAN NORM VAN BROCKLIN

**Comments:**

Once again, we are reminded of the beautiful artwork featured on many of these vintage football issues, primarily Bowman issues. One of the key areas, really in any collectible field, is eye-appeal. When a collector buys a card, an autograph, a bat or a jersey, they are usually drawn to it based on visual appeal. It's one main reason why a 1941 Play Ball Ted Williams card sells for more than his rookie card, a card made two years earlier. Collectors are drawn to what looks good. On that basis alone, early football issues, like this Norm Van Brocklin rookie, should enjoy increased demand as collectors educate themselves about sportscard collecting and the reality that many vintage football cards are actually tougher than their baseball counterparts.

## 1951 Bowman #20 Tom Landry

### Importance:

This is the only recognized rookie card of legendary coach Tom Landry. Landry started his career as a player but his coaching is what made him a legend. For 29 straight seasons, the head coach of the Dallas Cowboys was Tom Landry. During that time, the Cowboys won 13 division titles, five conference titles and two Super Bowls. The Cowboys would finish better than .500 for 20 straight seasons from 1966-1985, quite possibly Landry's most significant statistic as head coach. In 1990, he was elected to the Hall of Fame and this card is one of the keys to the 1951 Bowman set.

### Difficulty:

The vintage Bowman issues have three major problems that prevent most examples from reaching the upper echelon of the grading ranks. Those three obstacles are staining on the reverse, print defects and poor centering. The grey-colored backs, just like the early Bowman baseball issues, are often found with dark staining from wax. Wax can be fairly easily removed from the surface on the front of most cards but the reverse is an entirely different story. The wax penetrates the cardboard, causing a deeper stain. Print defects are nothing new to the vintage Bowman issues as a variety of spots, usually black, can spray the image.

Finally, and perhaps most importantly, centering is tough due to the very narrow borders. The white borders are very narrow and contrast greatly with the framed image. This causes the slightest centering problem to appear worse than it actually is. There's no place for the centering shift to blend in. It can blend in on some issues like the 1955 Topps baseball cards that have yellow backgrounds (the frame appears less defined there).

1951 BOWMAN TOM LANDRY

## Comments:

Landry is one of the few coaches to make the list. All right, so he was a player as well, but he made the top 200 list for his unreal record at the helm. While his 1952 Bowman Large and Small are technically more valuable, this card is his true rookie and, in terms of importance, it rises above the popular 1952 Bowman Landry cards. Coaches, no matter how great, do not receive the fanfare that the players do and that is something to consider. On the other hand, when you have risen to the top one or two coaches in football history, the concern of demand is virtually nonexistent. Landry was the head coach of "America's Team" for almost 30 years, what else do you need to know?

## 1952 Bowman Small and Large #1 Norm Van Brocklin

### Importance:

This is a key card of this legendary quarterback in one of the most popular football issues ever produced. Norm had the uncanny ability to perform under pressure. In the 1951 NFL Championship, he threw a famous 73-yard bomb to receiver Tom Fears to win the game and defeat the Cleveland Browns. That same year, he threw for 554 yards in one game. Amazingly, he didn't even lead his own team in passing that year due to the coach's insistence that Norm share time with quarterback Bob Waterfield.

Eventually, it was Van Brocklin who would have the last laugh. After the Los Angeles Rams no longer wanted him, Van Brocklin led the lowly Philadelphia Eagles to the 1960 crown. The small and large variations are both considered to be amongst the most popular football issues in the hobby.

### Difficulty:

To begin with, this card is a short print. Then add in the fact that it is also the first card in the set, the subject of major collector abuse over time. Finally, the issue as a whole is considered very condition sensitive anyway. Boy, this card is really tough. The vintage Bowman issues have three major problems that prevent most examples from reaching the upper echelon of the grading ranks. Those three obstacles are staining on the reverse, print defects and poor centering. The grey-colored backs, just like the early Bowman baseball issues, are often found with dark staining from wax. Wax can be fairly easily removed from the surface on the front of most cards but the reverse is an entirely different story. The wax penetrates the cardboard, causing a deeper stain. Print defects are nothing new to the vintage Bowman issues as a variety of spots, usually black, can spray the image.

Finally, and perhaps most importantly, centering is tough due to the very narrow borders. The white borders are very narrow and contrast greatly with the framed image. This causes the slightest centering problem to appear worse than it actually is. There's no place for the shift to blend in. It can blend in on some issues like the 1955 Topps baseball cards that have yellow backgrounds (the frame appears less defined there).

**1952 BOWMAN NORM VAN BROCKLIN**

## Comments:

Many collectors realize the importance of number one cards but, when you combine that fact with a great player and a tremendous set, the importance rises to a whole new level. This card is not just the first card in the most popular vintage football set of the 1950's; it also features a legendary quarterback. With baseball cards, the premiums placed on number one cards can sometimes be staggering but, with football cards, while the premium exists, it isn't nearly as dramatic. This offers a nice opportunity for collectors to acquire a key number one card without having to pay the requisite premium applied to baseball cards. This card has a great deal going for it.

## 1952 Bowman Small and Large #16 Frank Gifford

### Importance:

This is the only recognized rookie issue of this all-purpose Hall of Famer. It's hard to imagine today but many of the players from football's past played on both sides of the field, Gifford was no exception. After being named All-American at USC, Gifford went on to a standout career in the NFL. Gifford's accomplishments include being named All-NFL four times, selected to the Pro Bowl 7 times and he was named the NFL Player of the Year in 1956. As an offensive player, Gifford totaled almost 10,000 combined yards, with 3,609 yards and 367 receptions as a receiver. As one of the keys to, arguably, football's most desirable set, this Gifford rookie enjoys great demand.

### Difficulty:

The vintage Bowman issues have three major problems that prevent most examples from reaching the upper echelon of the grading ranks. Those three obstacles are staining on the reverse, print defects and poor centering. The grey-colored backs, just like the early Bowman baseball issues, are often found with dark staining from wax. Wax can be fairly easily removed from the surface on the front of most cards but the reverse is an entirely different story. The wax penetrates the cardboard, causing a deeper stain. Print defects are nothing new to the vintage Bowman issues as a variety of spots, usually black, can spray the image.

Finally, and perhaps most importantly, centering is tough due to the very narrow borders. The white borders are very narrow and contrast greatly with the framed image. This causes the slightest centering problem to appear worse than it actually is. There's no place for the shift to blend in. It can blend in on some issues like the 1955 Topps baseball cards that have yellow backgrounds (the frame appears less defined there).

1952 BOWMAN FRANK GIFFORD

## Comments:

Gifford makes this list as a versatile Hall of Famer player in the hobby's best football set from the 1950's. Gifford isn't going to be remembered for his numbers, although impressive, because he did not play a position that is judged by raw numbers. What Gifford does offer the collector is a very recognizable name, a name that may even outshine his actual performance and that is not a bad thing at all. When you are considering the purchase of a vintage card, no matter what sport, you have to consider whether or not the name of the player involved is easily identifiable. This card is a prime example of name power.

## 1952 Bowman Large #144 Jim Lansford

### Importance:

This is the most notorious condition rarity in the football card hobby. Along with the 1952 Topps #1 Andy Pafko card, this is the only other non-star sportscard to make this prestigious list. This is the final card in perhaps the most beautiful football card set ever produced. Some will argue that this set is the most beautiful set of any sport and, if you ask me, that argument is pretty strong. The large design, detailed artistry and bold colors give this Lansford the kind of eye-appeal that few cards can compete with, no matter what issue. The image is extremely powerful. While Jim Lansford was not a major star, this card, in hobby circles, has created a legend all its own. No need for career highlights here, the card speaks for itself, maybe even more so than the Pafko.

### Difficulty:

If this card wasn't incredibly difficult in high-grade, the card would have never been considered for the list to begin with. As the most noteworthy condition rarity in football card collecting, this Lansford is subject to many condition obstacles but one takes precedence over them all. Centering. Due to the location of this card on the 1952 Bowman sheet, placed at the extreme bottom right, the card is almost always found with horrific centering. Whether it's the very bottom border or the right edge, this card was doomed from the start.

Reverse staining was also a problem, a flaw found on many early Bowman issues. In addition, due to the large size of the issue, general wear is often a problem as many collectors had a difficult time preserving the edges and corners. The overall difficulty of this card in high-grade cannot be underestimated, it's the key reason why this card made the list.

| PSA | |
| --- | --- |
| 1952 BOWMAN LARGE | #144 |
| JIM LANSFORD | NM-MT 8 |
| | 03004331 |

JIM LANSFORD
U. of TEXAS

## 1952 BOWMAN JIM LANSFORD SP

## Comments:

While it's true that many non-star rarities have limited collector appeal, a few cards have the ability to cross-over into mainstream acceptance. The 1952 Bowman Large Lansford is one of them. The key is the overall importance and popularity of the set. Football card collecting has a lesser following than baseball cards do but keep in mind that this is *THE CARD* in *THE SET* within that niche of the hobby. This is really the only football equivalent to the 1952 Topps Pafko. Every single time someone attempts to build this beautiful set, the card that will be the biggest challenge is the Lansford. This factor causes an unusual flurry of demand. The image is a classic and the condition rarity is legendary.

# 1955 Topps All-American #37 Jim Thorpe

## Importance:

This is a key football card of, perhaps, the greatest pure athlete of the 20th Century. Considered the second most desirable card in the All-American set, this card captures the most versatile athlete of his day and, maybe, ever. Thorpe's contribution to the game of football cannot be measured by raw statistics, it can only be measured by the impact he made.

Football, in the early part of the 20th Century, was lacking in mainstream acceptance and support but Thorpe, and his incredible athleticism, was able to bring football into the limelight. As a player and coach, Thorpe won championships in 1916, 1917 and 1919. He could pass, run, throw, kick and tackle with anyone in the game. There will never be another one like him.

## Difficulty:

The 1955 Topps All-American issue has always been tough as a result of two main condition obstacles, poor centering and print defects. The horizontal cards have a well-defined frame surrounding the image, with the exception of the bottom area, making it clear to the viewer whether the centering is solid or not. The great contrast between the white borders and the bold-colored frames make it difficult to hide any centering imperfections unlike the subtle contrast on a 1958 Topps Ted Williams for example.

In addition, that same contrast also contributes to the possibility of noticeable print defects. There's a great deal of white on the face of the card, leaving the perfect "canvas" for colored print marks. This issue is not quite as tough as the National Chicles or Leafs but very tough for a 1950's issue.

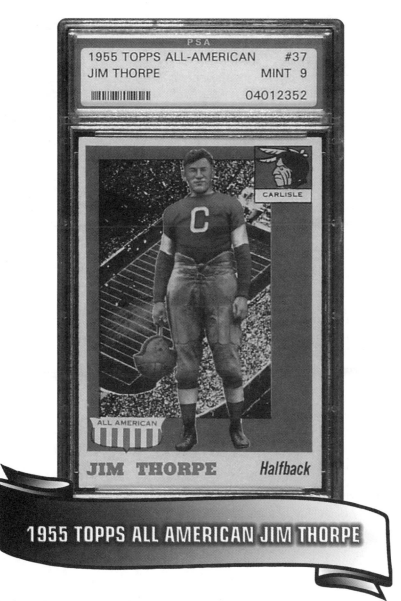

1955 TOPPS ALL AMERICAN JIM THORPE

## Comments:

Jim Thorpe's significance as an athlete is virtually unmatched in the 20th century and this is one of the few sportscards that features the phenomenal sports figure. Along with the 1933 Goudey Sport King Thorpe, this is one of the only cards to feature Thorpe as a football player. With so few Thorpe sportscards to choose from, this example takes on major significance. This colorful issue has great eye-appeal and the set features some outstanding cards including another major card on this list, the Four Horsemen (#68). Thorpe doesn't need any help with demand but the popularity of this particular issue doesn't hurt.

## 1955 Topps All American #68 Four Horsemen

### Importance:

This is one of the most popular cards in the football hobby and the key to the 1955 Topps All-American set. Knute Rockne, the legendary coach of Notre Dame University, was a believer in brains over brawn when it came to strategy on the field. The "Four Horsemen," which made up the backfield for the Fighting Irish, were the perfect example of Rockne's philosophy.

Elmer Layden, Jim Crowley, Harry Stuhldreker and Don Miller made up the fearsome foursome, nicknamed after the four horsemen of the apocalypse. Smaller than most of their opponents, the "Four Horsemen" helped lead their team to the Rose Bowl in 1925. This card was one of the first football cards to feature more than one player on the front and it remains a hobby favorite.

### Difficulty:

The 1955 Topps All-American issue has always been tough as a result of two main condition obstacles, poor centering and print defects. The horizontal cards have a well-defined frame surrounding the image, with the exception of the bottom area, making it clear to the viewer whether the centering is solid or not. The great contrast between the white borders and the bright-colored frames make it difficult to hide any centering imperfections unlike the subtle contrast on a 1958 Topps Ted Williams for example.

In addition, that same contrast also contributes to the possibility of noticeable print defects. There's a great deal of white on the face of the card, leaving the perfect "canvas" for colored print marks. This issue is not quite as tough as the National Chicles or Leafs but very tough for a 1950's issue.

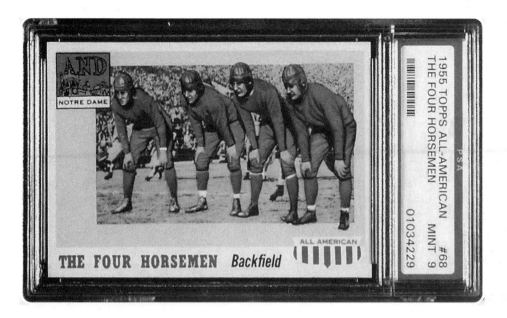

1955 TOPPS ALL AMERICAN FOUR HORSEMEN

## Comments:

This card features one of the most classic images in the football card hobby. If you are familiar with vintage football cards at all, you should be familiar with this legendary example. The interesting aspect to this card is the fact that it features four collegiate players. In the modern market, a card featuring a college player would not result in high demand but this card was made during a different era. Knute Rockne and Notre Dame were so popular that professional football took a back seat to these guys. Regardless of an individual's view of college versus professional football, this is just one of those cards that, by image alone, ranks amongst the very best on this list in terms of significance. If you are a football history buff or vintage card collector, you just have to own this card.

## 1957 Topps #119 Bart Starr

### Importance:
This is the only recognized rookie card of this legendary winner and one of the major keys to an extremely popular set. Bart Starr knew how to win, plain and simple. During 1956-1971, Starr would lead the Green Bay Packers to six division, five NFL and two Super Bowl titles. In fact, he was the Most Valuable Player in Super Bowls I and II. During the regular season, Starr was named MVP once in 1966 and was a three-time passing champion.

As far as Starr's numbers are concerned, he finished with nearly 25,000 passing yards, 152 touchdowns and a completion percentage of 57.4. The numbers are not what made Starr great, it was his ability to rise to the occasion and lead his team to victory, the true measure of any quarterback.

### Difficulty:
The 1957 Topps cards are known for their great star selection and beauty but they are also, unfortunately, known for their difficulty and this card resides in the tough high-number series. These horizontal cards have an extremely defined frame on the front and, when you factor in the narrow white borders, centering will always be an issue. There is great contrast between the solid, bold colors and the white borders leaving no chance for poor centering concealment.

In addition, print defects plague these potentially beautiful cards but the print defects that do the most damage here are slightly different from many of the other vintage football cards. With this issue, instead of dark print spots, you will usually see print "snow". These are the light colored, nearly white print spots that plague cards with darker backgrounds. They can present a real distraction and, in turn, the card can receive a serious downgrade if they are severe. In other words, beware of print "snowstorms."

Finally, much like the 1948 Leaf cards, these cards seem to come with a variety of eye-appeal because of the washed-out look many of the cards have. The examples with bright borders and bold color can make a world of difference.

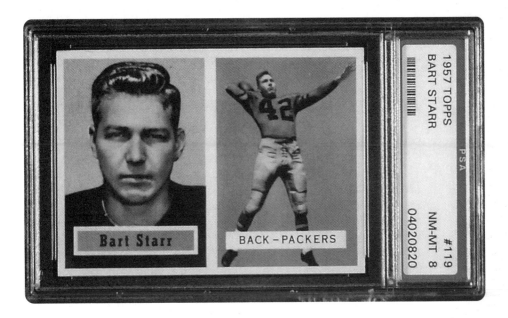

## 1957 TOPPS BART STARR

## Comments:

The Green Bay Packers, at one time, were a dominant force in the NFL. There were two major reasons for such dominance, the coaching of Vince Lombardi and the leadership of Bart Starr. Starr was a part of one of the most talked about teams, not only football history, but in sports history as well. Now that sports fans have seemingly endless access to vintage football footage on cable networks and video, the image of Starr leading the Packers down the field can be replayed over and over again. This set is, without question, one in high demand and it features two of football's most legendary quarterbacks. While the Johnny Unitas rookie card is the most sought-after card in the set, the Starr rookie is not far behind.

## 1957 Topps #136 Johnny Unitas

### Importance:

This is the only recognized rookie card of the quarterback legend and the key to the 1957 Topps set. Johnny Unitas struggled to make it in the NFL. After a couple of tough breaks, Unitas got his chance and never let go. After he retired, Unitas held virtually every major record for a quarterback. Unitas threw for 40,239 yards, completed 2,830 passes, had 26 games with 300 or more yards passing, 290 touchdown passes and 47 consecutive games with a touchdown pass. He will forever be remembered as the man who, by himself, led the 1958 Baltimore Colts to the title with a late drive to tie the game and an even longer drive to win it in overtime.

### Difficulty:

The 1957 Topps cards are known for their great star selection and beauty but they are also, unfortunately, known for their difficulty and this card resides in the tough high-number series. These horizontal cards have an extremely defined frame on the front and, when you factor in the narrow white borders, centering will always be an issue. There is great contrast between the solid, bold colors and the white borders leaving no chance for poor centering concealment.

In addition, print defects plague these potentially beautiful cards but the print defects that do the most damage here are slightly different from many of the other vintage football cards. With this issue, instead of dark print spots, you will usually see print "snow". These are the light colored, nearly white print spots that plague cards with darker backgrounds. They can present a real distraction and, in turn, the card can receive a serious downgrade if they are severe. In other words, beware of print "snowstorms."

Finally, much like the 1948 Leaf cards, these cards seem to come with a variety of eye-appeal because of the washed-out look many of the cards have. The examples with bright borders and bold color can make a world of difference.

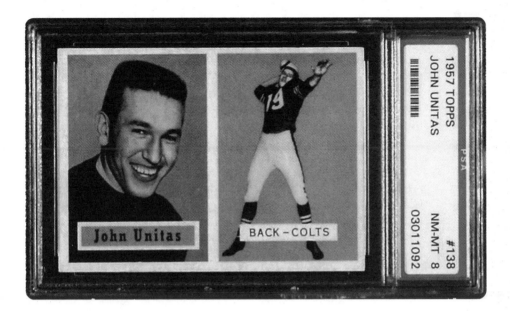

1957 TOPPS JOHNNY UNITAS

## Comments:

Within each sport, there are a few cards that are considered classics. This Johnny Unitas rookie is one of them. If you are compiling a vintage football collection, this is just one of those cards that you have to own. Statistically, Unitas had no match during his reign at quarterback as he destroyed the record books with his powerful right arm. The card itself has wonderful eye-appeal with a great orange/green background and the fact that the card resides in one of the all-time most popular football sets doesn't hurt either. Very few cards on this list have ultimate appeal from all angles but this card has all the qualities you would hope for in a card. Visual appeal, athlete significance, set popularity, player popularity and genuine difficulty. It's all here.

# 1957 Topps #151 Paul Hornung

## Importance:

This is the only recognized rookie card of this charismatic football legend. Paul Hornung was a multi-talented athlete who could do just about anything on the field. In college, at Notre Dame, Hornung won the Heisman Trophy in 1956 for his ability to excel at different spots on the field. He could throw, kick, catch and run.

As a member of the Green Bay Packers, Hornung excelled at halfback and kicker. In fact, his point total of 176 in 1960 remains a NFL record despite the fact that the league has added 4 more games since his historic season. Hornung would lead the league in scoring three years in a row, winning two MVP Awards along the way. As part of the most dominant football team of the 1960's, Hornung would go on to set other records including most points in a championship game with 19. His only rookie card is one of three major keys to one of the most popular football sets in the hobby.

## Difficulty:

The 1957 Topps cards are known for their great star selection and beauty but they are also, unfortunately, known for their difficulty and this card resides in the tough high-number series. These horizontal cards have an extremely defined frame on the front and, when you factor in the narrow white borders, centering will always be an issue. There is great contrast between the solid, bold colors and the white borders leaving no chance for poor centering concealment.

In addition, print defects plague these potentially beautiful cards but the print defects that do the most damage here are slightly different from many of the other vintage football cards. With this issue, instead of dark print spots, you will usually see print "snow". These are the light colored, nearly white print spots that plague cards with darker backgrounds. They can present a real distraction and, in turn, the card can receive a serious downgrade if they are severe. In other words, beware of print "snowstorms."

Finally, much like the 1948 Leaf cards, these cards seem to come with a variety of eye-appeal because of the washed-out look many of the cards have. The examples with bright borders and bold color can make a world of difference.

1957 TOPPS PAUL HORNUNG

## Comments:

Paul Hornung was one of the biggest draws in the NFL during the 1960's. His rookie card is featured in a tremendous set that also includes key rookie cards of Bart Starr and Johnny Unitas. The colorful designs make this issue one of the hobby's best productions from the 1950's. As a player, Hornung does not have the overwhelming career numbers that other Hall of Famers do but his rookie card has two great things going for it, popularity and team affiliation. Collectors are drawn to charismatic players and even more drawn to key figures on legendary teams. Hornung gave us both and his card is a key on most collector wantlists.

## 1958 Topps #62 Jim Brown

### Importance:

This is the only recognized rookie card of football's most feared fullback back of all-time. This 3-time NFL MVP was simply devastating. His speed and power went unmatched is his day, it was as if no one could stop him. He would lead the NFL in rushing in all but one season during his career. He would also rush for 1,000 yards or more in seven seasons despite the fact that there were only 12 games on the schedule the first few years of his career.

Brown retired after a mere 9 seasons but, to this day, he still holds the record for most yards per carry with 5.2. No running back in history, with 1,000 carries or more, has ever really challenged that number. This card is a classic and one of the most recognizable cards in the entire hobby.

### Difficulty:

The three major condition obstacles with regard to this key rookie card are reverse chipping, poor centering and print defects. The back edges, that frame Jim Brown's statistics, are red in color and, therefore, very susceptible to chipping. While reverse chipping will not cause a card to receive a major downgrade, it can prevent an otherwise Mint card from reaching that status. On the front, a solid black border frames the classic image of Brown. It is that solid frame, against the white borders, that makes the slightest centering imperfection easily detectable by the naked eye.

White print defects can often be found inside the black frame, but that beautiful black frame can also be responsible for stray dark print spots in the sky and grass behind the NFL great. One other condition problem of note would be the coloring of the borders. Many of them are somewhat toned but make sure they are not bordering on a brown color. You don't want Brown to be surrounded by brown.

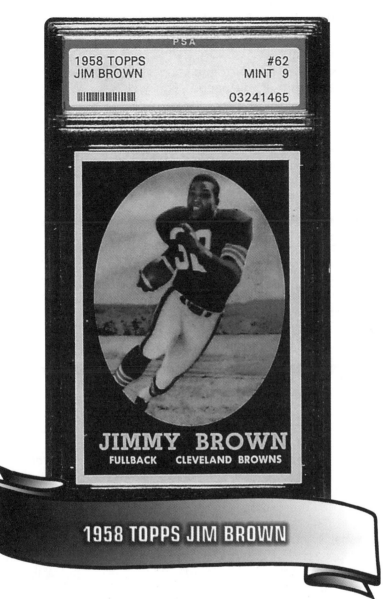

## 1958 TOPPS JIM BROWN

## Comments:

Brown is simply one of the most popular athletes on this list despite the existence of a somewhat controversial reputation. Why? Brown was so dominating on the field that it would be hard to comprehend that kind of domination today. This guy was so fast, so strong and so agile that he turned most defensive lines into Swiss cheese. This card, while it might not be the most valuable on the list, is perhaps the most recognizable football card image in the entire hobby. The image of a fierce Brown in full stride is a menacing yet graceful look at the most proficient running back in football history. By the way, "The Dirty Dozen" is still one of my favorite movies.

## 1962 Topps #1 Johnny Unitas

### Importance:

This is the first card in a tough, black-bordered set and it features Hall of Fame legend Johnny Unitas. Whether you are focusing on that famous crewcut or his cannon of an arm, this guy is immediately recognizable. Unitas wasn't chosen high in the NFL draft. As a 9th round pick, Unitas was cut so fast that he didn't even get a chance to throw one single pass for the team that drafted him, the Pittsburgh Steelers. After playing in a semi-pro league, Unitas was finally given an opportunity to play for the Baltimore Colts. Needless to say, he never looked back.

Unitas was, and still is, the inspiration for all of those athletes who struggle for the chance to prove themselves. He is proof that you should never give up hope. After 40,000-plus yards and almost 300 touchdown passes later, he made the Steelers look like fools for letting him go.

### Difficulty:

As the first card in the set, this Unitas key has a condition obstacle all its own. As you may have read, in regards to other cards on this list, number one cards were often overhandled and abused for a variety of reasons. If you chose to organize your set with the help of rubber bands, the first card took the brunt of the damage because it was at the top, in direct contact with those lethal rubber wraps. Other collectors chose to place their cards in shoeboxes. The number one card, being located at the top of most card stacks, came into direct contact with the box and would often get abused when the cards would get crammed due to overstuffing.

That's just the beginning of this card's problems. The 1962 Topps issue is one of the most condition sensitive issues on the list and that has a lot to do with its great popularity as a set. The main condition obstacle is centered on those pesky black borders. They help put a beautiful frame around the card but they easily show the slightest bit of wear. Beware of chipping and the fact that card "doctors" will often try to re-color the edges to conceal the damage. Centering is also an issue along with the fact that those black borders contribute to the possibility of noticeable print defects in the light-colored backgrounds. The 1962 Topps examples rank high on the condition sensitivity list but this Unitas is the toughest of them all.

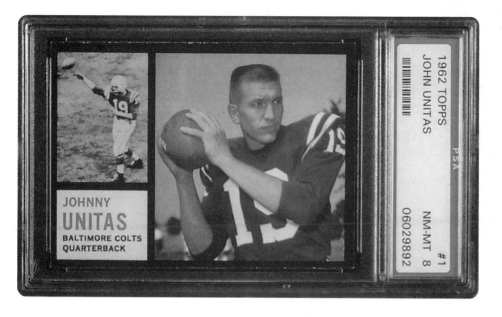

JOHNNY
UNITAS
BALTIMORE COLTS
QUARTERBACK

## 1962 TOPPS JOHNNY UNITAS

## Comments:

The 1962 Topps football set is, without question, one of the best football sets of the 1960's and Topps filled the set with great stars and key rookie cards. As the number one card in the set, you cannot overlook this example. Many baseball cards from the number one slot receive a multitude of collector attention even if the card features a common player. In this case, you have the greatest quarterback of his generation in that slot and the set is overwhelmingly popular, what a combination.

What collectors are drawn to, regardless of the sport, are the athletes who defied the odds to rise to the top of the game. Johnny Unitas was one of those guys. Scouts simply didn't think much of Johnny's potential, boy were they wrong. He didn't just become star, he became the best of his generation. Like overachieving Pete Rose in the baseball world, Unitas has a strong following. It may not be his rookie but this card has many things going for it. At this point in time, the card seems overlooked in comparison to other comparable number one examples.

## 1962 Topps #17 Mike Ditka

### Importance:

This is a key rookie card of legendary tough guy Mike Ditka. The slicked back hair, the mean stare and the nickname "Iron Mike" all point to one man, Mike Ditka. Many modern football fans recognize Ditka as the fiery coach of the modern game, the coach that led the Chicago Bears to victory on many occasions. What they should see is the legendary tight end that helped redefine the position. He was the first tight end ever selected to the Hall of Fame and for good reason.

Ditka's offensive numbers, coupled with his devastating blocking ability, made Ditka a standout. He finished with 427 receptions, 5,812 yards and 43 touchdowns as a professional. In 1963, Ditka led the Bears to a championship as a player and, 23 years later, he did it again as head coach. They never won a Super Bowl in between.

### Difficulty:

This card might be as sensitive as Ditka was tough. The 1962 Topps issue is one of the most condition sensitive issues on the list and that has a lot to do with its great popularity as a set. The main condition obstacle is centered on those pesky black borders. They help put a beautiful frame around the card but they also show the slightest bit of wear. Beware of chipping and the fact that card "doctors" will often try to re-color the edges to conceal the damage.

Centering is also an issue along with the fact that those black borders contribute to the possibility of noticeable print defects in the light-colored backgrounds. This issue ranks high on the condition sensitivity list and that factor has made this issue one of the hottest football card issues in the hobby. This card represents a true challenge for the high-end football card collector.

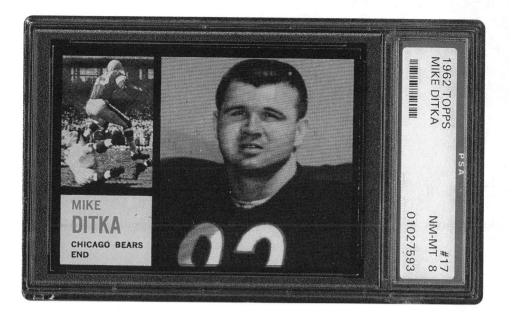

1962 TOPPS MIKE DITKA

## Comments:

His face is one of the most recognizable in all of sports. Like Babe Ruth's cartoonish grin or Kareem's trademark goggles, Ditka's slicked hair and mean stare are as memorable as his play on the field. He had the same haircut then as he does now. One of the most positive aspects to collecting his cards is that he is constantly on television. First he was a player, then a coach and now he can be occasionally seen as a commentator for NFL games.

Ditka is also one of the most impersonated figures, by comedians, in sports today. His frequent appearance serves as a constant reminder of the significance of Ditka as a player and a coach. As mentioned before, the 1962 Topps set is one of the most popular sets in the vintage football card market and, as one of the keys to the set, the Ditka rookie should enjoy great future demand.

# 1962 Topps #28 Jim Brown

## Importance:

This is a very tough issue of football's most devastating ball carrier. Jim Brown ended his football career early and pursued a career in Hollywood as an actor. Before he made the transition from fullback to a member of The Dirty Dozen, he left opposing players bruised, bloodied and battered.

Usually, it is the defensive player, such as a linebacker, who inflicts pain. Men tried to tackle burly Jim, but he would swat them away like miniscule flies and step on them on his way to the goal line. With so much vicious body contact, you would think he would have been injured at some point in his career. It never happened. Maybe he was the Terminator?

Along the way, Brown went to the Pro Bowl 9 straight years and was named Pro Bowl MVP twice. In fact, Brown ended his career with a 3-touchdown performance in the 1966 Pro Bowl. Brown's accomplishments are seemingly endless for someone who had such a short career. His 1963 record rushing total of 1,863 yards lasted for two decades. In addition, Brown scored 126 total touchdowns (106 rushing) and, after his very first year, *The Sporting News* named him both the Rookie of the Year and Player of the Year in 1957. He would be named Player of the Year by *The Sporting News* two more times (1958 and 1965). What a player.

## Difficulty:

The 1962 Topps issue is one of the most condition sensitive issues on the list and that has a lot to do with its great popularity as a set. The main condition obstacle is centered on those pesky black borders. They help put a beautiful frame around the card but they also show the slightest bit of wear. Beware of chipping and the fact that card "doctors" will often try to re-color the edges to conceal the damage.

Centering is also an issue along with the fact that those black borders contribute to the possibility of noticeable print defects in the light-colored backgrounds. This issue ranks high on the condition sensitivity list and that factor has made this card one of the most popular football card issues in the hobby. This card represents a true challenge for the high-end football card collector.

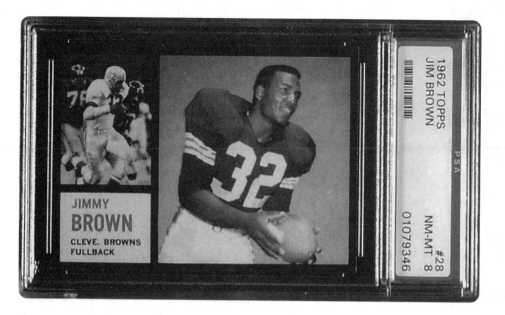

1962 TOPPS JIM BROWN

## Comments:

Despite not being a rookie card, this Jim Brown example is certainly one of the most desirable cards in the set. Brown always seemed to be so poised and professional when it came to his demeanor on the field. Even on this card, you can see the desire in his eyes. That's what made Brown such an unstoppable force. Very few football players, even Hall of Famers, have the crossover appeal that Brown has despite his somewhat controversial reputation. In other words, he was so impressive in his sport that fans of other sports still recognize him without any problem. Like Magic and Jordan, Mantle and Ruth, Brown is at the top. This card offers a positive outlook for all of the above reasons.

# 1962 Topps #90 Fran Tarkenton

## Importance:

This is the only recognized rookie card of one of the NFL's most prolific passers. Fran Tarkenton let the fans know early that he was going to be a star at quarterback during his very first game. In 1961, Tarkenton threw for four touchdowns as a member of the Minnesota Vikings. At the end of his career, he was the most prolific passer in the history of the NFL. Even though his numbers were eventually eclipsed by a few others, Tarkenton finished with 6,467 attempts, 3,686 completions, 47,003 passing yards and 342 touchdowns.

Despite phenomenal passing statistics, Tarkenton was probably best known for his quick feet and great scrambling ability. In fact, he rushed for 3,674 yards and 32 touchdowns. Tarkenton, a four-time All-NFL and nine-time Pro Bowl selection, led his team to the Super Bowl three times but never won the big game. He was, however, one of the most agile and entertaining quarterbacks to ever suit up

## Difficulty:

The 1962 Topps issue is one of the most condition sensitive issues on the list and that has a lot to do with its great popularity as a set. The main condition obstacle is centered on those pesky black borders. They help put a beautiful frame around the card but they also show the slightest bit of wear. Beware of chipping and the fact that card "doctors" will often try to re-color the edges to conceal the damage.

Centering is also an issue along with the fact that those black borders contribute to the possibility of noticeable print defects in the light-colored backgrounds. This issue ranks high on the condition sensitivity and that factor has made this issue one of the hottest football card issues in the hobby. This card represents a true challenge for the high-end football card collector.

## Comments:

What haunts Tarkenton is the fact that he never won a Super Bowl and, if he did win the big game, his card would probably be worth even more than it currently is. Quarterbacks are, unfortunately at times, judged by the amount of Super Bowls that they won. While it seems unfair to judge one player by the success of his entire team, it is a part of the game. In Tarkenton's case, his numbers are so incredible that it is basically irrelevant. If he were a borderline Hall of Famer, then it would matter.

When you rank as high as he does on the career passing list, there is no questioning his place in history. Tarkenton did lead his team to three Super Bowls so he was a winner, his team just never won the title. The Tarkenton example is the key rookie card in the set and the set is tremendous. This guy even had a key spot on the hit show *That's Incredible*, how can you not like him?

## 1965 Topps #122 Joe Namath

### Importance:

This is a hobby classic featuring the only recognized rookie card of "Broadway Joe." You might get an argument from Jim Brown rookie card supporters, but this card might be the most recognizable card in the entire football card hobby. The beautiful oversized issue is tough and very popular, just like the player it features.

Namath will probably be most remembered for his Super Bowl "guarantee" in Super Bowl III when his team was a near 20-point underdog against the Baltimore Colts. Namath's New York Jets went on to beat the Colts 16-7. Namath was also the first quarterback to amass 4,000 yards in a season and, despite nagging injuries, he was able to pile up passing yards at a tremendous rate. Namath was a real superstar of the sport.

### Difficulty:

This Namath rookie card, like all the cards in the popular 1965 Topps football set, presents a solid challenge to those who seek high-grade copies. These "Tall Boys," as collectors refer to them, are tough by virtue of their size alone. Much larger than the regular 2 ½ by 3 ½ cards we normally see, these cards were hard to store and, in turn, hard to protect from general wear. These cards were also notoriously cut off-center and the extremely narrow borders won't help conceal the slightest centering imperfection.

Finally, speaking of concealment, it's hard to conceal any print defects in a bright yellow background. All print spots are easily visible to the naked eye. Keep in mind that there is a print mark, located on Joe's hand, which is occasionally found and referred to as the "butterfly" variation. That mark is not considered a negative defect by collectors.

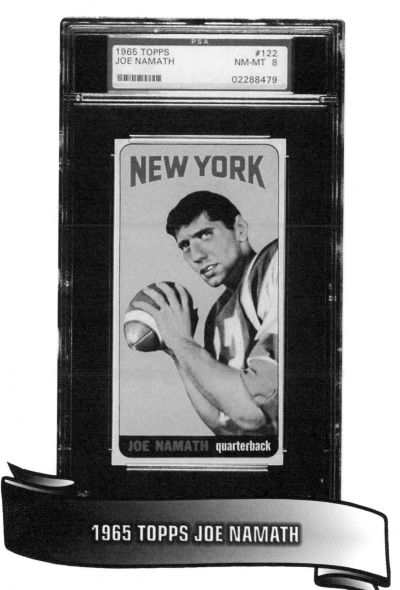

PSA
1965 TOPPS      #122
JOE NAMATH      NM-MT   8
02288479

NEW YORK

JOE NAMATH quarterback

## 1965 TOPPS JOE NAMATH

## Comments:

With the possible exception of the 1958 Topps Jim Brown rookie, this Namath rookie card is the most recognizable image in all of vintage football card collecting. The card, with its oversized design, great eye-appeal and underappreciated difficulty is a hobby classic. If there ever was an athlete that could appeal to almost anybody, it was Joe Namath. He was much more than just a sports celebrity, he was one of the most recognizable faces on the planet. Other quarterbacks had better numbers but "Broadway Joe" was an icon, somewhat like Joe DiMaggio in baseball. They were both much larger than their numbers. If you want a representative collection of key football cards, this card is a must.

## 1966 Philadelphia #31 Dick Butkus

### Importance:

This is the only recognized rookie card of the greatest linebacker to ever play the game. If you want mean, you want a card of Dick Butkus. Even his name sounds mean. Many opposing players had their life flash before their eyes when they saw Butkus coming at them with a head full of steam.

His 22 interceptions and 25 fumble recoveries were records when Butkus retired in 1973. In 9 years, Butkus was selected to 8 Pro Bowl teams. A model of work ethic and consistency, many football experts chose Butkus as the number one choice for the player they would most like to build a team around during an NFL poll. On defense, Butkus just made things happen.

### Difficulty:

High-grade examples of the 1966 Philadelphia issue seem to rarely come up for sale and for good reason. Good luck finding one! One condition obstacle, unique to this issue, is the fact that the reverse is framed by solid green edges. As you might imagine, those edges are prone to chipping and wear. Reverse chipping alone will not severely downgrade a card in most cases but it can prevent the card from reaching true mint status.

In addition, print defects can be a problem due to the contrasting dark and light areas on the face of the card. The sky, in the background, is most susceptible to stray dark print spots. Finally, the centering on these cards has always been an issue. Even most mint copies are not found with perfect centering, they are rarely dead-on.

**1966 PHILADELPHIA DICK BUTKUS**

## Comments:

Usually, defensive players do not excite the fans or collectors to the extent that the quarterbacks and running backs do. In this case, Butkus defied the odds. Die hard football fans always like a good tough guy, it brings back memories of the way the game used to be played. Players didn't use as much padding and the helmets were not as protective as they are today, it was just a different era. Butkus was the king of the tough guys, no one put more fear into opposing players than he did. Besides, he has the best name in football, maybe in sports. The toughest man in one of football's toughest sets, what a combination!

## 1966 Philadelphia #38 Gale Sayers

### Importance:

This is one of the most dazzling running backs in NFL history on his only recognized rookie card. Before there was Walter Payton, there was a man by the name of Gale Sayers whose brief career was filled with spectacular punt returns and dazzling ground moves.

Sayers wasted little time, bursting onto the scene by scoring 22 touchdowns and amassing 2,272 yards in his first pro season. In his seven years as a pro, Sayers was named All-League five times. Unfortunately for Sayers and his fans, injuries eventually took their toll. The great running back was forced to leave the game early becoming the youngest man ever inducted into the Hall of Fame.

### Difficulty:

High-grade examples of the 1966 Philadelphia issue seem to rarely come up for sale and for good reason. They are just really tough! One condition obstacle, unique to this issue, is the fact that the reverse is framed by solid green edges. As you might imagine, those edges are prone to chipping and wear. Reverse chipping alone will not severely downgrade a card in most cases but it can prevent the card from reaching true mint status.

In addition, print defects can be a problem due to the contrasting dark and light areas on the face of the card. The sky, in the background, is most susceptible to stray dark print spots. Finally, the centering on these cards has always been an issue. Even most mint copies are not found with perfect centering, they are rarely dead-on.

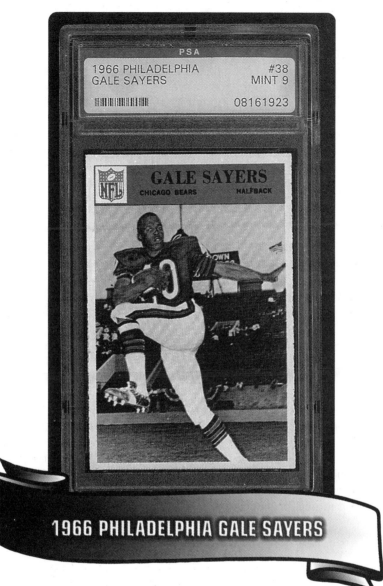

**1966 PHILADELPHIA GALE SAYERS**

## Comments:

A mention of Sayers brings to mind the age-old question, "What if?" What if Sayers remained healthy? What type of career numbers would he have? It's a question that comes up with many athletes such as Sandy Koufax, Ralph Kiner or even Bill Walton. At least, with Sayers, he was able to make his mark before the injuries took their toll on his body. When you talk about the greatest running backs in football history, the five guys that come to mind are Jim Brown, Walter Payton, Emmitt Smith, Barry Sanders and Gale Sayers. Many have argued that it was Sayers who may have been the most exciting of the five. While the set is not in major demand, the Sayers rookie card is a key for any serious vintage football collection.

## 1971 Topps #156 Terry Bradshaw

### Importance:

This is the only recognized rookie card of perennial winner Terry Bradshaw. Bradshaw's career didn't start out smoothly. High expectations led to major pressure on the new Pittsburgh Steelers quarterback but, after a few seasons, Bradshaw would routinely lead his team to postseason play. Bradshaw led the Steelers to eight AFC Central titles and four Super Bowl championships during his 14-year career. He also amassed 27,989 passing yards and threw for 212 touchdowns.

Bradshaw, a clutch postseason performer, threw 30 touchdowns in playoff and championship play. Fittingly, on his last throw in the NFL, Bradshaw completed a touchdown pass to end his career. What a way to go.

### Difficulty:

This Bradshaw rookie card is as tough as the "Steel Curtain." The main condition obstacle is found on the front. The card is framed with red borders that are very susceptible to chipping and wear, much like the black- bordered 1971 Topps baseball cards are.

One thing to keep in mind is that 1970's Topps cards, no matter what sport, seem to suffer from poor quality control in general. The seemingly lack of care put into the manufacturing process then has created a condition rarity today. Another interesting aspect to this card is that you don't seem to find this card offered all that often in any grade. Maybe Bradshaw's offensive line is still protecting him from blitzing card collectors?

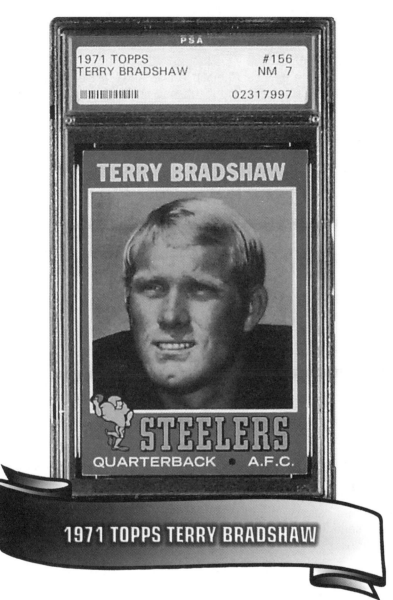

1971 TOPPS          #156
TERRY BRADSHAW      NM 7

02317997

TERRY BRADSHAW

STEELERS

QUARTERBACK ● A.F.C.

1971 TOPPS TERRY BRADSHAW

## Comments:

Bradshaw was not known for his arm in the way that a John Elway or Johnny Unitas were. He was not a standout quarterback simply because of a powerful right arm, it was Bradshaw's ability to win that made him a legend. Other quarterbacks have more passing yards and touchdowns but few have led their teams to victory as often as Bradshaw did. Now a respected broadcaster and comedian, Bradshaw remains in the spotlight and many consider him to be a likable, genuine guy. His appeal has helped the popularity of his sportscards and his rookie is no exception. As the general of the devastating Steelers Dynasty, Bradshaw should enjoy solid demand for years to come.

## 1972 Topps #200 Roger Staubach

### Importance:

This is the only recognized rookie card of Dallas Cowboy legend Roger Staubach. Staubach had to be patient at first, serving several years in the Navy before getting an opportunity to play football in the NFL. After two seasons as a backup, Staubach burst onto the scene in 1971. In his first full season, Staubach was the NFL Player of the Year, the Super Bowl MVP and he won the passing title.

During the mid to late 1970's, he would lead the Cowboys to another Super Bowl victory in Super Bowl XII in addition to three NFC championships. Staubach's "Hail Mary" pass in a 1975 playoff game versus the Minnesota Vikings is still considered one of the most exciting plays in football history. His rookie card is, by far, the most valuable card in the popular 1972 set.

### Difficulty:

This 1972 Topps Staubach rookie card is another victim of the doomed decade of card manufacturing. I am still looking for an answer but 1970's Topps cards, in all sports, were seemingly produced with little to no quality control. By the 1970's, you would figure that they could get it right but luckily, for those who appreciate condition difficulty, the cards were subject to a host of condition problems.

Some collectors have labeled 1970 as the year that cards became easier to acquire in high-grade. I don't see how that can be if 1970's cards were, in some cases, produced with evidently less care than some 1960's issues. This Staubach has to contend with poor centering, the major condition obstacle for those collectors that seek high-grade examples, and staining on the reverse to a lesser extent.

1972 TOPPS ROGER STAUBACH

## Comments:

Much like Terry Bradshaw but to a lesser degree, Staubach was the leader of a great dynasty during the 1970's. While Staubach may have lacked the number of Super Bowl victories that Bradshaw could claim, Staubach was at the heart of perhaps football's most popular team. In baseball, it's the New York Yankees. The accomplishments of Yankee players always seem to be magnified. Whether it's fair or not is another story entirely but, as collectors, I think it is important that you recognize the effect. Popularity might be the most significant factor in determining card desirability and demand. Accomplishments are important but, in many cases, popularity takes priority. Staubach will never lack in that department.

## 1976 Topps #148 Walter Payton

### Importance:

This is the official rookie card of the running back they called "Sweetness." When you watch video tape of Payton running, it looks so smooth, graceful and effortless. That is why they called him "Sweetness." Payton was a one man wrecking crew. He could run, block and catch with great skill.

During his 13 years with the Chicago Bears, Payton would set multiple rushing records. He finished his career as the NFL's all-time leading rusher with 16,726 yards, 3,838 carries and 110 rushing touchdowns. He also scored 15 more touchdowns as a receiver. Amazingly, even though he handled the ball so many times, he only missed one game in his whole career. Durable, powerful and humble, that was Walter Payton.

### Difficulty:

There's one major condition obstacle that has continued to haunt this card and high-grade collectors looking for this card. That obstacle would be centering. The poor centering associated with this card is often the main reason why so few gem mint examples have been located.

You can find this card with sharp corners and edges but great centering is the ticket to higher ground. More likely than not, the poor centering is altering the image from left to right and not from top to bottom (although that type of poor centering is certainly found as well). This card does not rank very high on the list of pure difficulty but it is semi-challenging for a post-1975 issue.

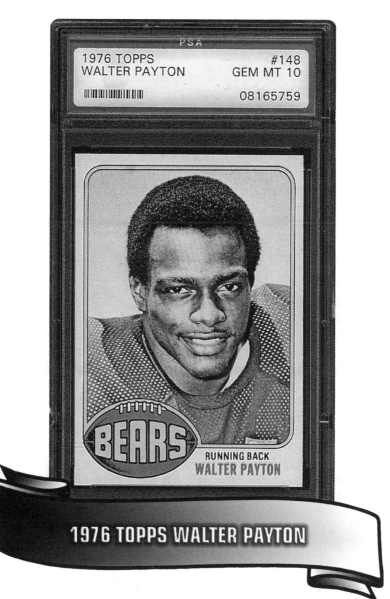

1976 TOPPS WALTER PAYTON

## Comments:

It's amazing that someone so soft spoken could be so deadly on the field but that is part of Walter Payton's appeal. When he passed away, not too long ago, fans were devastated because they had lost such a class act in a time when heroes are somewhat hard to find on the field. Even his rookie card captures the persona of this football legend, he just looks like a nice guy. That's probably not what his opponents were thinking after he ran them over on his way to a touchdown. No card in the set comes even close, in terms of demand, to this key rookie. If there is such a thing as a modern classic, this is it. The Walter Payton rookie card is a must for any serious card collector.

## 1981 Topps #216 Joe Montana

### Importance:
This is the rookie card of quarterback legend Joe Montana. Montana did not possess the greatest arm strength or the quickest feet but he did possess the unmatched leadership qualities that helped make the San Francisco 49ers the powerhouse team of the 1980's. The 49ers didn't simply beat teams, they destroyed them.

During his 14 seasons with San Francisco, he led the team to 10 postseason berths, 8 division championships and four Super Bowl victories. Montana was also named Super Bowl MVP on three different occasions which is still a NFL record. He finished with 40,551 yards passing and 273 touchdown passes.

### Difficulty:
All three rookie cards, featuring the legendary quarterbacks of the modern era, suffer three major condition obstacles. The first obstacle is print defects. The print defects in question are usually of the print "snow" variety where light or white-colored print spots sprinkle the background or image. The same problem that is very common on vintage issues, like 1957 Topps football, are also common here nearly 30 years later. So much for technology!

Centering is also a contributing obstacle, stopping many copies from reaching the elusive Gem Mint category. Finally, staining was still a problem in the 1980's. Whether it was a result of wax or that brick-like gum, the damage was done. This example is not very tough in NM-MT condition but true mint and gem mint copies are highly desirable.

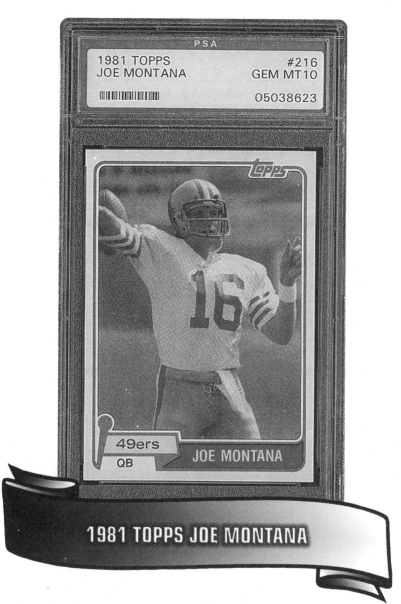

## Comments:

Joe Montana is, without a doubt, one of the most popular figures in NFL history. All this guy did was win and, to top it off, Montana just happened to be a very likable person. Montana has a reputation as being very personable and having a great sense of humor, have you seen that famous jock itch commercial? From his days at Notre Dame to his run as part of one the most dominant teams of the 1980's, Montana has enjoyed a great following. You can't go wrong with his rookie card. Even though it is modern and not as rare as some of the other gems on this list, Montana's popularity clearly takes care of that.

## 1984 Topps #63 John Elway

### Importance:

This is the rookie card of legendary comeback specialist John Elway. Elway knew how to rally his team to victory and he did it with a rocket arm and excellent mobility. In fact, with over 40 recorded 4th quarter comebacks, Elway stands alone in the record books. For seven straight seasons, Elway would pass for at least 3,000 yards and rush for 200 more. He was also named NFL MVP in 1987 and the AFC Player of the Year in 1993. After 8 playoff berths, 7 AFC Western Division titles and four AFC championships, Elway and the Denver Broncos finally won a Super Bowl when they upset the Green Bay Packers in Super Bowl XXXII and then repeated that feat the very next year against the Atlanta Falcons.

### Difficulty:

All three rookie cards, featuring the legendary quarterbacks of the modern era, suffer three major condition obstacles. The first obstacle is print defects. The print defects in question are usually of the print "snow" variety where light or white-colored print spots sprinkle the background or image. The same problem that is very common on vintage issues, like 1957 Topps football, are also common here nearly 30 years later. So much for technology!

Centering is also a contributing obstacle, stopping many copies from reaching the elusive gem mint category. Finally, staining was still a problem in the 1980's. Whether it was a result of wax or that brick-like gum, the damage was done. This example is not very tough in NM-MT condition but true mint and gem mint copies are highly desirable. Keep in mind that this card has been heavily counterfeited, so beware!

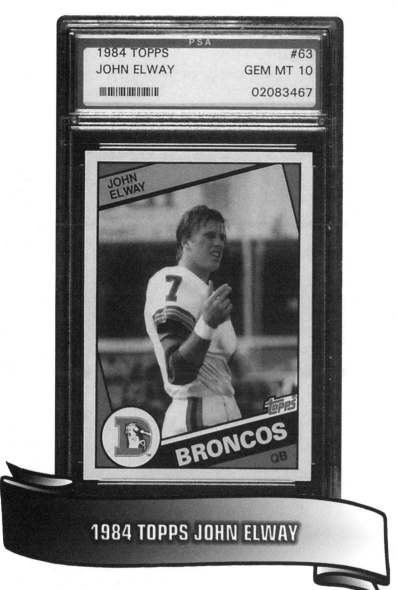

1984 TOPPS JOHN ELWAY

## Comments:

Elway was the equivalent in football of a Mark McGwire in baseball in one sense. In baseball, there are a few guys who have awesome power and then there's McGwire. Nobody can touch "Big Mac" in that department. In football, during Elway's era, it was similar situation. Other quarterbacks had great arms but Elway had a cannon for an arm that went unmatched in the league. A model of perseverance, Elway and his Denver Broncos took a lot a bashing over the years for not winning the Super Bowl. When Elway finally did it, it was like the whole world was celebrating with him. The wait just made it that much sweeter. This is a great card of a modern icon, not overly tough, but a key to any collection.

## 1984 Topps #123 Dan Marino

### Importance:

This is the rookie card of the NFL's most prolific passer. What can you say about this guy? In his first year, Marino led the AFC in passing and started the Pro Bowl. In his second year, he made his first year look like a joke. Just look at these numbers. Marino completed 362 passes, threw for 5,084 yards, threw 48 touchdowns passes and led his team to the Super Bowl. Even in the Super Bowl, he set records for attempts and completions. Needless to say, Marino holds numerous passing records including career passing yards and touchdowns. He is now the standard for passing in the NFL.

### Difficulty:

All three rookie cards, featuring the legendary quarterbacks of the modern era, suffer three major condition obstacles. The first obstacle is print defects. The print defects in question are usually of the print "snow" variety where light or white-colored print spots sprinkle the background or image. The same problem that is very common on vintage issues, like 1957 Topps football, are also common here nearly 30 years later. So much for technology!

Centering is also a contributing obstacle, stopping many copies from reaching the elusive gem mint category. Finally, staining was still a problem in the 1980's. Whether it was a result of wax or that brick-like gum, the damage was done. This example is not very tough in NM-MT condition but true mint and gem mint copies are highly desirable. Keep in mind that this card has been heavily counterfeited, so beware!

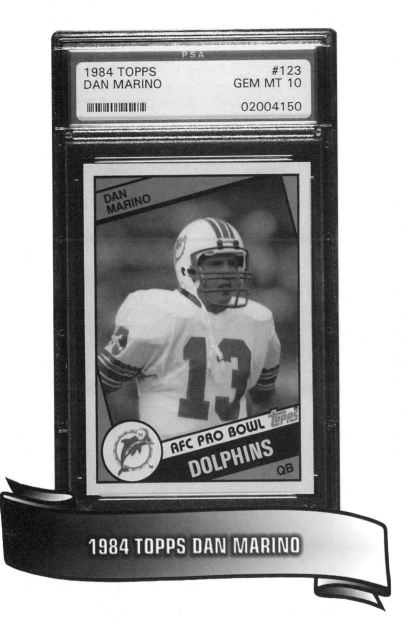

1984 TOPPS DAN MARINO

## Comments:

It was sad to see this great quarterback leave the game, but Dan Marino stayed on long enough to obliterate the record books with his powerful arm. All future quarterbacks will be compared to Dan Marino, plain and simple. Much like other quarterbacks on the list, Marino offered the total package as an athlete. He was a marketing dream, a great athlete, a likable man and he even had a flashy smile. Do you remember those Isotoner commercials? In true mint condition, this card is very desirable. It might be a modern card but it is overwhelmingly popular. With the current lack of talent at the quarterback position, it makes you wonder if anyone can approach Marino's numbers.

# 1986 Topps #161 Jerry Rice

## Importance:

This is the only recognized rookie card of the NFL's most prolific receiver. Montana to Rice and then Young to Rice are words that most football fans are familiar with. If you were a fan of the San Francisco 49ers, this was music to your ears. If you were rooting for the opponent, it was a horrible, gut wrenching sound. These two receiver/quarterback combos earned a few trips to the Super Bowl over the years and Rice still holds several Super Bowl receiving records.

Jerry Rice also holds almost every important receiving record in NFL history. Some of his records are so impressive that the runner up, in some categories, is not even remotely close to Rice. Rice's records include the most 1,000-yard receiving seasons (13 and counting including 11 consecutive), the most receiving yards in a season (1,848), the most touchdowns in a season (22), the most consecutive 100-catch seasons (3), the most career receiving yards (20,386 and counting), the most career receptions (1,364 and counting) and receiving touchdowns (185 and counting).

Rice keeps himself in such tremendous physical condition that he continues to perform despite closing in on 40 years of age. The numbers will continue to pile up unless he retires or finally loses NFL level skill. When it comes to wide receivers, there is simply no one that compares to Rice. This tough modern rookie card is a hobby favorite.

## Difficulty:

Chipping, chipping, chipping - Did I mention chipping? The green colored borders on this Rice rookie prevent many examples from reaching true mint status. Even cards straight from the pack often come with the obvious signs of edge or corner wear. NM-MT Rice rookies are abundant but it might take some time finding a mint copy, one that doesn't show a hint of white against the evil green edges. Centering, in addition to the easily chipped borders, can prevent a sharp example from reaching gem mint status. This is a tough card, by modern standards, in strict mint condition.

1986 TOPPS #161
JERRY RICE GEM MT 10
05005034

**1986 TOPPS JERRY RICE**

## Comments:

Jerry Rice might be part of the most popular quarterback/wide receiver tandem in football history. It's true that the quarterback position is given most of the glory when a team becomes a winner but Rice certainly gets his share. Like Dan Marino at quarterback, Rice has become the standard that all future wide receivers will be measured against. To add to the desirability of his rookie card, even though it is a modern one, it is very difficult to find in pristine condition due to those nasty green edges mentioned above. As far as modern cards are concerned, very few can claim to be as well-rounded as this one is.

## 1989 Score #257 Barry Sanders

### Importance:

This is a key rookie card featuring the most dominant running back of his era. Barry Sanders, despite a shocking retirement from the game in 1999, had a 10-year run of epic proportions. For 10 straight seasons, Sanders would rush for 1,000 or more yards (the first man to ever accomplish the feat) proving that he was not only quick and powerful but durable as well. Sanders reached that mark despite missing five full games in 1993. He would also become only the 3rd player in NFL history to rush for 2,000 or more yards in 1997 when he gained 2,053 yards on 6.1 yards per carry. Sanders was awarded the NFL MVP that year.

His career mark of 15,269 yards rushing ranks 3rd all-time behind Emmitt Smith and Walter Payton but Sanders, like Jim Brown, had a better YPC (yards per carry) average during his career at 5.1. The argument will continue but this former Heisman Trophy winner will forever be considered one of the very best at his position. Sanders does have other rookie cards produced by companies like Pro and Topps, but this is his most desirable.

### Difficulty:

The two major condition obstacles for this card are poor centering and chipping. The chipping is probably what prevents more Sanders rookie cards from reaching gem mint status than any other factor. Green borders, that allow the slightest touch of wear to be seen by the naked eye, surround the card. The left to right centering may also be a contributing factor to a potential downgrade but the colored borders are very sensitive.

1989 SCORE BARRY SANDERS

## Comments:

For whatever reason, Barry Sanders called it quits long before his skills seemed to be eroding and that factor can be a double-edged sword. On the one hand, we can envision what might have been. Without much of a stretch, he seemed destined to break Payton's all-time rushing mark before Emmitt Smith came along. On the other hand, too many athletes hang around too long and their diminished skills are on display, taking away from the legend they created in the first place. Sanders never let that happen. He rushed for over 1,400 yards his first year and, his last year, showed no signs of slowing. For fans and collectors, the memory of Sander's greatness remains strong like the legs that powered him down the field.

# 1990 Score Supplemental #101T Emmitt Smith

## Importance:

This is the most popular rookie card of football's future all-time leading rusher. Emmitt Smith seemed to sneak up on the career rushing mark and seems to ready to break Payton's mark during the 2002-2003 season. Smith has been consistent and durable, perhaps part of the reason why he went unnoticed for some time. He didn't possess the flash of a Bo Jackson or Barry Sanders but he never let up.

In 1991, Smith would start a streak of 11 straight 1,000 rushing yard seasons, peaking in 1995 with 1,773 yards and 25 touchdowns (the 25 touchdowns established a NFL record that year). Smith's five straight seasons of 1,400 rushing yards (1991-1995) was also a NFL record.

In addition, Smith has already been a Rookie of the Year (1990), MVP (1993), Super Bowl MVP (1993), and a Pro Bowl selection several times during his outstanding career. The rushing record is one of the most hallowed records in the game's history making this rookie card of the utmost importance. Smith does have other rookie cards produced by companies like Fleer, Pro and Topps, but this is his most desirable.

## Difficulty:

There are two major condition obstacles with this Smith rookie card. First of all, the card is surrounded by dark-colored borders so many of you will know what that means. Chipping and general wear are hard to avoid with the slightest touch revealing the white cardboard underneath. In addition, these cards were only available through factory distribution. Most of the factory cards were manufactured and packaged in such a way that, more times than not, prevented the Smith rookie from ever reaching true mint status. This card poses a solid challenge for serious, high-end modern card collectors.

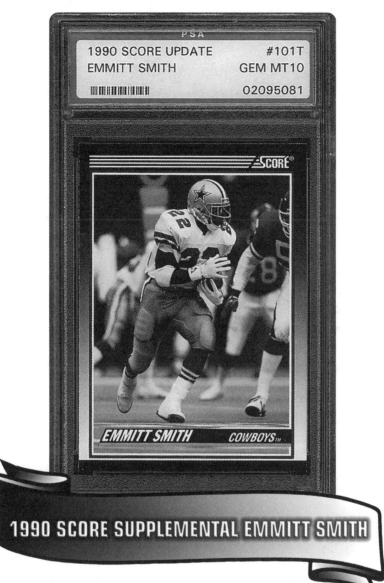

## 1990 SCORE SUPPLEMENTAL EMMITT SMITH

## Comments:

In all sports, certain career records are given elevated importance. In baseball, you have Hank Aaron's home run record. In hockey, you have Wayne Gretzky's goals scored record. In basketball, you have Kareem Abdul Jabbar's scoring record. All those records, as well as a few others within those sports, have been given this sort of blessing by fans. In football, one may argue that the career passing record or receiving record would be tops but the career rushing record should not be underestimated. In fact, it might be, according to many fans, the most appealing of the three. Even if Smith somehow falls short of the record, his place in history is solid but, let's face it, Emmitt's on the way.

## 1951 Parkhurst #4 Maurice Richard

### Importance:

The only recognized rookie card of one of hockey's best offensive players. Maurice "The Rocket" Richard of Montreal Canadien fame had one objective, to score as many goals as he possibly could. With surprising strength and tremendous quickness, Richard was able to land plenty of pucks beyond the goalie's reach.

Richard would finish his career with 8 Stanley Cup Championships, 544 regular season goals, 14 All-Star game selections and one Hart Trophy. In fact, when he retired, he had set 17 NHL records including his 50 goals in 50 games performance during the 1944-45 season, a feat that would not be repeated until 1981! While some of his records have been surpassed, Richard is still considered by many to be one of the most charismatic players to ever step on the ice.

### Difficulty:

As with most vintage hockey issues, finding the Richard rookie is tough enough in itself. Hockey cards, unlike baseball issues, were not distributed or protected to the degree of baseball cards, not even close. In regards to condition obstacles, there are a few to consider. First of all, the cardboard used in production on these blank-backed cards was very poor in quality and it fails to hold up well over time.

Second, "bleeding" is another obstacle, which is often associated with early Goudey baseball issues. When the sheets of cards were laid on top of each other, the moist ink would sometimes stick to the reverse of the cards above. It can make for a real distraction if the "bleeding" is significant. The color will sometimes spread on the surface as well. Then you have to acknowledge the fact that many copies exhibit very poor registration.

Finally, and most notably, the centering on this issue is very inconsistent, causing most of these cards to grade below Near Mint levels. Remember that these 51-52 Parkhurst cards have a natural toned look to them. All early Parkhursts are very tough.

PSA
1951 PARKHURST #4
MAURICE RICHARD NM-MT 8
04007734

MAURICE "ROCKET" RICHARD ----Mont. Canadiens
Right Wing. 1950-51 Record:---Goals 42
Assists 24, Points 66, Min. in Penalty 97
Born Montreal, Quebec, Aug. 4, 1921
NO. 4 PARKIE 1951-52 Hockey Series

## 1951 PARKHURST MAURICE RICHARD

## Comments:

Collectors are drawn to offensive players in virtually every sport. That is why Jordan, Ruth and a slew of quarterbacks are so popular within their sport. If you want to own a card of the first dominant offensive hockey player, you have to add this Richard to your collection. In addition to Richard's great offensive output, he was also a major winner. His eight Championships rank high on the list for any sport and everybody likes a winner. This is a key component to any vintage hockey collection.

## 1951 Parkhurst #61 Terry Sawchuk

### Importance:

This is the only recognized rookie card of one of hockey's greatest goalies. Terry Sawchuk overcame multiple injuries early in his career to become a mean force in front of the net. In fact, he had 103 shutouts in his career, an amazing mark that has yet to be approached at the time of this publication. His awesome goalie play led him to 3 Vezina Trophies, as the best NHL goalie, in his first 5 years as a pro. In addition, Sawchuk had a string of five straight seasons with a goals-against average of less than 2.00. Keep in mind that he owned the all-time win record until 2001.

While he was seemingly unstoppable on the ice, his temper and depression would lead him to his tragic and untimely death. After a bout with depression over his failed marriage in 1970, he started a fight with his roommate. During the fight, Sawchuk fell over a barbecue pit and was severely injured. He was on his way back to recovery when, during surgery to repair his liver, a blood clot caused his heart to stop according to reports.

### Difficulty:

As with most vintage hockey issues, finding the Sawchuk rookie is tough enough in itself. Hockey cards, unlike baseball issues, were not distributed or protected to the degree of baseball cards, not even close. In regards to condition obstacles, there are a few to consider. First of all, the cardboard used in production of these blank-backed cards was very poor in quality and it fails to hold up well over time.

Second, "bleeding" is another obstacle often associated with early Goudey baseball issues. When the sheets of cards were laid on top of each other, the moist ink would sometimes stick to the reverse of the cards above. It can reduce eye-appeal if the "bleeding" is significant. The color will sometimes spread on the surface as well. Then you have to acknowledge the fact that many copies exhibit very poor registration.

Finally, and most notably, the centering on this issue is very inconsistent, causing most of these cards to grade Near Mint or lower. Remember that these 51 Parkhurst cards have a natural toned look to them. All early Parkhursts are very tough.

## 1951 PARKHURST TERRY SAWCHUK

## Comments:

Besides the offensive stars of the game, fans and collectors seem to be drawn to the net-minders of hockey. There is a special quality about these menacing figures. Whether it's the special face masks or the fact that these guys can withstand an entire season of a 100-mph pucks being drilled at their noggin, the goalie is a special breed of athlete. Many of these guys are amongst the most colorful characters in the game, Sawchuk was hockey's first standout of the modern era. Remember that he guarded the net without a facemask for much of his career! He was a tough man and this is one tough card.

## 1951 Parkhurst #66 Gordie Howe

### Importance:
This is the only recognized rookie card of "Mr. Hockey" and the key to the set. Gordie Howe, at one time, held virtually every major offensive record until a guy named Wayne Gretzky came along. While Howe's numbers have been overshadowed by Gretzky's, Howe's ability to dominate for such a long period of time makes him a wonder.

Some of Howe's more notable achievements include ranking in the top five in scoring for 20 straight years, 6 Hart Trophies as the league's MVP, 6 Art Ross Trophies for leading the league in scoring, he scored at least 23 goals per season for 22 straight years and he was selected to 21 All-Star teams (12 First Team and 9 Second Team All-Star squads). The list of accomplishments goes on and on and the demand for his cards ranks at the top of all hockey lists.

### Difficulty:
As with most vintage hockey issues, finding the Howe rookie is tough enough in itself. Hockey cards, unlike baseball issues, were not distributed or protected to the degree of baseball cards, not even close. In regards to condition obstacles, there are a few to consider. First of all, the cardboard used in production on these blank-backed cards was very poor in quality and it fails to hold up well over time.

Second, "bleeding" is another obstacle, which is often associated with early Goudey baseball issues. When the sheets of cards were laid on top of each other, the moist ink would sometimes stick to the reverse of the cards above. It can reduce the eye-appeal if the "bleeding" is significant. The color will sometimes spread on the surface as well. Then you have to acknowledge the fact that many copies exhibit very poor registration.

Finally, and most notably, the centering on this issue is very inconsistent, causing most of these cards to grade Near Mint or lower. Remember that these 51 Parkhurst cards have a naturally toned look to them. All early Parkhursts are very tough.

PSA

1951 PARKHURST                    #66
GORDIE HOWE                   NM-MT 8

07009575

GORDON HOWE        —Detroit Red Wings
Right Wing        1950-51 Record.—Goals 43
    Assists 43, Points 86, Min. in Penalty 74
    Born: Floral, Sask., Mar. 31, 1928
No.   66   in the "PARKIE" 1951-52 Hockey Series.

## 1951 PARKHURST GORDIE HOWE

## Comments:

Wayne Gretzky may have broken many of Howe's offensive records but many fans believe that Gordie Howe is the symbol of hockey, not Gretzky. While that is certainly debatable, Howe's importance is not. There are only a few major figures in hockey history known to the mainstream public and Howe is one of them. While the 1954-55 Topps Howe is very popular, this Parkhurst example is his only recognized rookie. This is an ultra-important hockey card. There is only one "Mr. Hockey."

## 1953 Parkhurst #27 Jean Beliveau

### Importance:

This is a tough, key rookie card featuring hockey's most successful team captain. Jean Beliveau, "Le Gros Bill," (nicknamed after a popular French song of the day) was a player who combined size, grace and instinct with precision stickhandling. At 6'3, 205 pounds, he represented the prototype for all future hockey players, size plus skill. Amongst Beliveau's more notable accomplishments are 507 goals, 712 assists, (1,219 total points), 10 All-Star selections (6-First Team and 4 Second Team), 2 Hart Trophies, 1 Ross Trophy, 1 Conn Smythe Trophy and 10 Stanley Cup Championships with the Montreal Canadiens.

During his 18 seasons with Montreal, Beliveau was much more than a skilled player. He was a leader who helped bridge the gap between management and the players, he was the guy everyone went to for advice. This card is not only an extremely important rookie card, it is also considered one of the most beautiful postwar issues in all of sportscard collecting.

### Difficulty:

Toning, toning, toning, did I mention toning? Due to the paper stock on all 1953 Parkhursts, the borders on these gems are virtually always found with toning and, sometimes, major toning. In fact, the toning is so prevalent on this issue that cards which exhibit some toning (though not severe) will usually not be downgraded. Just make sure that the eye-appeal is not affected tremendously. Otherwise, if the toning becomes an distraction, the card could suffer. Of course, this card is also subject to the typical vintage card condition obstacles such as poor centering, print defects (especially with the light-colored backgrounds and edges) and general wear. Overall, this card is very tough to locate in high-grade with toning being the major problem.

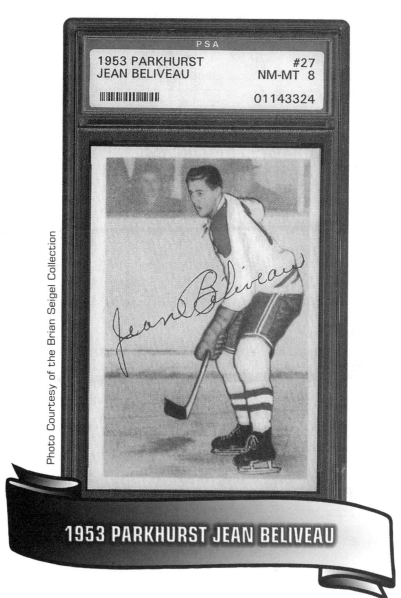

PSA

1953 PARKHURST #27
JEAN BELIVEAU NM-MT 8

01143324

## 1953 PARKHURST JEAN BELIVEAU

## Comments:

Widely considered one of the toughest vintage hockey issues ever produced, this Beliveau rookie card has a lot going for it. Beliveau is regarded
by most to be one of the 10 best players to ever take the ice and that is
important to the long-term demand of this example. While it is true that
hockey collecting has nowhere near the following that baseball collecting
does, vintage hockey cards offer a level of scarcity that few baseball issues
can compete with as they were produced in much lower numbers. Real
potential does exist as population numbers continue to steer the collector
demand. This card is ultra-attractive in top condition.

# 1954 Topps #8 Gordie Howe

## Importance:

This is the first Topps issue to feature this legendary hockey icon. When it comes to hockey cards, this one is at or near the top of virtually everyone's list. The beautiful colors and great photo of a young Howe make the image a classic. His career numbers are tremendous but it was Howe's production at the late stages of his career that separates him from all other legends of the game. At the age of 41, he scored 44 goals during the regular season.

At the age of 42, he finished second on the team in goals scored. Overall, Howe scored more goals after the age of 30 than he did prior to 30. After spending 6 years in the World Hockey Association, Howe returned for one last NHL hurrah at the age of 52. He went on to score 15 goals that year! Howe has set the standard for longevity for all sports.

## Difficulty:

This card can look absolutely fantastic when found in high-grade but that's the problem. This card rarely comes up for sale in NM-MT or better condition; it's a true high-grade rarity. The blue bottom border is extremely susceptible to chipping and, just above the blue, is a strip of red that is also prone to edge wear. That factor alone keeps most of the existing Howe rookies below NM-MT levels.

The strong colors near the base have been known to bleed and the centering, like most vintage issues, is very inconsistent to say the least. Finally, the white background provides a haven for dark print defects and, with the assortment of colors found on the front, don't be surprised if defects are present.

**1954 TOPPS GORDIE HOWE**

## Comments:

This card is definitely more visually attractive than his Parkhurst rookie and the fact that this card was Howe's first Topps example makes it very desirable. I liken this card to the 1952 Topps Mickey Mantle in the sense that, even though Mantle had a true Bowman rookie card the year before, the Topps issue has always received "rookie-like" attention. This card has such outstanding eye-appeal that it is no wonder why this card remains at the top of most vintage hockey wantlists. The image of Howe gliding across the ice combined with the red, white and blue colors is simply stunning.

## 1955 Parkhurst #50 Jacques Plante

### Importance:

This is a key rookie card of one of the NHL's greatest goalies. Jacques "Jake the Snake" Plante was an intense and focused athlete. He came to the ice to perform; Plante was not interested in partying after the game or socializing with members of his team. Plante wanted to win, that's all that mattered to him. His daring style was innovative; he would often leave the safety of the net to gain control of the puck. Plante was also the first goalie to regularly wear a mask in the early 1960's.

Plante's accomplishments were abundant. Plante won 7 Vezina Trophies for his work as a goalie, one Hart Trophy as the league's best player, 6 Stanley Cup Championships and was selected to 7 All-Star Teams (three First Team and four Second Team squads). After 17 seasons, Plante called it quits but his legacy remains.

### Difficulty:

Centering, chipping, bleeding and toning are all condition obstacles for this Plante rookie card. As with most early Parkhurst issues, the edges are almost always found with some degree of toning. The key is to make sure that the toning does not exceed the average degree of toning for this particular issue. Try to locate as many 1955 Parkhurst examples as you can so you can compare for yourself. There's no substitute for self education. Centering difficulties, with the exception of general wear, is probably most responsible for grade deductions.

Finally, the red bottom border is very susceptible to chipping and causes cardboard bleeding onto the reverse, making it virtually impossible to find true high-grade copies. All early Parkhurst cards are challenging and this one is widely considered one of the scarcest.

## 1955 PARKHURST JACQUES PLANTE

## Comments:

Plante was a true innovator and a fierce competitor on the ice. He is one of those athletes that cannot be judged by mere statistics because his contribution to hockey was much greater than that. His rookie card is, quite simply, the most dominating force in the set. In fact, it enjoys nearly twice the demand of the next most significant card in the set, the Maurice Richard example. As one of the few true legendary goalies, this gorgeous, action-packed card becomes extremely important.

# 1958 Topps #66 Bobby Hull

## Importance:

This is the only recognized rookie card of the "Golden Jet," one of the most powerful slapshot artists the NHL has ever seen. When you can strike a hockey puck with the force that Bobby Hull had, he was clocked close to 120mph routinely, you are going to score a lot of goals and provide nightmares for any opposing goalie. His unreal power led to 7 goal -scoring titles, four 50-goal seasons, 12 All-Star selections (10 First Team and 2 Second Team squads) and two Hart Trophies as the league's MVP.

Despite winning only one Stanley Cup Championship, Hull won three Ross Trophies and one Byng Trophy. Hull was also an anti-violence advocate for the sport. He was very outspoken about the rising levels of hockey violence during the 1970's and he is partially responsible for the decrease today.

## Difficulty:

This card, like most 1958 Topps cards, is very tough to find in high-grade, but it also has an additional problem - centering. In fact, the Hull card was the corner card on the uncut sheet, creating this centering problem. The card is often found with 70/30 centering or worse, damaging the eye-appeal. It's the biggest condition obstacle for this great rookie card. As the last card in the set, this card was also subject to the handling abuse often associated with number one and last cards in sets.

The lime green and yellow background, which can provide a stunning backdrop to the image of Hull, is an unfortunate magnet for dark print defects. Finally, the paper stock was very poor on the 1958 Topps hockey cards just like it was for the baseball issue. Finding true high-grade copies of this rookie card is a real chore.

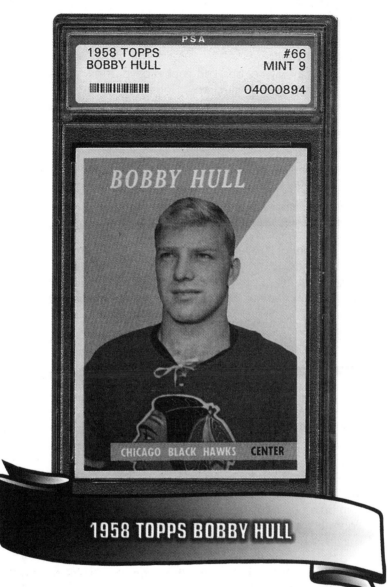

**1958 TOPPS BOBBY HULL**

## Comments:

This guy was a scoring machine. In terms of his offensive dominance, leading the league in scoring for 7 years is really an amazing accomplishment considering how difficult that is in all the other major sports. If you lead the NBA in scoring, you have to be a Michael Jordan-type player. To lead MLB in home runs for 7 years, you have to be an almost Mark McGwire-type player. Hockey is so overlooked that players like Hull don't get the respect they deserve from collectors but, when it comes to pure historical importance, this man is at the top. His rookie card not only dominates the set, but it is also one of the most significant rookie cards in the hobby. Overall, this is simply a tremendous and tough card.

# 1966 Topps #35 Bobby Orr

## Importance:

This is the only recognized rookie card of hockey's most legendary defenseman of all-time. Bobby Orr was so fast that he always seemed to be around the puck whether he had it in his possession or was trying to take it away from someone else. Like the famous movie character "The Terminator," no matter what you did to try and stop him, Orr just kept on coming. This guy has more trophies than you could possibly imagine, there are 16 in all. Orr's trophies include three Hart, two Ross, two Smythe, one Calder and 8 Norris!

When it comes to pure numbers, Orr's track record is amazing. It took Doug Harvey 18 years to break the assist record for defenseman, it only took Orr 7 ½ to break that mark. For six straight years, Orr reached at least 100 points, scoring at least 30 goals in each season with the exception of one (that year he scored 29). More importantly, Orr reinvented his position and no defenseman is emulated more than Mr. Orr.

## Difficulty:

Designed very much like the 1955 Bowman baseball issue, this Topps Orr rookie card is super sensitive to general wear. Dark brown, wood grain style borders surround the card. The slightest touch will be revealed, causing the card to show white and, in turn, the card will immediately be downgraded after inspection.

The centering (from top to bottom), due to the TV-style design, can often be difficult to decipher. Make sure that there is some room between the name and the bottom border. That way, the card will have a balanced look with some border at the top and at the bottom, a nice even balance. Overall, this is a very challenging card in high-grade. At the time of publication, no Mint 9's have been graded.

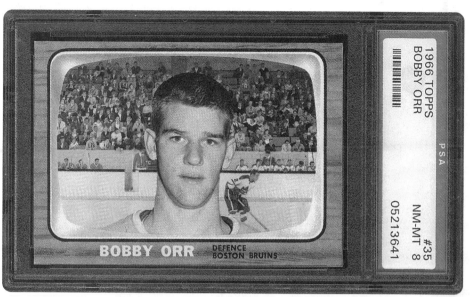

## 1966 TOPPS BOBBY ORR

## Comments:

Orr is widely regarded as one of hockey's very best players, ranking nearly as high as Gretzky and Howe on the all-time list. At his position, he simply has no comparable player, from any generation. Orr, like Plante for goalies, reinvented the position with reckless abandon. Paul Coffey did break Orr's scoring records but Orr was the innovator. Even though his numbers and athletic accomplishments are incredible, it is his appeal as a person that makes his cards an even more desirable choice. As one of hockey's most popular players, this rookie card dominates the set. Like the Hull rookie card, there is no comparable key. The set, as well as many hockey collections, revolve around this hockey legend.

# 1979 O-Pee-Chee #18 Wayne Gretzky

## Importance:

This is the key rookie card of hockey's greatest player. When you talk about the great players from each sport, Babe Ruth, Michael Jordan and Muhammad Ali come to mind but it is arguable that no athlete ever dominated his sport as much as Wayne Gretzky did.

Gretzky holds over 60, that's 60 NHL records at the time of publication. Let's take a look at some of his statistical prowess. Gretzky finished with 894 goals and 1,963 assists (2,857 career points), 15 All-Star selections (8 First Team and 7 Second Team squads), 9 Hart Trophies, 10 Ross Trophies, two Smythe Trophies and four Byng Trophies. Wow!

Gretzky was also part of four Stanley Cup Championship teams. His regular season records of 92 goals, 163 assists and 215 total points seem unreachable. Number 99, A.K.A. "The Great One", stands alone and his rookie card is clearly the most popular hockey card in existence, with the O-Pee-Chee (Canadian) issue having a huge edge over the Topps issue.

## Difficulty:

Good luck finding this card without flaws, it is very tough. The O-Pee-Chee (Canadian) example is much tougher than the Topps Gretzky rookie. The O-Pee-Chee version is almost always found with a rough-cut along the edges. This is very common for the issue. The colored borders, which are very susceptible to chipping and edge wear, make this card even more challenging.

In addition to the potential defects above, poor centering is a common condition obstacle. Most examples are found with at least 60/40 or worse centering side to side. Printing defects, in the surrounding blue border, are also commonly found. Even the focus of the image can be an issue here. If a gem mint Gretzky ever surfaced, the sky would be the limit. This O-Pee-Chee rookie card certainly provides a strong challenge by modern sportscard standards.

1979 O-PEE-CHEE WAYNE GRETZKY

## Comments:

What can you say about this player or this card? Gretzky, as a player, was as dominant on the ice as they come and the card is as desirable as cards get in the sport of hockey. Now it's true that an easier Topps Gretzky rookie was produced the very same year but the O-Pee-Chee rookie is the version most collectors clamor for due to its difficulty. Very few sportscards produced in the modern era generate the interest that this card does. Along with the Jordan rookie, this card symbolizes modern sportscard collecting. The bottom line is that you have to own this card if you are a sportscard collector of legends, regardless of sport.

## 1985 O-Pee-Chee #9 Mario Lemieux

### Importance:

This is the most important rookie card of, arguably, hockey's most talented player in history. Besides hockey's Wayne Gretzky, no other modern player was as much of a draw as Mario Lemieux. Lemieux's combination of size and skill made him the most feared player in the league and the heir apparent to Gretzky as the NHL's best player.

Despite a few nagging injuries, eventually being diagnosed with Hodgkin's disease and an early retirement after lingering effects from radiation and back problems, Lemieux piled up very impressive numbers. In fact, he is adding to those numbers after another comeback in 2000-2001.

After his 1997 retirement, he was only the second player in hockey history to average over 2 points per game. In addition, he won six scoring titles, he was selected to 8 All-Star Teams (5 First Team and 3 Second Team squads), he won three MVP awards and 13 Trophies overall (3 Hart, 6 Ross, 2 Smythe, 1 Calder and 1 Masterton). His story isn't over quite yet but he has already cemented his position as one of the game's true legends. There was a Topps issue produced during this same year but the O-Pee-Chee issue has a big edge.

### Difficulty:

The reality is that this card is probably one of the easiest cards to find in high-grade on the list. The O-Pee-Chee (Canadian) version is certainly tougher than the Topps version as most O-Pee-Chee cards are in the 1970's and 1980's. With the exception of a slight rough-cut and centering problems, problems that might prevent the card from reaching gem mint levels, this card does not provide a great challenge in near mint to mint or mint condition but, then again, difficulty is not the reason why this card made the list.

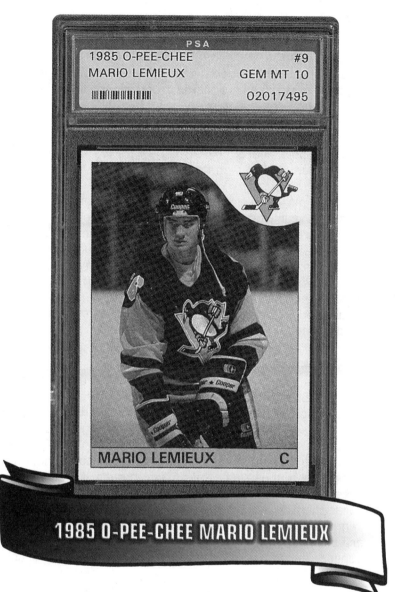

MARIO LEMIEUX          C

**1985 O-PEE-CHEE MARIO LEMIEUX**

## Comments:

Mario is considered hockey's most gifted physical specimen. Even Wayne Gretzky could not claim to have the physical gifts of this Pittsburgh legend. If Mario were to never play another game, his place in hockey history is etched in stone. It's too bad that Mario missed so many games due to a variety of injuries. Who knows what he might have done? In his injury prone career, Mario accomplished so much that it is hard to comprehend. While this card is not nearly as difficult as the rest of the vintage beauties on this list, Mario's importance and popularity make him an easy choice. A humble and likable guy, Mario is a collector favorite.

# 1932 U.S. Caramel #3 Bobby Jones

## Importance:

This is a key card of golf's first true superstar. The 1932 U.S. Caramel set is often overlooked in comparison to the 1933 Goudey Sport Kings set but it really is a classic. In fact, it is actually much more difficult than the Goudey issue. Despite so many star athletes in the set, the Jones remains a major key. This frail, temperamental boy turned into a well-liked golf champion before most young men finish college.

By the time he retired at 28, he had experienced more than most 80 year olds. In 1930, Jones would become the only man to ever win golf's version of the Grand Slam (U.S. and British Opens as well as U.S. and British Amateurs). Furthermore, Jones wasn't just a winning golfer, he embarrassed competitors with his skill. In fact, during a 36-hole playoff early in his career, Jones beat his opponent by 23 strokes! This tough, scarce issue is one of only a few mainstream Jones sportscards to ever be produced.

## Difficulty:

This issue is extremely challenging. If it were not for a "find" of 1932 U.S. Caramels a few years back, there probably wouldn't be any high-grade copies in existence. Major toning problems, inconsistent print quality and general wear issues make any of these U.S. Caramels a virtual impossibility in high-grade. Many of these examples are seen with very bland color and, due to the packaging process, the cards never seem to be found sharp. They are believed to be scarce partly due to the fact that the cards themselves could be redeemed for baseball balls and gloves. I am sure the cards are worth a lot more than the balls or gloves are today but who knew? Examples that exhibit a bright, fresh appearance sell for noticeable premiums in the marketplace.

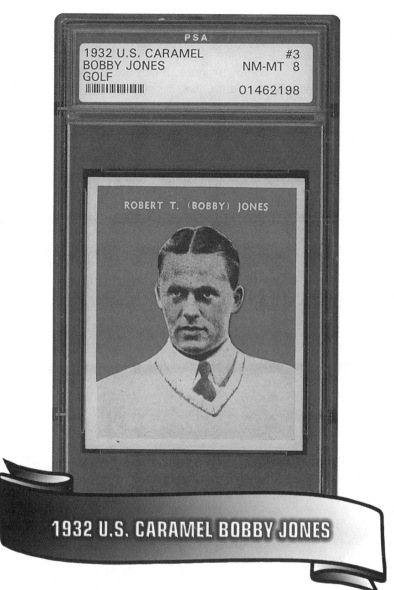

1932 U.S. CARAMEL BOBBY JONES

## Comments:

The story of Bobby Jones is one that will live on forever. Jones was told that he was a failure so many times as a youth that he drove himself to excellence. The funny thing was that, before the age of 30, he had basically accomplished everything that he set out to do as a golfer. With Jones, due to the emergence of golf as a major sport today, his cards have major potential. The more popular golf becomes, the more exposure golf history enjoys and the more attention Jones will receive. More and more, collectors are focusing on rarity and, if that trend continues, the 1932 U.S. Caramel Jones should enjoy great future demand.

## 1933 Goudey Sport Kings #38 Bobby Jones

### Importance:

This is the most popular vintage golf card in existence and a key to the set. Bobby Jones was the first dominant force that the world of golf had ever seen. He was young, confident and showed amazing poise for a golfer with such limited experience. Between the years of 1923 and 1929, Jones was an unstoppable force on the golf course and this dominance started at the age of 21.

What is perhaps even more amazing is the fact that he retired at the age of 28 after winning 13 majors, a record that stood for over 40 years. This is an astonishing number considering that most professional golfers today don't reach their peak until they are well past the age of 28. Keep in mind that Jones only entered 21 championships during that time. He was so dominant that his closest competitors, Walter Hagen and Gene Sarazen, never won a British or U.S. Open while Jones was playing. This Jones example is a classic. The classic swing, the slick-backed hair and the eyes of intensity form the image of a true legend.

### Difficulty:

The 1933 Goudey Sport King set is subject to a variety of condition problems with toning and bleeding at the forefront. The edges, as with the U.S. Caramels, can really alter the eye-appeal if they are toned which is, unfortunately, the condition you find most examples in. In addition, the reverse can often show signs of bleed-through. When the sheets of cards were laid on top of each other, the moist ink would sometimes stick to the reverse of the cards above. Now, it is true that this defect is found on the reverse but the bottom line is that collectors seem to care. If the bleeding is not severe, then it should not detract from the value in a substantial way. Remember that many of the Goudeys were not cut with razor-sharp, pointed corners so focus on corner wear not corner shape. This is a tough issue with a limited amount of high-quality examples in existence.

## 1933 GOUDEY SPORT KINGS BOBBY JONES

**Comments:**

Simply put, this 1933 Sport Kings Bobby Jones card is one of the most significant sportscards on this entire list. When you consider the overwhelming popularity of the sport today, with more and more youngsters picking up golf clubs, this card and this man become even more important. The focus on golf will only bring more attention to the history of the game and the players who excelled decade to decade. Jones was the first man to raise golf, as a sport, to another level. Baseball had Ruth, football had Grange and golf had Jones, his stardom was a breakthrough for the sport. This card is one of a few keys to perhaps the hobby's most intriguing set; the potential for increased demand on this card is outstanding.

## 1998 Champions of Golf/Master Collection Tiger Woods

### Importance:

This is a modern condition rarity featuring the most popular active athlete since Michael Jordan. Tiger Woods is so dominating that it is hard to comprehend. When you consider how young he is, the question arises, "Is this guy going to get even better?" The scary answer to this question is, most likely, yes. I could take up pages of this book listing Tiger's accomplishments. He already has over 20 PGA Tour victories under his belt and he is not even 30 yet! Woods completed his first career Grand Slam by the age of 24 with his British Open victory in 2000, the youngest ever to do so. Woods destroyed the record books with a 15-shot margin of victory at the U.S. Open in 2000.

Also in 2000, Woods became just the second man to win the U.S., British and Canadian Opens in the same year and just the second man to win three majors in one season. By the way, he won The Masters again in 2002. What else can you say? Tiger Woods is the sole reason why golf is so popular among our country's youth today.

### Difficulty:

Not many modern issues are legitimately tough, but this is certainly one of them. This issue was shrink-wrapped in a tight fashion. Guess who was at the bottom of the stack? You guessed it, Tiger Woods. The result is corner damage because the wrap caused most of the Woods cards to enter the world with blunting or lifting at the corners.

In addition, the card is surrounded by black borders. These borders can be chipped fairly easily, even when they are pulled straight from the factory set. This might be the toughest modern card on the list to find in gem mint condition. Please beware of sheet cut examples, they are not considered nearly as desirable.

## Comments:

This card, along with the 1996 SI for Kids issue, has a future that could be filled with great appreciation or one that could be hindered by unreal expectations. I chose this card over the SI for Kids Tiger example because this card has far better eye-appeal and will probably be more widely accepted as a mainstream issue in the future. Collectors seem to really enjoy this particular card for its larger design and reasonable difficulty, the combination gives the card some real credibility in a modern hobby filled with suspect cardboard. As one of Tiger's best looking and most difficult cards, the future looks good for this black-bordered beauty.

# 1887 N-28 Allen & Ginter John L. Sullivan

## Importance:

This is the first boxing card of major importance. With his huge, crossed arms, John Sullivan looks like a guy you would not want to mess with. Born in Boston, Sullivan became a professional fighter in 1878 after gaining a fierce reputation as the "Boston Strong Boy." Four years later, Sullivan would win the bare-knuckle heavyweight championship by knocking out Paddy Ryan in 9 rounds and he held that title until his death.

Starting in 1882, some of the Sullivan's matches were fought with gloves under new boxing rules. The last bare-knuckled championship bout was held in 1889. During that fight, Sullivan pummeled Jake Kilrain after 75 rounds of pure pain! That's right, 75 rounds. In 1892, Sullivan fought James Corbett for the heavyweight championship of the world under the new "glove" rules. Corbett knocked out Sullivan in 21 rounds and that remained the only blemish on his career record.

## Difficulty:

The early Allen & Ginter boxing cards, much like the baseball counterparts, are very rare and tough for a multitude of reasons. Each card, from the 50-card "World Champions" set, was packaged inside boxes of Allen & Ginter cigarettes. As you might imagine, tobacco stains are extremely common on these cards and, when you consider the fact that these cards were produced on bright white card stock, the combination is lethal. Any evidence of staining will be readily apparent and you often find staining on the reverse.

Corner and edge wear are both common due to the way in which they were packaged. In addition, the reverse of the cards features a checklist so don't be surprised if you come across examples that have notations placed on the back (most collectors would actually use the checklists in order to keep track of their sets). Finally, toning is a common condition obstacle when it comes to many vintage issues so look for discoloration around the edges, it can be a distraction.

1887 ALLEN & GINTER JOHN SULLIVAN

## Comments:

Some readers, not familiar with boxing or boxing card history, might be asking themselves, "Why is this card on the list?" I will tell you why. Boxing was the premier sport in our country during the 19th and early 20th Century. This card is a symbol, a time capsule, as the first boxing card of substantial importance and it happens to reside in one of the most beautiful sets ever issued. John Sullivan was a true American idol before other major sports like basketball and football began to take shape in our culture. Just looking at this card will create a time warp. It takes you back over 100 years to a time when bare-knuckled gladiators entered the ring with brutal intentions. This card made the list on almost pure importance alone.

## 1948 Leaf #1 Jack Dempsey

### Importance:

The first card in a very tough set featuring the "Manassa Mauler." In order to step into a boxing ring, you have to be tough; it's inherent in the sport. Jack Dempsey gave the word "tough" new meaning and became one of the first true stars of the sport. On July 4, 1919, Dempsey brutalized Jess Willard to claim the heavyweight title. Willard, the man responsible for ending Jack Johnson's reign as the champ, was left with broken ribs, a broken jaw and even partial loss of hearing as a result of Dempsey's punching power. This damage was inflicted after only three rounds. Many fighters would meet a similar fate at the hands of Dempsey.

In 1926, Dempsey would finally lose his title after facing a determined Gene Tunney in front of the largest crowd in boxing history. In the rematch, Dempsey would knock Tunney down in the 7th round but Dempsey failed to retreat to a neutral corner and, in turn, Tunney received a long count and was able to get to his feet before the count of 10. Tunney would end up winning by decision that day. Dempsey would finish his illustrious career with a 64-6-9 record with 49 of his wins coming by way of knockout.

### Difficulty:

As the first card in the set, this Dempsey card is a true condition rarity. Often the subject of collector abuse, the first cards were damaged by rubber bands and general exposure due to their location at the top of the stack. Like the baseball and football Leaf issues from the same year, this Leaf boxing issue suffers from a variety of condition obstacles. The three biggest concerns are toning, centering and print quality. The borders on this issue can be found with an almost brown color and this can really hinder the eye-appeal. You may not be able to find examples with truly white borders, but off-white will do.

In addition, many of these cards were cut with tilts and, in turn, are found off-center. Centered copies will, without question, sell for a premium. Last but not least, the overall print quality is very inconsistent on this issue, possibly more inconsistent than any issue on the list. Stray print defects and poor registration are just two examples of how a poor printing process reduced the number of quality examples. This is a very tough card overall.

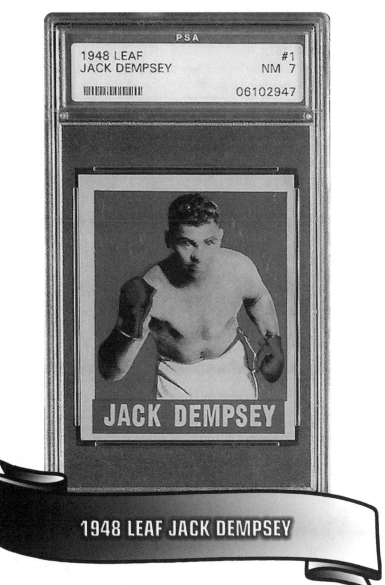

1948 LEAF JACK DEMPSEY

## Comments:

With Dempsey, the choice was tough. Should I list his 1933 Goudey Sport Kings card? Should I list his 1932 U.S. Caramel card? Both are significant sportscards but I came back to the 1948 Leaf Dempsey in the end. This set was devoted to boxers, it's the first card (the card that is always a notorious condition rarity) and the card itself is one of two major keys, along with the Louis. In the other two sets, Dempsey is lost in a sea of sports superstars like Ruth and Cobb. During the early part of the 20th Century, fans would pay up to $100 to watch Dempsey fight. Do you realize what $100 represented in 1920? Along with Rocky Marciano, Dempsey was, and still is, the prototypical tough guy and this card captures a key figure in boxing history.

## 1948 Leaf #48 Joe Louis

### Importance:

A key card of the man they called the "Brown Bomber." Jackie Robinson is usually given the credit for breaking color barriers and changing the way people viewed African-Americans in the athletic arena, but it was Joe Louis who made the biggest impact. Louis was, without question, the first African-American to gain widespread acceptance and superstar status in a segregated society. He was a hero to all and he handled himself with dignity and grace during an era when racial lines were drawn.

Louis held the heavyweight title for 12 years, a record that has yet to be approached in the sport. Perhaps his most memorable moment came when he avenged a loss to Germany's Nazi hero Max Schmeling. As a United States symbol and a symbol against oppression, Louis destroyed Schmeling with a right hand early in the fight. The legend of Joe Louis was complete. He finished with a 68-3 record, with 54 knockouts.

### Difficulty:

Like the baseball and football Leaf issue from the same year, this Leaf boxing issue suffers from a variety of condition obstacles. The three biggest concerns are toning, centering and print quality. The borders on this issue can be found with an almost brown color and this can really hinder the eye-appeal. You may not be able to find examples with truly white borders but off-white will do. In addition, many of these card were cut with tilts and, in turn, are found off-center. Centered copies will, without question, sell for a premium.

Last but not least, the overall print quality is very inconsistent on this issue, possibly more inconsistent than any issue on the list. Stray print defects and poor registration are just two examples of how a poor printing process reduced the number of quality examples. This is a very tough card overall.

1948 LEAF                                    #48
JOE LOUIS                           NM-MT  8

                                           06102945

**1948 LEAF JOE LOUIS**

## Comments:

This set, like its baseball counterpart, is very tough and in high demand. The combination of difficulty and beauty makes this set, and more importantly this card, a very popular choice. The bright background provides a wonderful frame for the menacing image of the heavyweight champ. When it comes to Louis as an athlete, I cannot tell you how underrated this man is. Not only as a boxer, but as a national hero and significant figure in our country's history. Imagine being the best fighter in the world but you can't eat at certain restaurants because of the color of your skin. Before there was Jackie, there was Joe.

## 1948 Leaf Boxing #50 Rocky Graziano

### Importance:

This card is the ultimate boxing rarity, the T206 Honus Wagner of boxing cards. Rocky Graziano was the Middleweight Champion of the World for a time and his three fights with Tony Zale were legendary. Despite losing to Zale twice, the three battles resulted in 7 knockdowns and an assortment of bumps and bruises. More importantly, these fights solidified Rocky as one of the most vicious brawlers of his day. With 67 career victories (52 coming by way of knockout), it is clear that Rocky was a dangerous opponent in the ring.

Rocky punished many of his victims with a relentless offensive attack, much like another Rocky named Marciano. The 1948 Leaf boxing set is filled with a few major stars that would otherwise overshadow Mr. Graziano like Jack Dempsey (a brutally tough #1 card) and Joe Louis. The fact remains, however, that it is Rocky that stands above the rest in terms of pure rarity and market value.

### Difficulty:

The bottom line with this card is that there are only three known examples at the time of this writing. In comparison to the 40-50 known T206 Honus Wagners, this Graziano card is one of the hobby's ultimate rarities. There are rumors that the rarity may stem from a contractual dispute but no one seems to know for sure. Even if you do happen to find an example in the marketplace, all of the tough 1948 Leaf condition obstacles apply. Poor paper quality, print defects, centering troubles and toning are amongst the culprits. All in all, this card so incredibly difficult that the chances of ever seeing one in person are few and far between.

**1948 LEAF ROCKY GRAZIANO**

## Comments:

The good news is that rarity is an increasingly important factor in the hobby as collectors search for the best and the rare. The bad news is that this happens to be a boxing card and not a baseball card. If this were a baseball card, of a player comparable to Graziano in terms of historical importance, the current market demand would be much higher than it is today. Not only is this card rare, the card features a true champion and a likable man, not just any boxer. This Rocky might not have the star power of Marciano or Balboa, but he sure is in a class in himself in terms of scarcity.

# 1951 Topps Ringside #32 Rocky Marciano

## Importance:

This is a key card from boxing's only retired, undefeated heavyweight champion. Rocky Marciano wanted to be a major league catcher but he was told that he lacked the physical skills needed for the position, then came boxing. Even when it comes to the sport that made him famous, professional scouts felt that Rocky lacked the physical gifts necessary to compete. He was shorter, lighter and slower than most heavyweight fighters were, he also lacked grace.

What scouts failed to see was his enormous heart and the power in his right hand. Marciano was the classic brawler, not very graceful, but a guy who seemed indestructible with his unreal ability to absorb punishment. He would take three or four punches just to land one of his own.

In 1952, Marciano would get the chance to fight for the heavyweight championship against Joe Walcott. After being knocked down in the first round and behind on the scorecards after 12 rounds, Marciano landed a thunderous right hand in the 13th round that drove Walcott to the canvas and ended the fight. After winning the championship, Marciano would defend his title six times. Marciano retired after going 49-0, with 43 of his wins coming by way of knockout.

Tragically, Marciano would perish in a plane crash in 1969 at the young age of 46. Despite his short life, Marciano left a lasting mark on the sport and, perhaps more than almost any other athlete; he personified the "American Dream." With a little talent and a lot of heart, Marciano rose to the top of his profession and left it with an unblemished record.

## Difficulty:

The biggest problem with this card is simply finding it at all. While the set is considered somewhat mainstream for boxing cards, it did not get distributed nearly to the degree of popular baseball issues of the day. Keep in mind that, during the era, boxing was still considered a very popular spectator sport so, in turn, these cards were probably physically handled nearly as much as any baseball issue. This issue is not quite as tough as the 1948 Leaf boxing production, but this Marciano is still very tough to locate in top grades.

## 1951 TOPPS RINGSIDE ROCKY MARCIANO

## Comments:

Marciano was a real fan favorite and he was able to elevate boxing to a new level. Other heavyweight champions have showed more skill or had more flash but Marciano remains the only champ to retire with an unblemished record. This card has a unique design and, while it is not as tough as the 1948 Leaf boxing set, it still remains a tough issue to locate in top grades. Marciano was also known as a compassionate man. In fact, after his knock-out victory over Joe Louis, Marciano went back to his dressing room and cried. Even in victory, he was devastated to see such a great man fall, Louis was one of his idols. Boxing, as a sport, is in a little trouble today but that makes fans yearn for the days of yesteryear. This card should remain in demand as one of the few mainstream boxing issues available.

## 1933 Goudey Sport Kings #6 Jim Thorpe

### Importance:

This is one of the most visually appealing cards in an incredibly popular set. This is another fan favorite. The bright colors and proud image of Thorpe create a classic, an image that many collectors recognize from the moment they lay eyes on it. Thorpe is still considered to be one of the greatest all-around athletes of all-time. In 1950, Thorpe was voted the greatest male athlete of the first half of the 20th Century, his ability and skill were legendary. He was able to succeed in a variety of sports including football, baseball and track and field.

Thorpe was an All-American halfback at Carlisle (twice in 1911 and 1912), the 1912 Olympic decathlon and pentathlon champion, a professional baseball player (featured on his M101-5 Sporting News card) and football player. In 1920, Thorpe became the first president of the American Professional Football Association, later known as the NFL. With this in mind, should Thorpe have been the first card in the set? If you think so, you will get no argument from me.

### Difficulty:

The 1933 Goudey Sport Kings are subject to a variety of condition problems. These cards, due to the narrow borders, are often found off center because the slightest shift to the left or right, top or bottom, can cause the card to lose eye-appeal. In addition, toning is very common for the issue as most Thorpe examples are found with some degree of discoloration along the edges.

The reverse is also subject to toning but, more importantly, it may suffer from "bleeding." When the sheets of cards were laid on top of each other, the moist ink would sometimes stick to the reverse of the cards above. If the bleeding is not severe, then it should not detract from the value in a substantial way. Finally, look out for varying degrees of color strength. Some of these Sport Kings were produced with very bland colors while others were bold. This is a reasonably tough vintage card overall.

1933 GOUDEY SPORT KINGS JIM THORPE

## Comments:

This Jim Thorpe example has many things going for it. The set, as a whole, is one of the most collectible sets from the era due to the wide variety of sports stars to choose from and the undeniable visual appeal of these miniature pieces of art. Thorpe is one of a few key football figures to be honored in the set, along with Rockne and Grange. Regardless of the set and Thorpe's mark on the sport of football, his mark on sports in general is far more significant. Thorpe will always be referred to as the "measuring stick" that all other multi-sport athletes are judged by. Thorpe opened the doors to popular modern athletes such as Bo Jackson and Deion Sanders. Thorpe will remain a key sports figure for decades to come.

## 1933 Goudey Sport Kings #45 Babe Didrickson

### Importance:

It would be hard to comprehend how dominating an athlete Babe Didrickson was. Much like male sports star Jim Thorpe, Babe could do it all. She excelled in every sport imaginable including track, basketball and golf during a time when women were discouraged from participating in athletic events. In fact, she was such a powerful hitter as a teen that boys nicknamed her "Babe" after the legendary baseball slugger. I guess her name, "Babe," was extremely appropriate considering how dominant that other "Babe" was.

This card, which is very tough to find in nice shape, represents one of only two female athletes featured in the set and Babe was the first female athlete to reach such lofty heights in the male-dominated sports world. Could you imagine the endorsements Babe would get today?

### Difficulty:

The 1933 Goudey Sport Kings suffer from a variety of problems and this Didrickson is no exception. More often than not, you see this Didrickson example with toned borders. The slightest yellowing of the edges can really be an eyesore so watch out. In addition, the narrow borders made it easy for poorly centered copies to be manufactured. Even if the card is just slightly off-center, it appears to be worse due to the small frame.

Finally, along with the obvious wear obstacles, "bleeding" on the reverse can be a problem. When the sheets of cards were laid on top of each other, the moist ink would sometimes stick to the reverse of the cards above. If the bleeding is not severe, then it should not detract from the value in a substantial way. This is a difficult card for sure.

# 1933 GOUDEY SPORT KINGS BABE DODRICKSON

## Comments:

Babe Didrickson was so dominant that it is hard to imagine an athlete today, male or female, with that kind of ability. Many sports experts argue that she might be the greatest pure athlete of the 20th Century considering her astounding athletic dominance, no other female athlete could match her skill and no other male athlete could claim to master so many sports. The 1933 Sport Kings set is extraordinarily popular due to the beautiful designs and variety of sports stars. The Didrickson card has long been considered one of the keys to the set and, in addition, the card is one of the set's tougher examples. As a woman, Babe will never get the respect of comparable male athletes but, then again, there are no comparable male athletes. She was one of a kind.

# The Cards that Just Missed the Cut

After reading through the card listings, I am sure many of you are asking, "Why didn't this card or that card make the list?" As mentioned earlier, this is part of what makes the hobby fun. You can ask 200 collectors to make a top 200 list and you will receive 200 different lists. Long after this book reaches the hands of collectors and becomes engulfed in dust on an old bookshelf, the debates will rage on.

What about those cards that just missed the cut?

As you might imagine, there were a host of cards that just missed the cut and each one could easily be justified as a member of this elite group. There were many incredibly rare vintage cards that were left off the list like Shoeless Joe Jackson's rookie card and the 1933 Goudey #1 Benny Bengough. Both examples are tremendous cards but the Jackson card is so rarely seen that only the most advanced collectors know what this card looks like, therefore, the overall popularity weans.

The Bengough card, while a very tough one, just missed the cut because the market for high-end copies is very thin. As the number one card in one of the most beautiful sets ever produced, the Bengough card receives a great deal of attention from some advanced collectors. On the other hand, as a common player, the card has very limited overall appeal unless you are trying to build a high-end set or simply collect condition rarities. It just missed inclusion on the list but a few other cards were stronger in other areas.

Popular athletes like Mickey Mantle and Michael Jordan will also be a subject of conversation. One could argue that every single card ever made of these guys could have made the list because their popularity is simply overwhelming. Keep in mind that popularity, while it is a very important aspect of a card, is only one aspect and we did not want to simply pro

duce a checklist for Mantle, Koufax, Jordan and Mays. Any cards of these icons could be argued as candidates for the list.

In addition, any cards, especially rookie cards, of any Hall of Famer would be candidates for an all-time list such as this. Great rookie cards like that of Joe Morgan, Robin Yount and Don Drysdale did not make it but are all wonderful cards. To take it a step further, any cards of any exclusive club members (3,000 Hits, 500 Home Runs, 300 Wins, etc.) are extremely popular and desirable. Great quarterbacks, All-Century Teams and Scoring Leaders might be other examples of popular collecting themes.

Modern stars like Randy Johnson, Pedro Martinez or overlooked players like Eddie Murray or Rafael Palmeiro were close calls as well. In basketball, there were borderline misses such as great centers like Hakeem Olajuwon and Patrick Ewing. In football, star quarterbacks like Troy Aikman and Brett Favre were also part of the *Just Missed Club*. With many modern athletes,

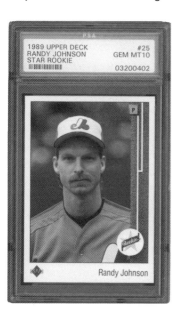

even retired ones, time will tell if they eventually make the list. It really depends on how history treats the player's accomplishments and their prized cardboard. A player like Randy Johnson may be a lock in a year or two but we will have to wait and see.

The bottom line, with all the near misses, is that there were a lot of them. It would be very easy to add 50 or 100 cards to this great list, there are so many interesting cards to collect in our hobby. With that in mind, realize that a near miss today might be a sure thing tomorrow as this exclusive club of elite cardboard is an ever-changing list as new heroes emerge and old ones fade from the limelight. Which ones will have the staying power to remain on the list over the long haul? We will all have to sit back and watch as history is reshaped and our hobby evolves but remember, there's always hope in case your card didn't make the list this time around.

# THE GALLERY

PSA
1887 N172 OLD JUDGE #
CAP ANSON NM-MT 8
01555301

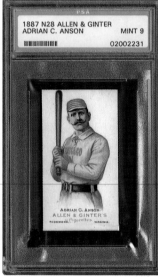

PSA
1887 N28 ALLEN & GINTER #
ADRIAN C. ANSON MINT 9
02002231

PSA
1888 N162 GOODWIN CHAMPS #
CAP ANSON NM 7
07042659

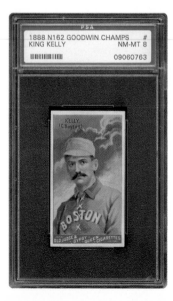

PSA
1888 N162 GOODWIN CHAMPS #
KING KELLY NM-MT 8
09060763

PSA
1909 RAMLY #
WALTER JOHNSON NM-MT 8
02043799

T206
TY COBB
PORTRAIT GREEN BACK

NM-MT 8

06005241

T206
TY COBB
PORTRAIT RED BACK

NM-MT 8

06031279

T206
TY COBB
BAT OFF SHOULDER

NM-MT 8

04368084

T206
TY COBB
BAT ON SHOULDER

NM-MT 8

06016970

T206
WALTER JOHNSON
HANDS AT CHEST

NM-MT 8

02076870

T206
WALTER JOHNSON
PORTRAIT

NM-MT 8

03386187

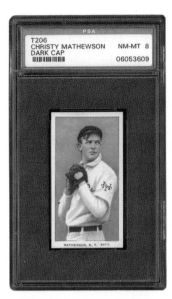

T206
CHRISTY MATHEWSON
DARK CAP
NM-MT 8
06053609

T206
CHRISTY MATHEWSON
PORTRAIT
NM-MT 8
09000591

T206
CHRISTY MATHEWSON
WHITE CAP
NM-MT 8
09005654

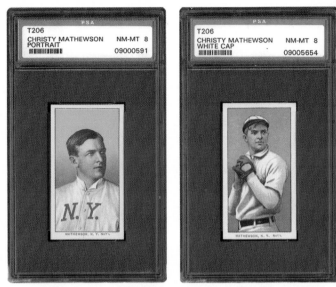

T206
EDDIE PLANK
NM-MT 8
02044145

T206
HONUS WAGNER
McNALL/GRETZKY
NM-MT 8
00000001

T206
TRIS SPEAKER
NM-MT 8
03000839

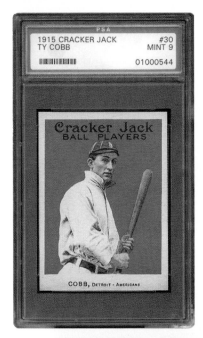

1915 CRACKER JACK #30
TY COBB
MINT 9
01000544

Cracker Jack
BALL PLAYERS

COBB, Detroit - Americans

1915 CRACKER JACK #57
WALTER JOHNSON
MINT 9
06012953

Cracker Jack
BALL PLAYERS

JOHNSON, Washington - Americans

1915 CRACKER JACK #68
HONUS WAGNER
NM-MT 8
07059222

Cracker Jack
BALL PLAYERS

WAGNER, Pittsburgh - Nationals

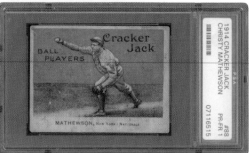

1914 CRACKER JACK #88
CHRISTY MATHEWSON
PR-FR 1
07116515

Cracker Jack
BALL PLAYERS

MATHEWSON, New York - Nationals

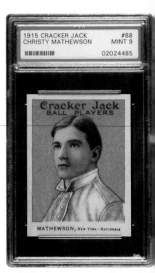

1915 CRACKER JACK #88
CHRISTY MATHEWSON
MINT 9
02024485

Cracker Jack
BALL PLAYERS

MATHEWSON, New York - Nationals

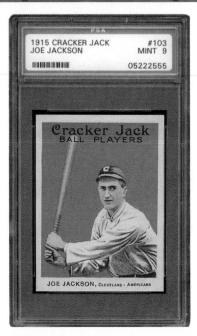

1915 CRACKER JACK #103
JOE JACKSON
MINT 9
05222555

Cracker Jack
BALL PLAYERS

JOE JACKSON, Cleveland - Americans

1915 M101-5 SPORTING NEWS #86
JOE JACKSON
NM-MT 8
06046685

JOE JACKSON
L. F.—Chicago White Sox
86

1915 M101-5 SPORTING NEWS #176
JIM THORPE
BLANK BACK
07002143

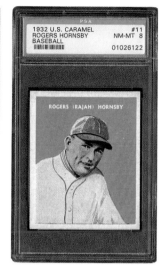

1932 U.S. CARAMEL          #11
ROGERS HORNSBY       NM-MT  8
BASEBALL
01026122

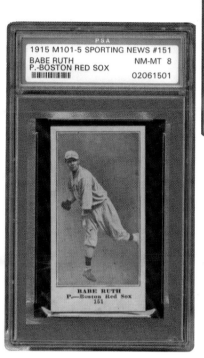

1915 M101-5 SPORTING NEWS #151
BABE RUTH            NM-MT  8
P.-BOSTON RED SOX
02061501

1932 U.S. CARAMEL          #14
TY COBB              MINT  9
BASEBALL
02017105

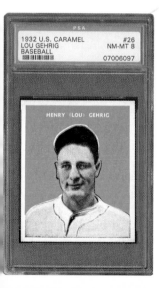

1932 U.S. CARAMEL          #26
LOU GEHRIG           NM-MT  8
BASEBALL
07006097

1932 U.S. CARAMEL          #32
BABE RUTH            NM-MT  8
BASEBALL
07029624

1933 DeLONG               #7
LOU GEHRIG           NM-MT  8
02112755

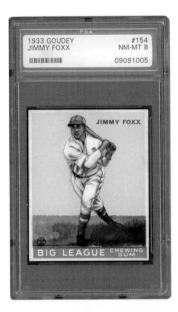

1933 GOUDEY #154
JIMMY FOXX NM-MT 8
09091005

1933 GOUDEY #53
BABE RUTH NM-MT 8
01248740

1933 GOUDEY #144
BABE RUTH NM-MT 8
02010419

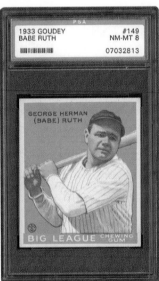

1933 GOUDEY #149
BABE RUTH NM-MT 8
07032813

1933 GOUDEY #181
BABE RUTH NM-MT 8
02012282

1933 GOUDEY #160
LOU GEHRIG NM-MT 8
01124237

1933 GOUDEY #106
NAPOLEON LAJOIE MINT 9
02024708

1933 GOUDEY #127
MEL OTT NM-MT 8
06025939

1933 GOUDEY #207
MEL OTT NM-MT 8
07053459

PSA
NM-MT 8 #230
05039819
1933 GOUDEY
CARL HUBBELL

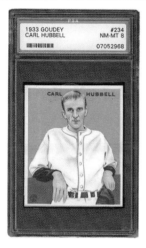

PSA
1933 GOUDEY #234
CARL HUBBELL NM-MT 8
07052968

PSA
1933 SPORT KINGS #1
TY COBB MINT 9
BASEBALL
04187736

PSA
1933 SPORT KINGS #2
BABE RUTH NM-MT 8
BASEBALL
04277059

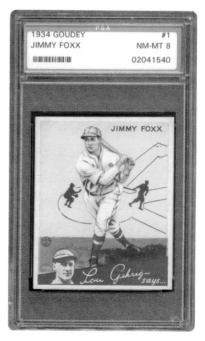

PSA
1934 GOUDEY #1
JIMMY FOXX NM-MT 8
02041540

1934 GOUDEY      #6
DIZZY DEAN      NM-MT   8
01052432

1934 GOUDEY      #37
LOU GEHRIG      NM-MT   8
01202208

1934 GOUDEY      # 61
LOU GEHRIG      NM-MT   8
02002339

1934 GOUDEY      #62
HANK GREENBERG      NM-MT 8
02018600

1934 DIAMOND STARS      #1
LEFTY GROVE      NM-MT   8
05020542

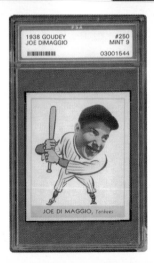

1938 GOUDEY      #250
JOE DiMAGGIO      MINT   9
03001544

1938 GOUDEY      #274
JOE DiMAGGIO      MINT   9
01043375

1938 GOUDEY #264
BOB FELLER
NM-MT 8
06023226

1938 GOUDEY #288
BOB FELLER
NM-MT 8
06359775

1939 PLAY BALL #26
JOE DiMAGGIO
MINT 9
02006056

1939 PLAY BALL #92
TED WILLIAMS
MINT 9
08142787

1940 PLAY BALL #1
JOE DiMAGGIO
NM-MT 8
08003483

1940 PLAY BALL #225
SHOELESS JOE JACKSON
NM-MT 8
01045049

1941 PLAY BALL #14
TED WILLIAMS
MINT 9
07036531

1941 PLAY BALL #54
PEE WEE REESE
MINT 9
08016746

1941 PLAY BALL #71
JOE DiMAGGIO
GEM MT 10
02025248

1948 BOWMAN #6
YOGI BERRA MINT 9
09093401

1948 BOWMAN #36
STAN MUSIAL MINT 9
03761768

1948 LEAF #1
JOE DI MAGGIO NM-MT 8
05012425

JOE DI MAGGIO

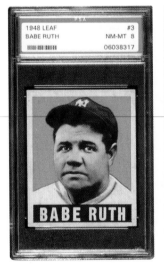

1948 LEAF #3
BABE RUTH NM-MT 8
06038317

BABE RUTH

1948 LEAF #4
STAN MUSIAL MINT 9
01022203

STAN MUSIAL

1948 LEAF #8
SATCHEL PAIGE NM-MT 8
08133425

LEROY PAIGE

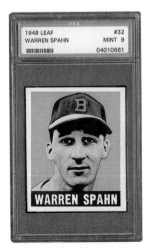

1948 LEAF #32
WARREN SPAHN MINT 9
04010661

WARREN SPAHN

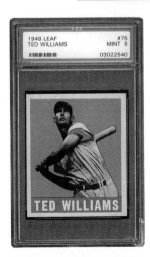

1948 LEAF #76
TED WILLIAMS MINT 9
03022540

TED WILLIAMS

1948 LEAF #79
JACKIE ROBINSON
MINT 9
07014078

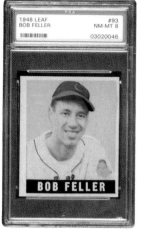

1948 LEAF #93
BOB FELLER
NM-MT 8
03020046

1949 BOWMAN #84
ROY CAMPANELLA
NM-MT 8
02079869

1949 BOWMAN #224
SATCHELL PAIGE
MINT 9
06012329

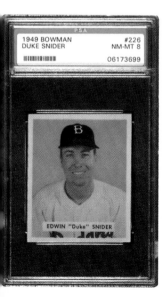

1949 BOWMAN #226
DUKE SNIDER
NM-MT 8
06173699

1950 BOWMAN #98
TED WILLIAMS
MINT 9
04010664

1951 BOWMAN #1
WHITEY FORD
MINT 9
07053831

1951 BOWMAN
MICKEY MANTLE
#253
PSA
GEM MT 10
02006022

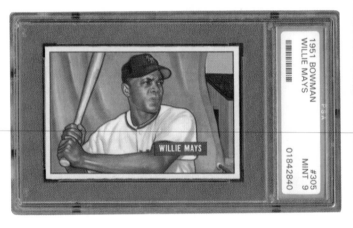

1951 BOWMAN
WILLIE MAYS
#305
MINT 9
01842840

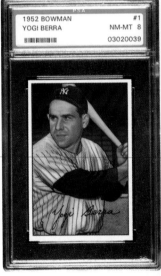

PSA
1952 BOWMAN
YOGI BERRA
#1
NM-MT 8
03020039

PSA
1952 BOWMAN
MICKEY MANTLE
#101
MINT 9
03537908

PSA
1952 BOWMAN
STAN MUSIAL
#196
MINT 9
05322035

PSA
1952 BOWMAN
WILLIE MAYS
#218
NM-MT 8
06019811

1952 TOPPS · #1 · ANDY PAFKO · PSA GEM MT10 · 02106023

1952 TOPPS · #191 · YOGI BERRA · PSA MINT 9 · 03025089

1952 TOPPS · #261 · WILLIE MAYS · PSA GEM MT10 · 05037628

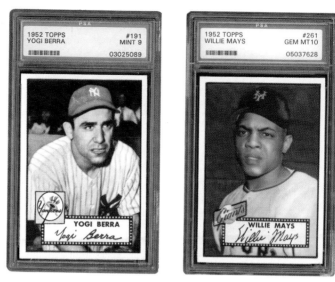

1952 TOPPS · #312 · JACKIE ROBINSON · PSA MINT 9 · 06048945

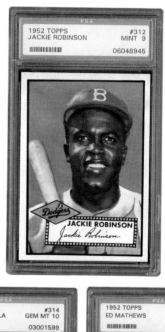

1952 TOPPS · #311 · MICKEY MANTLE · PSA GEM-MT 10 · 02006104

1952 TOPPS · #314 · ROY CAMPANELLA · PSA GEM MT 10 · 03001599

1952 TOPPS · #407 · ED MATHEWS · PSA NM-MT 8 · 06040559

1953 BOWMAN COLOR #33
PEE WEE REESE
MINT 9
09089668

1953 BOWMAN COLOR #153
WHITEY FORD
NM-MT 8
08009029

1953 TOPPS #1
JACKIE ROBINSON
MINT 9
02017086

1953 TOPPS #82
MICKEY MANTLE
MINT 9
05023067

1953 TOPPS #244
WILLIE MAYS
GEM MT 10
08011465

1954 BOWMAN #66
TED WILLIAMS
MINT 9
11077794

1954 DAN-DEE POTATO CHIPS
MICKEY MANTLE
MINT 9
01631115

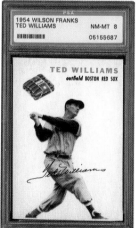

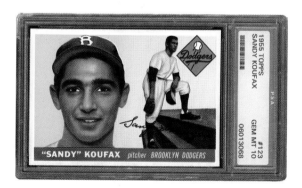

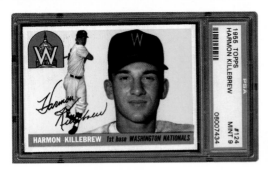

1955 TOPPS
HARMON KILLEBREW
#124
PSA
MINT 9
06007434

HARMON KILLEBREW 1st base WASHINGTON NATIONALS

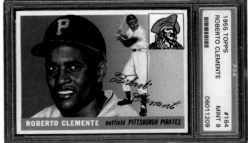

1955 TOPPS
ROBERTO CLEMENTE
#164
PSA
MINT 9
06011209

ROBERTO CLEMENTE outfield PITTSBURGH PIRATES

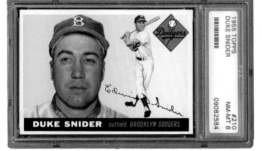

1955 TOPPS
DUKE SNIDER
#210
PSA
NM-MT 8
09082584

DUKE SNIDER outfield BROOKLYN DODGERS

MICKEY MANTLE
outfield NEW YORK YANKEES

1956 TOPPS
MICKEY MANTLE
#135
PSA
MINT 9
07115145

PSA
1957 TOPPS          #1
TED WILLIAMS    MINT 9
06174768

TED Williams
BOSTON RED SOX OUTFIELD

PSA
1957 TOPPS          #35
FRANK ROBINSON   MINT 9
02107733

FRANK Robinson
CINCINNATI REDLEGS O.F.

PSA
1957 TOPPS          #302
SANDY KOUFAX    MINT 9
04023912

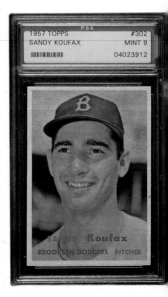

SANDY Koufax
BROOKLYN DODGERS PITCHER

1957 TOPPS #328
BROOKS ROBINSON
MINT 9
04134647

1957 TOPPS #407
YANKEES POWER HITTERS
MANTLE & BERRA
MINT 9
07046682

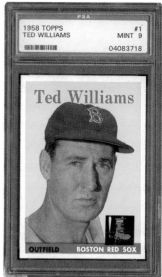

1958 TOPPS #1
TED WILLIAMS
MINT 9
04083718

1958 TOPPS #418
SERIES BATTING FOES
MANTLE & AARON
MINT 9
08162030

1959 FLEER TED WILLIAMS #68
TED SIGNS FOR 1959
MINT 9
07004323

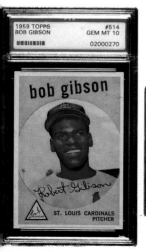

1959 TOPPS #514
BOB GIBSON
GEM MT 10
02000270

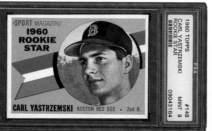

1960 TOPPS #148
CARL YASTRZEMSKI
ROOKIE STAR
MINT 9
09043164

1962 TOPPS #1
ROGER MARIS
MINT 9
09019744

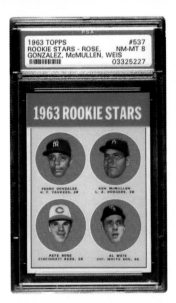

# 1963 ROOKIE STARS

PEDRO GONZALEZ
N.Y. YANKEES, 2B

KEN McMULLEN
L. A. DODGERS, 3B

PETE ROSE
CINCINNATI REDS, 2B

AL WEIS
CHI. WHITE SOX, SS

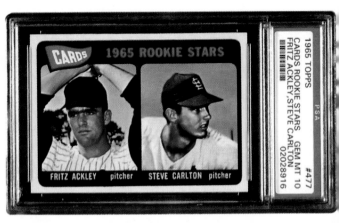

CARDS  1965 ROOKIE STARS

FRITZ ACKLEY  pitcher    STEVE CARLTON  pitcher

A. LEAGUE ROOKIE STARS

ROD CAREW • 2B      HANK ALLEN • OF
MINNESOTA TWINS     WASHINGTON SENATORS

METS  1967 ROOKIE STARS

BILL DENEHY • P      TOM SEAVER • P

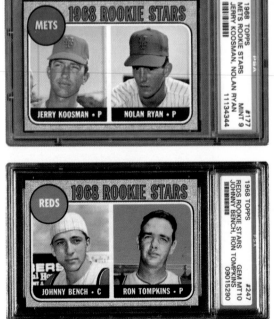

1968 ROOKIE STARS

METS

JERRY KOOSMAN • P    NOLAN RYAN • P

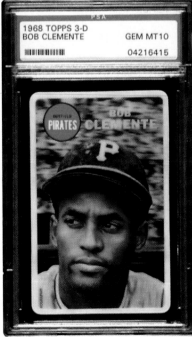

PIRATES  BOB CLEMENTE

P

1968 ROOKIE STARS

REDS

JOHNNY BENCH • C     RON TOMPKINS • P

1969 TOPPS     #260
REGGIE JACKSON
    MINT 9
02007819

1969 TOPPS     #500
MICKEY MANTLE
WHITE LETTERS
    MINT 9
02048284

1973 ROOKIE THIRD BASEMEN

1973 TOPPS
ROOKIE THIRD BASEMEN
CEY, HILTON, SCHMIDT
#615
MINT 9
01018423

1975 TOPPS MINI     #228
GEORGE BRETT
    MINT 9
08003437

1980 TOPPS     #482
RICKEY HENDERSON
    MINT 9
05101166

1982 TOPPS TRADED     #98T
CAL RIPKEN, JR.
    NM-MT 8
03236263

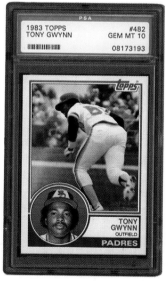

1983 TOPPS     #482
TONY GWYNN
    GEM MT 10
08173193

1984 FLEER UPDATE     #U-27
ROGER CLEMENS
    GEM MT 10
07091125

1948 BOWMAN #69
GEORGE MIKAN GEM MT10
02075060

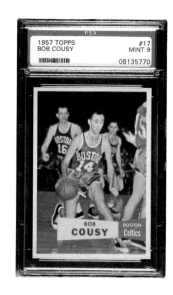

1957 TOPPS #17
BOB COUSY MINT 9
08135770

1957 TOPPS #77
BILL RUSSELL NM-MT 8
08135737

1961 FLEER #3
ELGIN BAYLOR NM-MT 8
08135720

1961 FLEER #8
WILT CHAMBERLAIN NM-MT 8
01428058

1961 FLEER #36
OSCAR ROBERTSON MINT 9
02319186

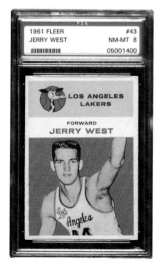

1961 FLEER #43
JERRY WEST NM-MT 8
05001400

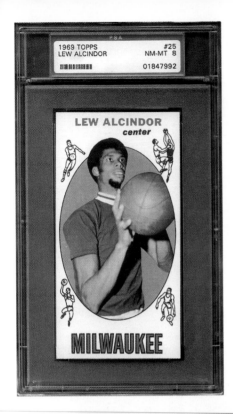

1969 TOPPS     #25
LEW ALCINDOR
01847992    NM-MT 8

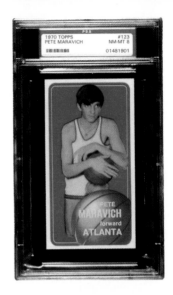

1970 TOPPS     #123
PETE MARAVICH
01481901    NM-MT 8

1972 TOPPS     #195
JULIUS ERVING
04057478    MINT 9

1980 TOPPS
SCORING LEADER
BIRD, ERVING, JOHNSON
06052909    MINT 9

1986 FLEER     #57
MICHAEL JORDAN
09047283    GEM MT10

1992 UPPER DECK     #1
SHAQUILLE O'NEAL
07079591    GEM MT 10

1996 TOPPS CHROME     #138
KOBE BRYANT
03219304    GEM MT10

1935 NATIONAL CHICLE #34
BRONKO NAGURSKI
NM-MT 8
06022843

1933 SPORT KINGS #4
RED GRANGE
FOOTBALL
NM-MT 8
05013108

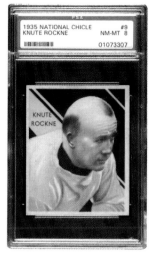

1935 NATIONAL CHICLE #9
KNUTE ROCKNE
NM-MT 8
01073307

1948 LEAF #1
SID LUCKMAN
EX-MT 6
03539072

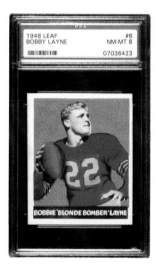

1948 LEAF #6
BOBBY LAYNE
NM-MT 8
07036423

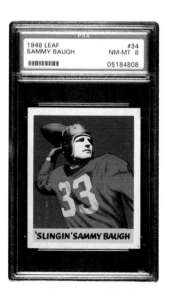

1948 LEAF #34
SAMMY BAUGH
NM-MT 8
05184808

1950 BOWMAN #5
Y.A. TITTLE
NM-MT 8
03386373

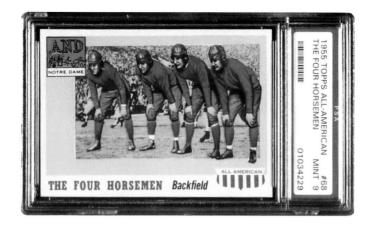

1955 TOPPS ALL-AMERICAN
THE FOUR HORSEMEN
#68
MINT 9
01034229

THE FOUR HORSEMEN  *Backfield*

NOTRE DAME

ALL AMERICAN

1957 TOPPS
BART STARR
#119
NM-MT 8
04020820

Bart Starr

BACK–PACKERS

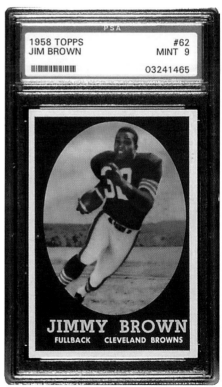

PSA
1958 TOPPS
JIM BROWN
#62
MINT 9
03241465

JIMMY BROWN
FULLBACK    CLEVELAND BROWNS

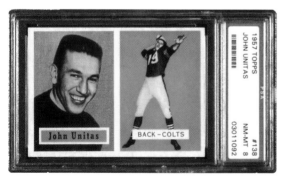

1957 TOPPS
JOHN UNITAS
#138
NM-MT 8
03011092

John Unitas

BACK–COLTS

1957 TOPPS
PAUL HORNUNG
#151
NM-MT 8
07001210

Paul Hornung

BACK–PACKERS

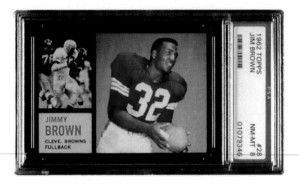

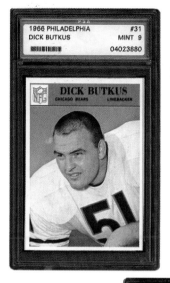

1966 PHILADELPHIA #31
DICK BUTKUS
MINT 9
04023880

DICK BUTKUS
CHICAGO BEARS · LINEBACKER

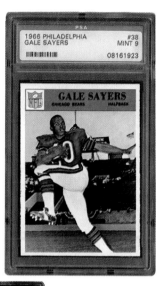

1966 PHILADELPHIA #38
GALE SAYERS
MINT 9
08161923

GALE SAYERS
CHICAGO BEARS · HALFBACK

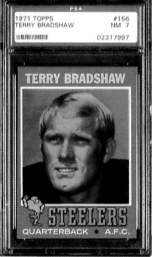

1971 TOPPS #156
TERRY BRADSHAW
NM 7
02317997

TERRY BRADSHAW
STEELERS
QUARTERBACK · A.F.C.

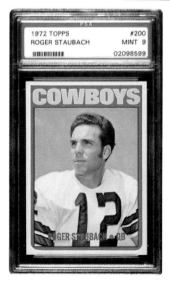

1972 TOPPS #200
ROGER STAUBACH
MINT 9
02098599

COWBOYS
ROGER STAUBACH · QB

1976 TOPPS #148
WALTER PAYTON
GEM MT 10
08165759

BEARS
RUNNING BACK
WALTER PAYTON

| 1981 TOPPS | #216 | | 1984 TOPPS | #63 | | 1984 TOPPS | #123 |
| JOE MONTANA | GEM MT 10 | | JOHN ELWAY | GEM MT 10 | | DAN MARINO | GEM MT 10 |
| | 05038623 | | | 02083467 | | | 02004150 |

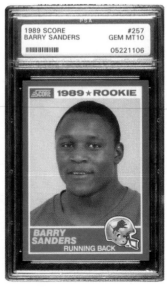

| 1986 TOPPS | #161 | | 1989 SCORE | #257 | | 1990 SCORE UPDATE | #101T |
| JERRY RICE | GEM MT 10 | | BARRY SANDERS | GEM MT10 | | EMMITT SMITH | GEM MT10 |
| | 05005034 | | | 05221106 | | | 02095081 |

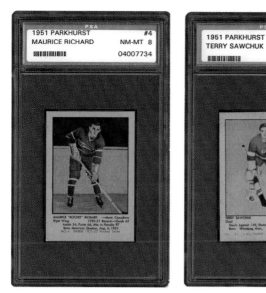

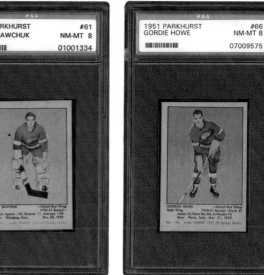

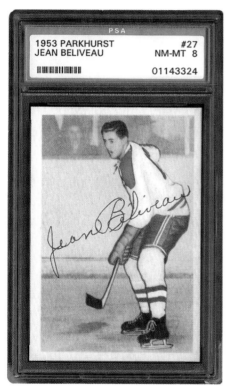

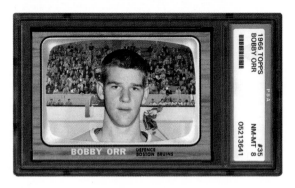

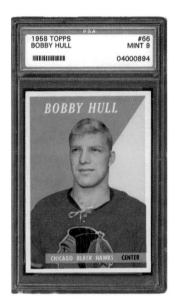

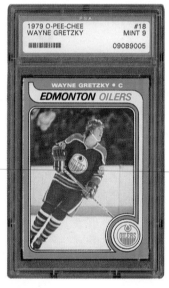

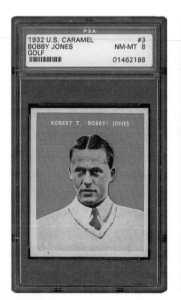

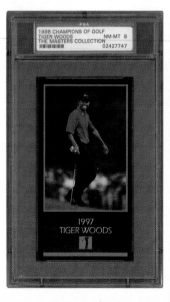

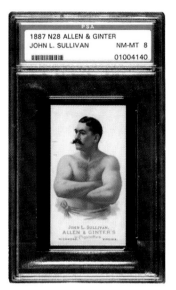

PSA
1887 N28 ALLEN & GINTER
JOHN L. SULLIVAN          NM-MT 8
01004140

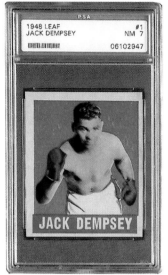

PSA
1948 LEAF                    #1
JACK DEMPSEY              NM 7
06102947

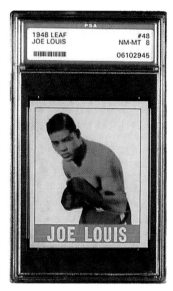

PSA
1948 LEAF                    #48
JOE LOUIS                  NM-MT 8
06102945

PSA
1948 LEAF                    #50
ROCKY GRAZIANO           VG-EX 4
07045755

1951 TOPPS RINGSIDE
ROCKY MARCIANO
#32
NM-MT 8
04211899

PSA
1933 SPORT KINGS             #6
JIM THORPE                NM-MT 8
FOOTBALL
08095196

PSA
1933 SPORT KINGS            #45
BABE DIDRICKSON          NM-MT 8
TRACK
04088607

# You Make The Call.
# We'll Help You Make The Cash.

## The most profitable way to sell your sportscards and memorabilia is also the easiest.

Give us just 10 minutes by phone and we'll give you an expert opinion on how much your vintage sportscards and memorabilia are likely to bring at auction. And not just any auction. Superior Sports Auctions — recognized as the nation's premier sports auction house. And the one that consistently attracts more serious buyers and record prices.

Of course, getting you the highest price is just the beginning. You can expect low commissions. Fast payments. Cash advances. PSA grading for your ungraded cards. And unmatched pre-auction marketing. Plus, we make the whole process as easy as "sending in your items and waiting for your check."

It's your call. Take your chances on selling your sportscards and memorabilia by yourself. Or call the experts proven to bring top dollar every time. Superior Sports Auctions. Take a few minutes to find out what your collection will bring at **Superior's next auction. Call us today at (231) 922-9862.**

COLLECTORS
UNIVERSE
NASDAQ: CLCT

A Division of Collectors Universe

Visit **www.superiorsports.com** or call (231) 922-9862

Mr. Wantlist!

YES, WE KNOW MR. WANTLIST IS POWERFUL,
BUT NO, IT CAN'T HELP YOU LOCATE YOUR MISSING SOCK.

Mr. Wantlist, Teletrade.com's unique technology allows you to tell us what cards you're looking for — then we'll find them for you! You don't even have to keep checking to see if we've found them yet. When we do find them, we'll shoot you an e-mail and let you know. All you have to do is gear up to place your bids.

**TELE TRADE**

WWW.TELETRADE.COM
800.232.1132

27 Main Street, Kingston, New York, 12401  Tel 845-339-2900  Fax 845-339-3288
Teletrade is a subsidiary of Greg Manning Auctions, Inc. NASDAQ Symbol: GMAI

# 1-800-350-2273

# Is It Real?

## Did I Get Scammed?

## Should I Toss It?

## Was It A Good Investment?

## Will It Sell For Record Price?

# You Have Genuine Questions.
# We Have Authentic Answers.

One of the most valuable names in sports history isn't Babe Ruth, Willie Mays, or even Honus Wagner. It's PSA/DNA — the leading sports autograph authenticator in the world.

Experienced collectors know that up to 70% of today's sports autographs are counterfeit — even those that are "certified." So they turn to PSA/DNA's experts, James Spence and Steve Grad, for authentication and verification that not only preserves their investment but also protects them from fraud. It's why the nation's leading auction houses and even federal law enforcement units look to our experts for unparalleled expertise and peace-of-mind.*

So before you buy or sell another autograph, make sure it is accompanied by an even more important one: a PSA/DNA Letter of Authenticity. For a fee schedule and submission information, go to **www.psadna.com** and click on Submission Center.

*"Babe-signed balls took three of the Top 10 spots this week, as baseball season kicked into its second month. It's interesting to note that all three Babe baseballs were PSA/DNA authenticated, perhaps signaling bidders' unwillingness to honor other certificates of authenticity with top bids in light of the federal government's reports of rampant forgery at online auction sites over the last 36 months."
"Auction Circuit", **Sports Collectors Digest**, June 7, 2002*

**PSA DNA**
AUTHENTICATION SERVICES
A Division of Collectors Universe

**COLLECTORS**
**UNIVERSE**
NASDAQ: CLCT

Visit **www.psadna.com** or call (888) 947-7788

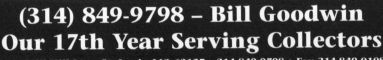